Tax Law and Digitalization: The New Frontier for Government and Business

Tax Law and Digitalization: The New Frontier for Government and Business

Principles, Use Cases and Outlook

Edited by

Jeffrey Owens
Robert Risse

Wolters Kluwer

Published by:
Kluwer Law International B.V.
PO Box 316
2400 AH Alphen aan den Rijn
The Netherlands
E-mail: international-sales@wolterskluwer.com
Website: lrus.wolterskluwer.com

Sold and distributed by:
Wolters Kluwer Legal & Regulatory U.S.
7201 McKinney Circle
Frederick, MD 21704
United States of America
E-mail: customer.service@wolterskluwer.com

ISBN 978-94-035-3403-9

e-Book: ISBN 978-94-035-3404-6
web-PDF: ISBN 978-94-035-3405-3

Editors

Prof. Dr Jeffrey Owens headed up the OECD's tax work for over twenty years. He trained as an accountant and economist. He has also published widely in the area of public finance. After retiring from the OECD in 2012, Prof. Dr Owens took up a post as Professor and Director of the WU Global Tax Policy Center at the Institute for Austrian and International Tax Law, WU (Vienna University of Economics and Business), a research fellowship at the European University Institute in Florence, a part-time position as a Senior Policy Advisor to the Global Vice Chair of Tax at EY, and he is an advisor to a number of governments and organizations.

Prof. Dr Robert Risse, lawyer and financial advisor, has been the head of the Tax and Trade department of Henkel AG & Co. KGaA since 2000 and is globally responsible for all topics and projects related to taxation and customs. From 1991 to 1998, Prof. Dr Risse was responsible for corporate group management in the areas of national and international tax law in the tax department of Mannesmann AG, and from 1997 to 1999, he was the head of the Tax and Risk Management department of Deutsche Post AG. Prof. Dr Risse is, among other things, on the board of the Rhein-Ruhr Discussion Group of the International Fiscal Association (IFA) (so-called IFA West), and is a member of the tax advisory examining board at the Ministry of Finance of North Rhine-Westphalia. Since August 2017, he has been Honorary Professor for Tax Compliance and Applied Tax Planning at the Institute of Accounting, Finance and Taxation at the University of Leipzig chaired by Prof. Carmen Bachmann. Since December 2017, he has been the Chairman of the board of directors for the WU Transfer Pricing Center at the Institute for Austrian and International Tax Law, WU (Vienna University of Economics and Business).

Contributors

Alexander Beuther has been a researcher at the Institute for Information Systems (IWi) at the German Research Center for Artificial Intelligence (DFKI) since 2019. He currently works in the Center of Competence for Tax Technology of IWi, DFKI, and more specifically on the VisEP project (visualization of decisions in processes), in which he is investigating the potential of business process management, process mining and artificial intelligence. He graduated from Saarland University in business informatics in 2019 with a master's degree in the research fields of process mining and software usability.

Jérôme Duperrut has been an Associate Director for economic analysis and international institutions at SICPA, a Swiss company dedicated to enabling trust in the physical and digital worlds, since 2015. His work ranges from assessing the fiscal benefit of digital tax stamps adopted by tax authorities for excise duty collection to addressing the usefulness of secure digital technologies, including blockchain, in the area of taxation. Previously, he was a Senior Advisor at the International Monetary Fund, Economist at the Swiss Federal Department of Finance, and Scientific Advisor at the Swiss Parliament. He has accumulated policy and practical experiences in the areas of domestic revenue mobilization, tax administration, and the digitalization of taxation.

Peter Fettke is a Professor of Business Informatics at Saarland University and principal researcher, research fellow and group leader at the German Research Center for Artificial Intelligence (DFKI), Saarbrücken. Mr Fettke, with his group of about 30 people, is interested in concepts, methods, and techniques at the intersection between business informatics and artificial intelligence, namely the modelling of computer-integrated systems, automated planning, and deep learning. He is the author of more than 150 peer-reviewed publications. His work is among the most-cited articles in leading international journals on business informatics, and he is one of the top five most-cited scientists at DFKI. He is also a sought-after reviewer for renowned conferences, journals, and research organizations.

André Flottmann holds an LLM in Taxation and works as a Global VAT and Sales Tax Manager at Henkel AG & Co. KGaA. In his role, he guides and structures SAP projects from a VAT perspective. His legal background and knowledge on process structures helps him to drive digitalization projects, such as process mining in VAT.

Matthias Gries, StB, graduated from the Otto-Friedrich University of Bamberg, Germany, with a Doctorate in Business Taxation. He works as in-house tax advisor in the Tax Digitalization/VAT department at Siemens and also as a lecturer at the University of Bamberg. Mr Gries previously worked as a tax advisor for Flick Gocke Schaumburg.

Karl Gürges has been with Henkel AG & Co. KGaA since 2016. He began as a master thesis student and later pursued a career in the Global Trade department of Henkel Global Supply Chain in Amsterdam, the Netherlands. His current role is in the Global Tax department based in Düsseldorf, Germany. Mr Gürges implements projects in the area of tax and customs digitalization, covering the whole range of technological applications.

Sascha Jafari holds a Master's in Taxation from the University of Maastricht, the Netherlands. In the past, Mr Jafari worked for Accenture in the financial services industry, and later for Deloitte in its Tax Management Consulting unit. His unique skill set allows him to build a bridge between IT and taxation. Although these two fields are not often combined, Mr Jafari has been writing software for many years and knows how to bring IT and taxation together. In the past, he built tax analytics software and internal fraud investigation tools for publicly listed companies. After years of research into cryptography, in 2017 he started 'summitto' to build a confidential real-time reporting system to prevent VAT fraud throughout the European Union and around the world.

Shimeng Lan is a tax consultant at KPMG in Switzerland and is pursuing a PhD in International Tax Law at the Institute for Austrian and International Tax Law, WU (Vienna University of Economics and Business). She studied at the University of International Business and Economics, China, where she graduated in law in 2016. She also holds an Advanced Master's in International Taxation from Leiden University, the Netherlands, and had practical experience with an international advisory firm and the Secretariat of the OECD-hosted Global Forum on Transparency and Exchange of Information for Tax Purposes.

Marta Olowska is a research and teaching associate at the WU Global Tax Policy Center at the Institute of Austrian and International Tax Law, WU (Vienna University of Economics and Business). She is a PhD candidate in the field of business law, with a primary focus on indirect taxation and new technologies, at WU. She holds a Master's in Law and a Bachelor's in International Relations from the University of Warsaw, Poland, and completed postgraduate studies in taxation at Warsaw School of Economics (SGH), Poland. She gained international experience participating in exchange programmes in Singapore and the United States. Before joining WU, she worked at Dentons' Warsaw office in the tax department.

Dennis Post is a tax partner with EY and the Global Blockchain Tax Leader. He is responsible for the development and deployment of blockchain solutions for tax as well as tax solutions for enterprise blockchains. He is part of the EY Advanced Technology Tax Lab, a global network of tax labs dedicated to solving tax problems through the application of advanced technologies. Mr Post heads the Dutch Tax Lab satellite office (Tax Lab NL) in Amsterdam and has more than nineteen years of experience in dealing with international tax matters. He holds a PhD in taxation, obtained at the University of Amsterdam. He has published several books on international tax-technical matters and articles in well-known (international) tax magazines and is a frequent speaker at (international) blockchain-related events. He is connected to Nyenrode Business University as well as the University of Amsterdam.

Sebastian Stephan has been a researcher at the Institute for Information Systems (IWi) at the German Research Center for Artificial Intelligence (DFKI) since 2018. He graduated from the Konstanz University of Applied Sciences, Germany, with a Master's in Informatics in 2017. He is interested in concepts, methods, and techniques at the intersection between business process management and artificial intelligence. The main part of his research focusses on topics related to the use of process mining and analytics in tax and auditing.

Helena Strauss holds a PhD in Accountancy at the faculty of Economic and Management Sciences (North-West University, South Africa). Her PhD focused on international tax, technology, and assurance. She holds a Master's in international taxation and a Bachelor's in Finance and Assurance. She is currently pursuing an MBA in Information Technology at the University of Cumbria, UK. She gained her experience as a senior manager: audit and consulting at KPMG after which she joined the South African Revenue Services as specialist and consulting lead in the field of tax administration within the digitalized economy. She is currently responsible for audit, consulting, and organizational development within an international organization. She is a member of SAICA, ISACA, and an affiliate member of the ACFE.

Philippe Thevoz has a PhD in Engineering, and has been at the forefront of digital transformation for the last thirty years, from numerical simulation and high-power computing in the nineties to blockchain technologies more recently. Since 2015, as an independent consultant, he has advised governments and businesses in their digital transformation, with a strong accent on blockchain technologies. Since 2017, as Executive Vice-President eGovernment Systems at SICPA, he has the responsibility to lead the development of new digital platforms for governments. This includes secure registries, next generation of digital signatures, and secure value documents, based upon data and process integrity, using the latest digital technologies, such as blockchain, cryptography, digital Identity, secure marking, and artificial intelligence. He is a member of the OECD Blockchain Expert Policy Advisory Board (BEPAB).

Michael Tobai heads the tax technology and digitalization activities at Siemens AG. Before that, he held various management positions in the areas of business process outsourcing, shared services, centre management, and process consulting for various domains. His academic background comprises a diploma degree in industrial engineering, and two MBAs with focus on general management and finance respectively.

Goran Todorov is a global consultant for the legal and technical certification of invoicing systems, advising on the implementation and certification of sales data controller systems. Mr Todorov has collaborated with many tax authorities to introduce a clearance model and the real-time audit of fiscal invoices, a technological innovation that triggered the online cash register movement worldwide. Mr Todorov actively conducts research on the advancement of fiscal device technology development and various invoice legislation concepts, and has published several papers describing the design of digital invoicing solutions (DICE) for preventing missing trader intra-community (MTIC) and VAT fraud between jurisdictions. He is Managing Director of Data Tech International.

Raul Zambrano is an IT engineer and Technical Assistance and Information Technology and Communication Director at the Inter-American Center of Tax Administrations (CIAT). He has managed modernization projects carried out by CIAT in eight countries, and has participated in developing and evaluating information systems as a consultant in more than twenty tax and customs administrations. He has lectured on the topic of databases, information systems management and tax administration and technology. He is a member of the Task Force on the Digital Economy (BEPS Action 1), and an author and editor of publications covering tax administration and information technology.

Summary of Contents

Table of Contents

Preface

New technologies are changing the way we work and live, and have the potential to help countries achieve the United Nations Sustainable Development Goals. They can also transform the way that tax administrations, taxpayers and their advisers interact, leading to a reduction in the compliance cost for taxpayers and the administrative cost for tax administrations, a level playing field for large and small businesses, and fewer opportunities to engage in aggressive tax practices. For countries that are able to harness these technologies, they will also – in the long run – offer them a competitive advantage in attracting investment and talented individuals.

What technologies are we talking about? We are referring to those which are already widespread, such as cloud computing; those which are increasingly being used by large MNEs and more advanced tax administrations, such as artificial intelligence, machine learning, and big data; and those which are still at a development stage, such as blockchain. The key challenge for both government and business is how best to combine these different technologies and how to manage the transition from the old to the new.

In recent years, the terms 'tax compliance' and 'digitization' have been widely used in public debate and professional literature. The initial question for this book was: Is tax compliance suitable for the technically digital innovations? The tension between a business perspective and a jurisprudential perspective as to what is meant by tax compliance is currently overlaid by the technical pressure to apply it, and to the digitalization of tax processes. Many business processes are carried out manually, and the use of Microsoft Excel spreadsheets can be seen as falling into this category. Entering the new digital world, where processes are supported by machines or even automated, is not easy, since questions arise on the conceptual content of compliance and how far compliance can be digitized.

The authors of the chapters in this book explore these issues from the perspective of how to achieve better tax compliance at a lower cost. What comes out from the chapters is that tax systems are on the verge of a true transformation but to successfully gain the full benefits will require unprecedented cooperation between government, business, and academia. Change is always painful, but the tax community must embrace the disruption to its traditional way of working and, in particular, move away from a confrontation to a more cooperative approach by all parts of this community.

The chapters in the book were presented at a conference held under the auspices of the Digital Economy Taxation Network (DET).[1]

It is part of a series of conferences[2] organized over the last four years based upon the research carried out by the DET partners. This Conference was hosted by the Institute for Austrian and International Tax Law, WU (Vienna University of Economics and Business) in December 2020 and brought together over 300 participants from government, business, and academia from 65 countries. The Conference was able to benefit from the work undertaken by the WU Transfer Pricing Center and the WU Global Tax Policy Center, as well as input from the Institute's newly created LLM program on tax and technology.

The editors would like to thank Philipp Walter Scharizer, Hedwig Pfanner, and Renée Pestuka for the preparation of this book, and Milena Jana Gegios for the organization of the Conference. Without their dedication, the success of the Conference and the completion of this book would not have been possible. The editors also wish to thank all of the contributors for their patience in revising their chapters, and Jo Hamilton-Bilijam who undertook the linguistic editing of the text.

1. The DET is made up of the Commonwealth Association of Tax Administrators (CATA), Inter-American Center of Tax Administrations (CIAT), the Inter-American Development Bank (IDB), the Intra-European Organization of Tax Administrations (IOTA), the World Bank (WBG), the Institute for Fiscal Studies (IEF), the Korea Institute of Public Finance (KIPF), the German Research Center for Artificial Intelligence (DFKI), the National University of Singapore (NUS), the University of Exeter (TARC), the University of New South Wales (UNSW), the University of São Paulo, the Singapore University of Social Science (SUSS), Xiamen University (CITACT-XMU), the University of Geneva, the Symbiosis Law School of Pune (SLS-P), and Revenu Québec.
2. '*Reimagining Taxation in the Age of Digital Disruption*' 5th High Level Conference: 3 December 2018, Georgetown/Washington DC, US; '*VAT/GST Challenges in a Digital Economy*' Workshop: 17-18 December 2018, Vienna, Austria; '*Application of Blockchain Technology in Tax Administration*' International Seminar: 8 November 2019, Hangzhou, China; '*Tax Compliance: Exploiting the potential of AI, Robotics and Data Analytics*' 6th High Level Conference: 9-10 October 2019, Geneva, Switzerland; '*Transfer Pricing, AI, Blockchain & Data Analytics*' Workshop: 22 February 2020, Vienna, Austria.

CHAPTER 1

Digitalization of the Tax and Trade Functions: An Overview of Tax Technology Trends from the Perspective of Business Informatics

Alexander Beuther, Sebastian Stephan & Peter Fettke

1 INTRODUCTION AND MOTIVATION

Tax departments are increasingly exposed to the dynamics of change associated with digitization. Enormous amounts of data (big data) must be processed, digitally prepared, and further processed. At the same time, tax departments are facing increasing digitization and cost pressure due to limited budgets. Tax departments cause considerable costs to the company. These costs are not offset by any direct revenues. In addition, the task portfolio of the tax department is continuously expanding. New technologies promise support in this area in terms of greater process and cost efficiency, but also in terms of ensuring complex legal regulations and compliance requirements are met. For this reason, the key to securing competitiveness is the consistent exploitation of new optimization potentials. Under the term 'tax technology' (tax tech), tools have become established that support tax departments in responding to these challenges, but the market for tax tech tools is very broad, diverse, and often confusing. The tools offered differ both in their range of functions and, due to the development history, in their solution approach. As an integration discipline as shown in Figure 1.1, tax tech stands at the interface with business taxation, tax law, and finance, and will advance the integration of these classically separate fields. Based on the intersection and tension between the different stakeholders, there is a wealth of possibilities for the application of information technology, like the use of electronic balance sheets, automated transmission to the tax authorities, or the use of innovative analytics applications to uncover unusual processes, unknown data patterns, or anomalies in tax transactions.[1]

Figure 1.1 Tax Tech Ecosystem

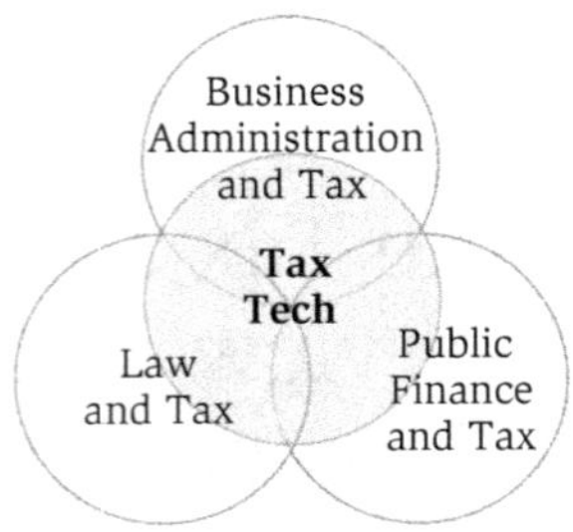

Source: Peter Fettke, *Der TaxTech-Würfel und das TaxTech-Haus zur digitalen Transformation der Steuerfunktion* (Tax Compliance, TLE-004-2020).

The selection of suitable software in the tax area does not differ from the general procedure in selecting software. Just as with the development of software: requirements catalogues, or specifications are created before the actual software selection process. These are based on previous company and process analyses and combine all the features required by the application from a functional as well as a technical point of view. On the one hand, this concerns specifications that result from the company's current IT situation, such as the operating systems, databases, architectures, or security standards used, and on the other hand, from the functional and non-functional requirements of the users. In contrast to customized software, standard software may not always fully comply with all the requirements of a particular company. Thus, dividing the specified requirements into 'mandatory' and 'optional' requirements is a suitable way to simplify the selection process when choosing from the range of different tax tech software on offer. Mandatory requirements are those requirements that are indispensable for achieving the intended goal, while optional requirements have a certain amount of leeway regarding their specification or existence for the achievement of the goals.

The market for tax tech tools is particularly heterogeneous and lacks transparency. In addition to large providers, there are numerous small and medium-sized providers. Many of them are specialized in particular areas, and thus provide dedicated solutions for special tax issues. However, these developments of tax tech tools are driven by the needs of individual tax departments and solve only specific problems. This market segment has been particularly dynamic in recent years: existing tools have been substantially developed, both technologically and functionally; various providers have established a variety of tools; and many new tools and providers have emerged.

1. Peter Fettke, *TaxTech – Die vierte Disziplin der Steuerwissenschaft* 19-24 (Der Betrieb, Sonderausgabe Nr. 01/2018).

Two factors are particularly worthy of note: first, there has been increasing cooperation between leading enterprise resource planning (ERP) and tax system providers; and second, individual industry solutions have been established by implementation partners. These factors are typical indictors of what is a growing and emerging market. This contribution aims to provide a high-level overview of the market as well as the technically supported functions. This chapter provides a structure of the market, and identifies technologies used, upcoming trends, and future perspectives.

This chapter is organized as follows: section 2 provides definitions of the required terms. Section 3 presents the approach, structure, and analysis method. Section 4 presents the key findings of the market overview carried out. Section 5 evaluates the results according to technologies, tax types, application areas, functions, and trends. Section 6 discusses one of the key findings of the market overview, the move towards tax platforms, in more detail. Finally, section 7 concludes.

2 DEFINITIONS

2.1 Information System

To understand the term 'information system', it is crucial to first of all understand the two terms that compose it: 'information' and 'system'. First, the term 'information' can be misleading, and it is often – wrongly – synonymously used in place of the words 'data' or 'knowledge'. 'Data' refers to syntax; 'information' refers to interpretation; and 'knowledge' refers to the usage of information. In that vein, the data element '01-03-2021' can be a string (data); but it can also be interpreted as a date (information); or, in a particular context, it can act as a due date for tax filing (knowledge). Second, the term 'system' generally describes an entity consisting of a set of components with different properties that are related to each other.

When these two terms are combined to create the term 'information system', it, thus, refers to 'a software system to capture, transmit, store, retrieve, manipulate, or display information, thereby supporting people, organizations, or other software'.[2] Further, it contains all intangible parts of a multi-part, computer-based system.

2.2 Software

'Software' is a generic term describing any program that can be executed on a computer. Drilling down further, a distinction can be made between 'application software' and 'system software'. Software – in a broad sense – is made up of intangible parts: objects, modules, components, etc. One specialization of the broad term of 'application software' is tax software or tax information systems, which address tax-relevant business tasks and processes within a tax department. In this contribution, the term 'tool' will be used synonymously with the terms 'software' and 'information system'. We also distinguish between the terms 'tool' and 'platform'. The main difference between a platform and a tool is that a platform provides an additional layer

2. Wil M. van der Aalst & Christian Stahl, *Modeling Business Processes. A Petri Net Oriented Approach* 4 (The MIT Press 2011).

for combining multiple software systems while a platform addresses not just one software application layer, but several, such as the data and application layers. This allows, for example, functions from different software systems to be orchestrated and processes to be mapped end to end.

2.3 Functions and Function Trees

A 'function' consists of one or more business tasks that are executed on a business object and which follow the main aim of supporting the business goals. A function can describe a task performed on tangible or intangible objects. It is triggered by certain conditions and is complete when the goal of the function is reached. Functions are elements of processes but have neither a control flow nor a time-related reference. A function can occur in different granularities: as elementary tasks (one business task); as sub-tasks; or as realizations of other tasks (more business tasks).

In this chapter, a distinction is made between 'tax functions' and 'software functions': tax functions are not only prescribed by law and tax office work, but also driven by the typical tasks within the tax department; software functions cover tax or business functions, as well as supportive, technical, and additional functions for the tax department or tax office workflows.[3]

'Function trees' are models that describe the function view of the business architecture. A function tree depicts a hierarchical list of all functions of a defined domain and provides an overview of the activities in this domain. The hierarchical order depends on the functional decomposition. Various elements represent the different granularities of the model's elements, including top-level functions, elementary functions, subfunctions, and an arbitrary number of layers in between. At the highest hierarchical level, functions are often equivalent to a domain, business division, or a life cycle stage, and describe primary function requirements. Functions with lower hierarchical positions are defined more precisely and represent the realization of upper nodes. The lowest-level functions are the elementary functions and cannot be broken down any further.[4] Figure 1.2 shows the concept of function trees for an enterprise.

3. William D. Samson, *History of Taxation* 21-41 (The International Taxation System 2002).
4. August-Wilhelm Scheer, *ARIS – Business Process Modeling* (Springer-Verlag Berlin Heidelberg 2000).

Figure 1.2 Exemplary Overview of the Function Modelling Approach[5]

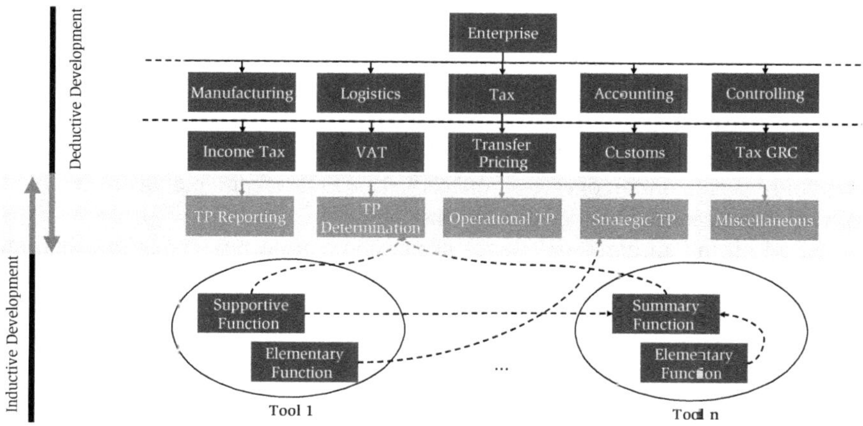

Source: Alexander Beuther & Peter Fettke, *Towards the Digital Transformation of Tax – Inductive Development of a Functional Reference Model for International Transfer Pricing* 3 (SIGASYS Pre-Workshop ICIS 2019)

3 MARKET OVERVIEW APPROACH

3.1 Structure

The identification of available solutions in the context of tax tech tool selection is currently a time-consuming and risky undertaking associated with vagueness. So far, hardly any comprehensive market overview is available that can be used both for an initial rough analysis and for a subsequent detailed investigation.[6] This particular contribution aims to fill that gap by pursuing the goal of providing an overview of tax tech tools from a functional and technical viewpoint. It is based on 102 tax-related tools or platforms of various sizes, namely in terms of users, geographical spread, and system size; 79 of the 102 tools studied are tax tools and 23 are tax platforms, which are analysed separately in section 6. This market overview focusses on the tax areas of value added tax (VAT), transfer pricing and (to a certain degree) customs, as well as solutions falling under the term 'tax platforms'. The period of research was from mid-2019 to early-2020. This market overview took the form of secondary research, performed using the internet and primary research (to a certain degree). The web-based research was conducted using publicly available information from company

5. Alexander Beuther & Peter Fettke, *Towards the Digital Transformation of Tax – Inductive Development of a Functional Reference Model for International Transfer Pricing* 3 (SIGASYS (Pre-Workshop ICIS) 2019).
6. PSP also provides a market overview about tax tech tools. It is more tool-based compared to this market overview, where the focus is more to provide a functional view: https://www.psp.eu/media/allgemein/tax-technology_markt-ueberblick.pdf (Accessed April 2021).

websites, brochures, manuals, and videos; the primary research took the form of information from conference contributions, conference stands, interviews and marketing materials. The assessment was performed by two researchers independently. This research method has both advantages and disadvantages: on the one hand, an open-source review can cover a large geographic area and a great number of tools and thus provide a relatively good overview of the current state-of-the-art as well as market developments; on the other hand, there is an element of subjectivity related the researchers themselves, something that cannot be avoided. Thus, the results obtained pertain only to this market overview and serve as a first screening of tax tech tools and platforms and should not be used in another context.

Based on the authors' experience of participating in tax-related projects, more than fifty-seven general (as opposed to company-specific) characteristics were identified for the selection of tools and technology applications. These characteristics were then compared with the functions available in the tools. The data about the individual characteristics can be found in the respective sections – *see* sections 3.2 and section 3.3.

A characteristic was either completely fulfilled or not fulfilled at all by the tool. While not all functions of a tool could be considered in the market overview, those functions that are directly tax-relevant were, indeed, considered. The focus of this market overview was to get an overview of the features described from a functional and technological perspective of the leading tax tech tools and platforms. Using the structured evaluation scheme described in Figure 1.3 and the defined characteristics allowed structured and consistent web searches to be performed. However, the data and information contained in this contribution are unverified, as the evaluation and assessment of the tools depended heavily on the quality and level of detail of the information provided about them.

Figure 1.3 Structured Evaluation Scheme for the Market Overview

[Name Software]	[Name Vendor]
Target Group	Sector Focus
System Size	
Basic information	
Software Type	
Market Position	
Tax Type	
Application Area	
Tax and technology-related information	
Tax Functions	
Technologies	
Trends	
Brief Description of the Software	
Vendor information	
Software Functionalities	
Address/Contact: Tel: Email: Web:	Business Type:

Source: Author's own research.

Each tool's information was captured and analysed according to the structured recording evaluation scheme depicted in Figure 1.3. Overall, the scheme consists of three sections: (1) basic information; (2) tax and technology-related information; and

(3) vendor information. Basic information and tax and technology-related information are described in sections 3.2-3.3.

3.2 Basic Information

Basic information gives a general overview of the application area of a tool. This includes target groups addressed, sectors focussed on, system size, software type, and market positions. These criteria help to categorize a tool according to general customer needs, as follows:

- *Target group* describes the type of users for which the tools are developed. Here, a distinction can be made between tax departments, consultants, and tax authorities. Even greater differentiation between the users would have been possible by defining users according to their roles – tax executives or tax managers, for example. However, the objective was to gain insights into the users and their interests in general.
- *Sector focus* describes the branch or industry in which the tool is applied.
- *System size* describes the capabilities of the tool. Suitable sub-criteria for system size are the volume of documents and master data that can be processed and the number of concurrent users.
- *Software type* helps to differentiate between generic tools, area-specific tools, and problem-specific tools. A differentiation between standard and customized tools as well as on-premises and cloud-based tools is also made.
- *Market position* determines a tool's uniqueness compared to its competitors. It includes the market penetration and market position of a tool. For example, the year in which a solution was first installed can be used to draw conclusions about its classification in the life cycle. Based on the year of market entry, the number of customers and the installation figures, initial conclusions and indications can be drawn about the development status and acceptance of the tool as well as the future growth potential of the provider. Furthermore, the market position is generally an appropriate way of assessing the geographical distribution and usage of the tool.

3.3 Tax and Technology-Related Information

Tax and technology-related information include the tax types, application areas, tax functions, technologies, and trends. The tax type describes the focus of the tool. The application area is a high-level categorization and is used to group capabilities that tools have in common. The tax function describes tasks that are addressed by the tax tech tool. Technologies cover those technologies currently used in the market and addressed by the current tool. Trends indicate upcoming technologies and technological developments that we will see in the (near) future and have emerged from the investigated tax tech tools. Figure 1.4 gives an overview of the tax and technology-related research fields (i.e., tax type, application area, etc.) and its criteria that describe the categories of each research field.

Figure 1.4 Overview of Tax and Technology-Related Research Fields and Criteria

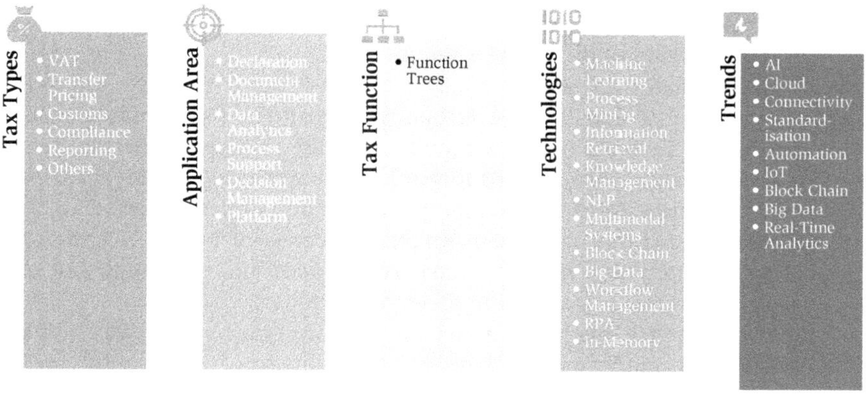

Source: Author's *own* research.

The remainder of this section provides a description of all investigation fields and their corresponding criteria, together with a brief definition of each

3.3.1 Tax Types

Tax types include all investigated types of taxation or closely related topics, as well as interdisciplinary topics. This includes VAT, transfer pricing, customs, tax compliance, and reporting, as well as other taxes that are not the focus of this market overview (examples of which are income tax or property tax). The reason for focussing on these tax types is the direct interaction between them.[7] For example, in the case of imports and materials, if an adjustment is made to transfer prices, the customs value and consequently the VAT assessment base also changes. A brief definition of each criteria of the aforementioned tax types follows:

- *VAT* is levied on supplies of goods and services for consideration. The basis for calculation is the invoiced amount that the recipient of the service must spend to receive the service. This means that tax is levied at all stages of the value chain. Through the so-called input tax deduction, a product or service remains completely tax free until it is delivered to the end customer. In this process, the VAT is set to zero at each stage and thus reimbursed to the company by the tax authorities.
- *Transfer pricing* occurs in multinational operating groups of companies of any size and which are subject to critical audits by local tax authorities. In tax terms, transfer prices are prices and conditions for cross-border business relationships between associated companies and between the head office and

7. Danny Beeton & Geo. Hopkins, *An Integrated Approach to Transfer Pricing, VAT and Customs Duty Planning* (Tax Planning International Transfer Pricing 2000).

permanent establishment. In other words, it is specifically about the value-added-adequate allocation of the tax substrate to the states involved in a transaction. However, the related tasks – the so-called transfer pricing management – comprise much more than the determination of the methodology or the preparation of the documentation.

- *Customs duties* are applied alongside import turnover tax to cross-border movements of goods. They are an instrument of foreign trade policy. A distinction is made between protection tariffs to protect selected domestic industries and punitive tariffs to ward off dumping and subsidy measures by third countries. Depending on the goods, customs duties are levied on units of a product (quantity, volume, mass) or a percentage of its value. The amount of duty is determined from the category of goods and the country of origin. Several national rules apply to the customs duties.
- *Tax compliance* refers to the establishment and maintenance of a system to ensure and comply with tax laws and requirements of the tax authorities. It is therefore better for companies to implement a system that functions, and to establish a corresponding organizational structure that complies with tax laws, takes advantage of tax structuring opportunities, and – at the same time – ensures the avoidance of risks for the company.
- *Reporting* includes all legally required reporting duties of a company and is mainly directed at addressees outside the company. A distinction is made between the two areas of declaration and reporting.

3.3.2 Application Areas

To categorize the tax tools, six areas of application were defined: declaration management, document management, data analysis, process management, decision management, and platform management/infrastructure. The goal was to gain an initial understanding of the level of coverage, and to identify those application areas that have received very little attention to date. A brief definition of each of the aforementioned areas of application follows:

- *Declaration management* describes solutions that help to prepare tax returns or other tax-related forms and documents more efficiently, accurately, or automatically. This includes, for example, the declaration of the content or value of a commercial or shipping good for the purpose of customs clearance.[8]
- *Document management* describes solutions for the database-supported management of electronic documents. Corresponding solutions include all functions for the management of tax-relevant documents (files), such as check-in/check-out functionality, versioning, editing, and organization of content.[9]

8. Margaret Cotton & Gregory Dark, *Use of Technology in Tax Administrations 2: Core Information Technology Systems in Tax Administrations* 1-13 (International Monetary Fund 2017).
9. Aleksei V. Azarkhin, *Problems of Digital Processing of Documents in Interaction Between Tax Relations Parties* 651-657 (Current Achievements, Challenges and Digital Chances of Knowledge Based Economy 2021).

- *Data analysis* describes solutions that derive new insights based on tax-related data and help to identify risks, errors, or inconsistencies in transaction and source data. For example, topics such as automated business document analysis (BDA) or anomaly detection fall under the scope of data analysis.[10]
- *Process support solutions* help to support the execution of a process by using technologies related to automation and data management to make the right information available to the right person at the right time and in the right place. Process support, thus, goes beyond the support of a single task. Examples of process support include the automated preparation of tax returns or advance VAT returns.
- *Decision management solutions* help to support all strategic, tactical, and operational activities and management tasks to enable an organization to make the best decisions in the long-term.
- *Platform management and infrastructure* describe solutions that ensure the interaction of individual solutions on a higher level. For example, they provide data, ensure a workflow, or form the infrastructure for the interaction between data and workflow. This also includes solutions that are based on existing solutions and provide additional functionalities (add-ons).[11]

3.3.3 Tax Functions

This criterion is used to collect information about the implemented functionalities within tax tech tools. Tax functions are structured and described according to the function trees as defined in section 2.

3.3.4 Technologies

The scope of the technologies investigated is based on the tax tech study conducted by the German Research Center for Artificial Intelligence (DFKI) and international tax advisory firm WTS in 2017.[12] Consequently, this study focusses on the following technologies: machine learning, process mining, information retrieval, knowledge management, natural language processing (NLP), multimodal systems, blockchain, big data, workflow management, robotic process automation (RPA), and in-memory database. However, the authors are aware that such a classification is in constant change. This means that the developed classification will not necessarily be fully relevant in the future, nor will all possible technologies be included in this classification. Furthermore, the criteria within the investigated field technologies are typically not disjunctive to each other. The criteria can be interpreted differently which leaves

10. Irish Mcintyre, *Data Analytics for Tax: A Primer* (Tax Executive, 69(1) 2017).
11. Mohanbir Sawhney, *Leveraged High-Variety Strategies: From Portfolio Thinking to Platform Thinking* 54-61 (Journal of the Academy of Marketing Science, 26(1) 1998).
12. Peter Fettke, Gerd Herzog, Johannes Lahann, Heiko Maus, Günter Neumann & Tim Niesen, Künstliche Intelligenz im Steuerbereich. Innovationsstudie zur Digitalisierung und den Potentialen Künstlicher Intelligenz im Bereich Steuer 1-96 (wts studie 2017).

some room for interpretation. A brief definition of each of the aforementioned technologies follows:

- *Machine learning* rests on the central idea of learning that starts with a rudimentary understanding of the world, generates experiences form events that occur, links them together, and thus gradually and continuously develops the machine's understanding of the world. Typical technologies are: classification, decision trees, regression analysis, logistic regression, support vector machines, autoencoders, and deep learning.[13]
- *Process mining* is a research discipline in the field of artificial intelligence (AI) that combines the areas of data mining and business process management.[14] It focusses on the systematic evaluation of large, process-aware data. The objective is the recognition of structures, correlations, and developments within the data.[15]
- *Information retrieval* uses different methods to the fields of AI and computational linguistics; the goal of information extraction is to construct systems that can specifically detect and structure domain-specific information from free texts, while at the same time 'reading over' irrelevant information.[16]
- *Knowledge management* describes several methods to manage and contribute the knowledge of both individuals and joint groups (e.g., business units). One major goal is the embedding of knowledge in processes for the realization of business process-oriented knowledge management. The knowledge base can be understood as all data and information, all knowledge, and all capabilities that the corresponding entity has or should have for solving its tasks. Examples are knowledge-based document analysis, semantic desktops, and case-based reasoning.[17]
- *NLP* is a branch of computer science and computational intelligence. In general, the term NLP is used as a generic term for different approaches, methods and techniques when it comes to processing natural language information with the help of a computer. This can range from text classification, machine translation and question-answering systems to complex deep

13. Peter Fettke, Gerd Herzog, Johannes Lahann, Heiko Maus, Günter Neumann & Tim Niesen, Künstliche Intelligenz im Steuerbereich. Innovationsstudie zur Digitalisierung und den Potentialen Künstlicher Intelligenz im Bereich Steuer 1-96 (wts studie 2017).
14. Wil M. van der Aalst, Hajo A. Reijers, Anton J. M. M. (Ton) Weijters, Boudewijn F. van Dongen, Ana K. Alvas de Medeiros, Minseok Song & Henricus M. W. (Eric) Verbeek, *Business Process Mining: An Industrial Application* 713-732 (Information Systems, 32(5) 2007).
15. Joerg Evermann, Jana-Rebecca Rehse & Peter Fettke, *Predicting Process Behaviour Using Deep Learning* 129-140 (Decision Support Systems, 100 2017), Nijat Mehdiyev, Joerg Evermann & Peter Fettke, *A Multi-Stage Deep Learning Approach for Business Process Event Prediction* 119-128 (IEEE 19th Conference on Business Informatics, 1 2017).
16. Harald Holz, Heiko Maus, Ansgar Bernardi & Oleg Rostanin, *From Lightweight, Proactive Information Delivery to Business Process-Oriented Knowledge Management* 101-127 (Journal of Universal Knowledge Management, 2 2005), Andreas R. Dengel, *Knowledge Technologies for the Social Semantic Desktop* 2-9 (International Conference on Knowledge Science, Engineering and Management 2007).
17. Uwe V. Riss, Alan Rickayzen, Heiko Maus & Wil M. van der Aalst, *Challenges for Business Process and Task Management* 77-100 (Journal of Universal Knowledge Management, 2 2005).

semantic and context-sensitive analysis to understand the semantics of the information given. The latter is also subsumed under the term 'natural language understanding' (NLU). For example, a user makes a request using text (input) to a chatbot, which then provides the most appropriate response to this request.[18]

- *Multimodal systems* are part of human-technology interaction where the use of special AI techniques aims to enable highly flexible user interfaces to make it easier for users to use the underlying IT-based systems. Multimodal systems include communication on all sensory levels, such as speech, eye movements, gestures, facial expressions, body posture, physical actions and biometrics. NLP, automatic speech recognition (ACR), and text to speech (TTS) also fall into the research area.[19]
- *Blockchain* describes the stringing together of transaction data records. Based on the three central building blocks (decentralization, cryptography, and the consensus-building model), the main goals in the use of blockchain technology are to verify data flows easily and to create transparency and security.
- *Big data technologies* encompass various technologies which focus on processing large quantities of data. The data structures usually vary, i.e., they can be structured, semi-structured, and unstructured. Due to the speed at which data is generated, there are additional requirements for processing and ensuring data quality in addition to the storage of this data, since it usually comes from different sources. With its focus not only on processing internal company data, but also on integrating data from external data sources to enrich the internal data, big data technologies go beyond traditional technologies such as standard technologies like relational or object-relational database management systems as well as data warehouse or reporting solutions.[20]
- *Workflow management* supports the modelling, simulation, execution, and monitoring of business processes at workflow-level. It allows to define, create, and manage the execution of workflows using a workflow engine. Such engines can interpret the process definition, organize the work according to the process participants, and, if necessary, orchestrate dedicated services from other distributed information systems.[21]

18. Lynette Hirschman & Rob Gaizauskas, *Natural Language Question Answering: The View from Here* 275-300 (Natural Language Engineering, 7(4) 2001).
19. Wolfgang Wahlster & Mark T. Maybury, *An Introduction to Intelligent User Interfaces* 1-13 (RUIU, San Francisco: Morgan Kaufmann 1998), Sharon Oviatt, Björn Schuller, Philip Cohen, Daniel Sonntag & Gerasimos Potamianos, *The Handbook of Multimodal-Multisensor Interfaces, Volume 1: Foundations, User Modeling, and Common Modality Combinations* (Morgan & Claypool 2017).
20. Vincenzo Morabito, *Big Data and Analytics. Strategic and Organisational Impacts* (Springer, 3rd ed. 2017).
21. Gregory Mentzas, Christos Halaris & Styliandos Kavadias, *Modelling Business Processes with Workflow Systems: An Evaluation of Alternative Approaches* 123-135 (International Journal of Information Management, 21(2) 2001).

- *RPA* is a technology that aims to automate 'highly repetitive and mindless' tasks.[22] In RPA, so-called software robots, acting as synthetic IT users, configure, manage, and automate highly repetitive, highly structured, high-volume tasks that require the use of existing IT systems. RPA technology provides a non-invasive alternative to coding automated business logic for simple processes in an application or service.
- *In-memory (computing)* refers to a database technology that stores data in random-access memory (RAM) rather than on hard disk drives. As a result, the higher data-access speed enables data to be processed much faster, often in real time.[23]

3.3.5 Trends

In the context of globalization and increasing digitalization, certain (global and emerging) technology and business trends can be observed, and this is also true of the tax tech environment. This overview examines to what extent the tools identified address the following trends: AI technologies, networking and connectivity, cloud computing, standardization, automation, internet of things (IoT), blockchain and smart contracts, big data, real-time analytics, and outsourcing.[24] A brief description of each of the aforementioned trends follows:

- *AI technologies*, in general, refer to technologies that attempt to emulate human-like intelligence, i.e., by building or programming a computer in such a way that it can process problems independently. As a subfield of computer science, the subject area of AI encompasses much more than purely computer science, and includes neuroscience, communication science, psychology, mathematics, and linguistics as well.[25]
- *Networking and connectivity:* Many buzzwords can be united under the term 'connectivity' – digitalization, IoT, and big data, to name but a few. Essentially, all of the above-mentioned trends pursue a similar goal, namely comprehensive networking based on modern internet and communication technologies. Connectivity, thus, describes the networking capabilities of electronic products, but also of people, companies, data, information, and other different entities within, for example, a business or industrial network.
- *Cloud computing* describes an approach in which an IT infrastructure (e.g., storage space or computing power) or application software is obtained from an

22. Constantin Houy, Marten Hamberg & Peter Fettke, *Robotic Process Automation in Public Administrations* 385-388 (Digitalisierung von Staat und Verwaltung 2011).
23. Hasso Plattner & Alexander Zeier, *In-Memory Data Management: Technology and Applications* (Springer Science & Business Media 2012).
24. Authors' own discretion of the 'trends' defined, in combination with Laurence Goasduff, *Top Trends on the Gartner Hype Cycle for Artificial Intelligence* (Gartner 2019), https://www.gartner.com/smarterwithgartner/top-trends-on-the-gartner-hype-cycle-for-artificial-intelligence-2019/.
25. Reid G. Smith & Joshua Eckroth, *Building AI Applications: Yesterday, Today, and Tomorrow* 6-22 (AI Magazine, 38(1) 2017).

external provider as a service via the internet. Often, the different types of service are subsumed under the term 'anything as a service' (XaaS).

- *Standardization* comprises all activities and measures to standardize processes or individual process steps according to predefined standards (e.g., ISO standards). Standardization is usually a prerequisite for automation through, for example, AI technologies.
- *Automation* refers to the ability of a system to perform certain tasks and activities through autonomous actions without human input or interaction to achieve a certain goal.
- *IoT* refers to a network of physical objects that incorporate embedded technologies (ubiquitous computing) to communicate and sense/interact with their internal states, or with the external environment.
- *Blockchain* describes technologies for exchanging data using a decentralized and distributed database. Blockchain is a network in which data is stored redundantly. In the blockchain itself, the data is written in 'blocks', which are interconnected in a constantly growing list. The most widespread application of blockchain is the cryptocurrency bitcoin.
- *Big data* is a way to describe mass data and refers to data volumes that are large, complex, and versatile. The term 'big data' subsumes methods and approaches to structure and process data. Within the field of tax tech, the term is often used together with 'tax data lakes'.
- *Real-time analytics* encompasses all technologies that enable all data and resources available in an organization to be analysed within seconds or minutes of the arrival of new data.[26] Well-known tools and technologies include Hadoop, Spark, and in-memory databases. In contrast to classic business intelligence approaches, real-time analyses involve a dynamic query and reporting process.
- *Outsourcing* generally refers to the outsourcing of individual activities or processes from an entity to an external entity.[27] According to the functional area to be supported (e.g., exemption certificate management), it encompasses the provision of the resources necessary for the execution of the tasks and the affected phases in the life cycle of the corresponding tasks (operation or monitoring, for example). In the context of this market overview, the focus is particularly on the resources, i.e., the underlying software and its range of functions (*see also* the description of cloud computing).

26. Laurence Goasduff, *Top Trends on the Gartner Hype Cycle for Artificial Intelligence* (Gartner 2019), https://www.gartner.com/smarterwithgartner/top-trends-on-the-gartner-hype-cycle-for-artificial-intelligence-2019/.
27. Randall C. Reid & Mario Pascalev, *Strategic and Ethical Issues in Outsourcing Information Technologies* 189-204 (Social Responsibility in the Information Age: Issues and Controversies 2002).

3.4 Tax Tool Search and Analysis Strategy

The tools that have been included in this market overview are tools produced by private companies of any size, but whose headquarters, significant development, and main distribution activities are in Europe. The selection process and the analysis can be summarized as follows:

- Tools were gathered from different public and private sources to create a longlist. 'Public sources' are commonly available information which include websites, brochures, manuals, videos, conference contributions, conference stands, and marketing materials. Private sources include networks and interviews (e.g., EY, Thomson Reuters). Public sources were primarily used to conduct this market overview. Information obtained from the authors' network mainly consisted of exchanging with the authors' project partners (e.g., WTS). Only a few interviews were performed, especially in the context of tax platforms.
- The market overview was conducted using a structured recording scheme (*see* section 3.1). This allowed the findings of the research to be presented clearly and in detail.
- The search for and identification of relevant tools continued throughout the entire market overview period (mid-2019 to early-2020).
- Every tool identified was placed on a longlist.
- The longlist was then split into two lists: one containing tools developed by large companies and another containing those developed by small and medium-sized companies.
- Each list was then analysed by the researchers independently.
- Each of the researchers peer-reviewed the results of the other. If the results were reproducible and transparent, the tool was then taken forward. This (re)search strategy resulted in 102 tax-related tools or platforms being identified: 79 tax tools (analysed further in sections 4.1-4.5) and 23 tax platforms (*see* section 6).

4 KEY FINDINGS

The key findings of the market overview about the tax tech tools are presented in sections 4.1-4.5 and are delineated according to the tax tech research fields and criteria as presented in section 3.3, namely according to tax types, application areas, tax functions, technologies, and trends. Each section starts with a quantitative analysis and is followed by a qualitative analysis. As previously stated, the aim of this study is to give a brief overview of the market as a whole; its purpose is not to provide a detailed description of each tool. Each tool can be assigned to multiple criteria, so the sum of all tools to criteria can exceed the total number of tools. This section does not include tax platforms, which are addressed in section 6.

4.1 Key Findings by Tax Type

Figure 1.5 shows the distribution of tax types: all investigated tax tools can be assigned to at least one tax type. The area most addressed by the tools is tax compliance with forty-one tools (52%) meeting this criterion, which is also one of the more controversial topics within tax tech. The joint-second most addressed areas are VAT and reporting, each with thirty tools (38%). Another twenty-four tools (30%) address 'other' topics, mostly as additional services closely related to their main tax type. Transfer pricing tools are less common with just twelve of the tools identified (15%) addressing this tax type. The areas of reporting and tax compliance are interdisciplinary, and the tools aimed at these specific functions may therefore also address the VAT, transfer pricing, and customs tax types. Thus, their occurrence tends to be higher than the direct tax types.

Figure 1.5 Distribution of Tax Types

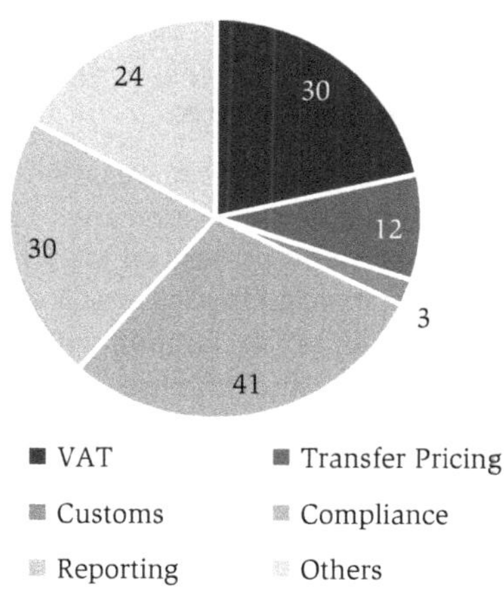

Source: Authors' own research.

Twice as many tax tools address the area of VAT compared to transfer pricing (thirty tools versus twelve tools respectively). System sizes range from small, single function tools (e.g., VAT ID checks) up to large, multi-function/complex tools, such as those that support processes end to end, like the purchase-to-pay process. Many VAT tools support the whole or part of the taxation process. Achieving an even higher level of process support, several tools have interfaces with common standard tools, or with e-commerce tools and platforms. Another focus is tax compliance for VAT, in particular cross-border transactions. Some VAT tools are part of bigger systems, which may also address the area of transfer pricing.

Transfer pricing tools are mostly part of bigger systems rather than stand-alone tools. Thus, there are only a few holistic transfer pricing suites which are enriched by some small, stand-alone tools, mostly used for documentation issues. Customs-specific tools were only partially focussed on within this market overview. Against this background, no representative information of the market and tools could be obtained.

Tax compliance is an issue that intersects with all tax types to some degree, even more so than reporting. Tax compliance includes rule checking, informing/warning those persons responsible for tax about violations, and mapping the compliance rules of different countries. Due to significant variations in compliance rules in different local areas, the tax tools addressing this issue are highly regionally adapted – take the considerable differences in tax risks in different countries, for example, the proactive risk control in Germany versus a more reactive documentation of occurred risks in Switzerland.

In summary, most of the tax tools identified address either one tax type (VAT, transfer pricing, or customs) or one specific task area (reporting or compliance). Thus, the tools studied are often isolated solutions to support dedicated functionalities. This might explain the organic development and increasing use of shadow IT within tax departments. In this vein, a move towards more integrated tools, often referred to as tax platforms, may thus be more desirable (*see* section 6).

4.2 Key Findings by Application Area

Figure 1.6 shows the distribution of application areas: seventy-seven out of seventy-nine tools can be assigned to at least one application area. The areas most addressed by the tools are those of data analytics and process support with fifty-three tools (67%) meeting these criteria. The second most addressed area is document management with thirty-eight tools (48%). The areas of tax declaration with thirty tools (38%), decision support with twenty-eight tools (35%), and infrastructure with twenty-five tools (32%) are all addressed by similar numbers of tools.

Figure 1.6 Distribution of Application Areas

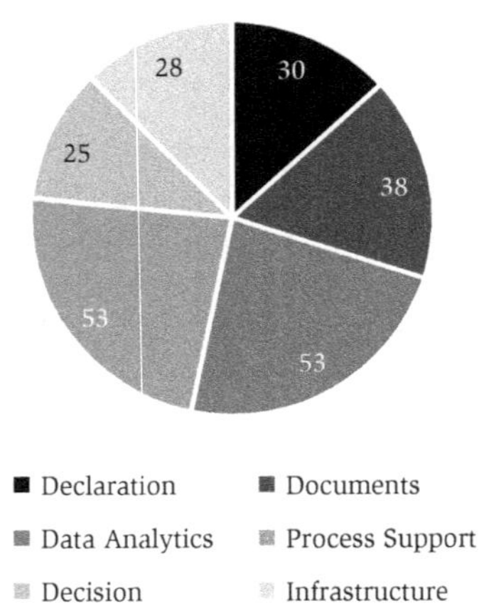

Source: Authors' own research.

The two application areas of data analytics and process support are by far the most diverse areas. Data analytics ranges from Excel analysis to advanced AI solutions. AI data analytics is often offered as separate apps and add-ons/expansions of tools. Process support ranges from the automation or acceleration of single tax processes by using workflow templates up to holistic solutions that enable tax departments to orchestrate services of the underlying information systems. However, also in this application area are many tools that provide support for dedicated tax-related functions. Regarding document management, there are solutions that provide a shared workspace for documents, as well as solutions where documents can be attached to to-do lists or tasks. In addition to the pure sharing of documents, repositories with forms and tax-relevant documents, including filing instructions and questionnaires, are also offered. Convenience features, such as intelligent search functions and roll-forward, try to set products apart from the competition. Declaration management supports or automates the filing workflows. It supports repetitive task like the file transformation and data transmission to and from tax authorities. Often, sources like tax balance sheets and manual questionnaires rather than operational data sources are used as input sources. Platforms focus on technology-independent solutions and micro services for specific tax issues. These are mostly provided in the form of services by consultancy firms. However, an integration into business tools' ecosystems is mostly not possible or requires huge integration efforts. This is also one of the main streams of tax tool solutions, and in-depth analysis and discussion is provided in section 6.

4.3 Key Findings Using Function Trees

For a better overview, this section distinguishes between the two tax types of VAT and transfer pricing, and integrates the two relevant interdisciplinary topics of tax compliance and reporting for each tax type. No functions for customs will be presented as it is not the focus of this study. The function trees for both VAT and transfer pricing are provided in Figures 1.8 and 1.10.

4.3.1 VAT Functions

To structure the functions and provide an appropriate framework, the researchers developed a VAT life cycle to order the functions in this field. As there is no commonly accepted VAT life cycle, a life cycle was assembled from different life cycles obtained from various companies and consultancy firms, for example, the Big Four (*see* Figure 1.7). These life cycle stages were used to allocate the functions of the investigated tools. The authors found a large intersection of deductively created life cycles and inductively assembled function trees. Both the theoretical and the practical life cycles were combined with the stages shown in Figure 1.7. They were put into a functional life cycle model which served as a reference point for deductive and inductive modelling.

Figure 1.7 VAT Life Cycle Stages

EY	VER TEX	TaxBPM	PWC	PWC	KPMG		VAT
Planning	Analytics		Strategy;	Analysis	Planning		Planning
Accounting	Determination	Calculation; Accounting	Accounting	Calculating	Accounting		Determination
			Tax Return	Filling			Declaration
		Report; Documentation				→	Reporting
Compliance	Compliance	Compliance	Compliance; Governance; Controls		Compliance;		Compliance
Controversy	Audit	Audit; Defence			Disputes		Audit
			Technology; Processes	Invoicing; Bookkeeping			Support

Source: Authors' own research.

The VAT function tree contains 120 functions (*see* Figure 1.8): one function is the field of VAT itself; six functions are the six life cycle stages as depicted in Figure 1.7; sixteen functions are high-level functions, which means that these functions consist of one or more subfunctions or elementary functions; ninety-seven functions are elementary functions. From the application view: eight functions are assigned to tax planning; thirty-one functions are assigned to VAT determination (which consists of twenty functions for VAT classification, two functions for VAT calculation, and six functions for VAT adjustments); thirteen functions are assigned to VAT declaration; fifteen functions are assigned to VAT reporting (which consists of nine functions for external VAT reporting, and four functions for internal VAT reporting); and a remarkable forty-five functions are assigned to VAT tax compliance (which consists of six functions for VAT risk monitoring, and fourteen functions for VAT risk management).

A summary follows for each life cycle stage. However, each stage can consist of a set of specific subfunctions. A short explanation of each stage is provided in Figure 1.8.

Figure 1.8 VAT Function Tree

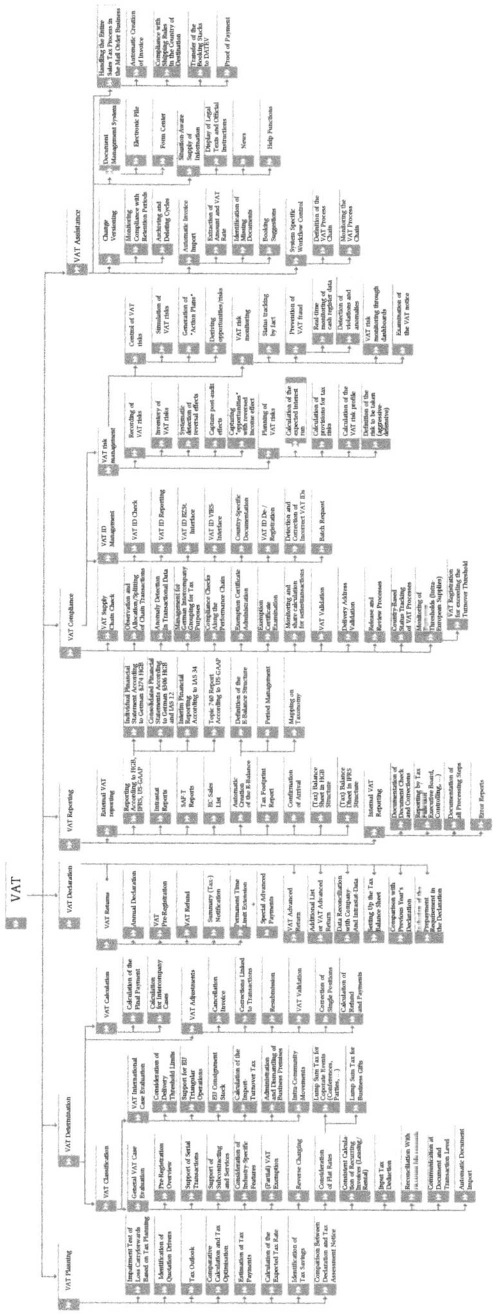

Source: Authors' own research.

- *VAT planning:* For VAT analysis, the tools provide overviews of specific issues and the identification of quota drivers. In addition to the analysis of the actual VAT situation, the forecasting supports the monitoring and planning of VAT processes. The impairment test of loss carry-forwards based on tax planning, a tax forecast, comparative calculation and tax optimization, calculation of the expected tax rate, and estimation of tax payments support companies in VAT decisions.
- *VAT determination:* When it comes to classification, it is important to determine the context of the transaction. Specific types of transactions must be considered, such as support for serial transactions, support for European Union (EU) triangular transactions, intra-Community movements, and the calculation of import VAT. Adjustments can be made in real time, and special cases (e.g., flat-rate tax) can also be recognized and considered retrospectively. Special businesses can also be considered, for example the consideration and dismantling of business premises, and so-called chargebacks. Regional 'features' can be handled, such as the calculation of (partial) sales tax exemptions in the United States and input tax deductions, where sales tax and not goods and services taxes (GST) is applicable.
- *VAT declaration*: Modern tax information systems cover many tasks related to the declaration processes. The main task is the VAT declaration itself, including VAT (pre-)registrations, VAT refunds, summary (tax) declarations, and the permanent extension of deadlines with their special advance payments. Various sub-tasks for VAT declaration exist - such as data processing and aggregation into a data format accepted by the government, taxable supplies, other services and unpaid VAT, tax-free supplies, supplementary information on turnover, and electronic transfer to the tax authorities - and support the main tasks.
- *VAT reporting:* External sales tax reporting supports the preparation of the annual financial statements. It shows the financial situation and the economic success of a company, and consists of a balance sheet and an income statement. On the one hand, the Intrastat declarations cover the statistical values and the European Community Sales List (ESL) report contains all transactions for imports and exports between the EU Member States. In the case of tax audits, on the other hand, the Standard Audit File for Tax (SAF-T) report is a specification of a machine-readable file for transmitting financial data to the tax authorities. The internal reporting system includes all reporting measures of a company that go beyond the required obligations. It is mainly aimed at internal company interests and consists of the documentation of internal processes, such as incoming inspection and corrections, as well as the documentation of all processing steps and error reports relevant to sales tax.
- *VAT compliance management*: One special topic in VAT compliance management is VAT ID management, which consists of VAT ID interfaces with the tax authorities and audits. Country-specific documentation, VAT ID (de-)registration, and the detection and automatic correction of invalid VAT IDs can also be considered. Other compliance tasks check correctness together

with workflows and supply chains. The detection of anomalies in transaction data and compliance checks together with the service chain directly or indirectly relate to transactions. Regional peculiarities are covered by the administration and checking of exemption certificates and the monitoring of sales thresholds.

- *VAT support:* The various functions are designed to support the VAT procedures within a company. On the one hand, there are solutions based on workflows, such as system-specific workflow control, which enables the VAT process chain to be defined and monitored. On the other hand, there are document-based solutions, such as document management systems (electronic files or form centres). There is also support for complete, end-to-end VAT process solutions in certain areas, especially for online transactions automatic invoice import. Besides, change versioning helps tax professionals monitor compliance and reproduce decisions.

4.3.2 *Transfer Pricing Functions*

Other than VAT, transfer pricing functions are oriented along the life cycle stages of transfer pricing: strategy and guidelines, operational transfer pricing, monitoring, documentation, and audit.[28] The audit stage also includes governance, risk, and compliance functions (*see* Figure 1.9).

Figure 1.9 Transfer Pricing Life Cycle

Source: Authors' own research.

Based on the life cycle, the transfer pricing function tree contains 127 functions (*see* Figure 1.10). From the top-level function (transfer pricing), five general functions are derived, namely 'Strategy & Guidelines', 'Operational Transfer Pricing', 'TP Documentation', 'TP Audit', and 'Transfer Pricing Miscellaneous'. Each function

28. Yair Holtzman & Paul Nagel, *An Introduction to Transfer Pricing* 57-61 (Journal of Management Development 33(1) 2014).

corresponds to one stage within the function tree. Different from the transfer pricing life cycle, 'monitoring' is a part of the 'operational transfer' pricing in the function tree. Additionally, 'transfer pricing miscellaneous' has been added as an own specialization in order to consider other, more unspecified, functions. The 121 functions left are elementary or 'lower-level' functions which concretize the top-level functions:

- *Strategy and guidelines*: 'Strategic transfer pricing' consists of not only preparing functions, like 'depicting enterprise structure' or 'definition of transfer pricing model', but also analytic tasks, like 'simulation of transfer prices on product level', 'simulation and comparison of transfer pricing strategies (intra-pricing strategies and operative structures)', or 'creation of internal transfer pricing guidelines'. It also subsumes planning tasks like 'tax optimization according to risk profile (aggressive/defensive)'. These functions are of a strategic nature and thus support experts within their decision-making process.
- *Operational transfer pricing:* The 'operational transfer pricing' can be further categorized into the functions 'pricing', 'monitoring', and 'adjustments'. Each of these functions also has different characteristics. For example, the function 'transfer pricing calculation' provides a logic for the selection of an appropriate method while it can consist of different subfunctions itself; the functions 'calculation of net margins' or 'transfer pricing benchmarks' are such subfunctions. While these functions are not elementary, they must be broken down to be applied to a concrete problem setting. 'Monitoring' describes the necessary functions for the operational execution of transfer pricing, such as the 'arm's length principle' and the 'adjustment of out-of-the-range prices'. It contains system-near-functions, such as 'real-time updated transfer pricing lists' and 'estimating the effects of transfer pricing adjustments'.
- *Documentation:* Documentation includes functions such as 'OECD documentation' with the specializations 'Master File', 'Local File', and 'country-by-country (CbC) reporting', or the 'automated data exchange with the tax authorities'. These functions follow the OECD (Organization for Economic Co-operation and Development) specification with its necessary documentation obligations. 'Master File', 'Local File', and 'CbC reporting' differ fundamentally in the data required, and thus in the underlying data and data preparation, but directly address the same business needs. Therefore, they belong to the same 'high-level' function. The automated information exchange with the tax authorities could be observed as an optional function, the existence of which depends on the technical implementation of other tax functions.
- *Audit:* This includes preventive measures to avoid tax audits as well as functions to support the tax-audit process. It is part of governance, risk, and compliance tasks for transfer pricing. It ensures that transfer prices comply with public and private guidelines, and warns relevant stakeholders when risks occur. It further supports tax audit by documenting the communication process with the tax authorities.

Figure 1.10 Transfer Pricing Function Tree

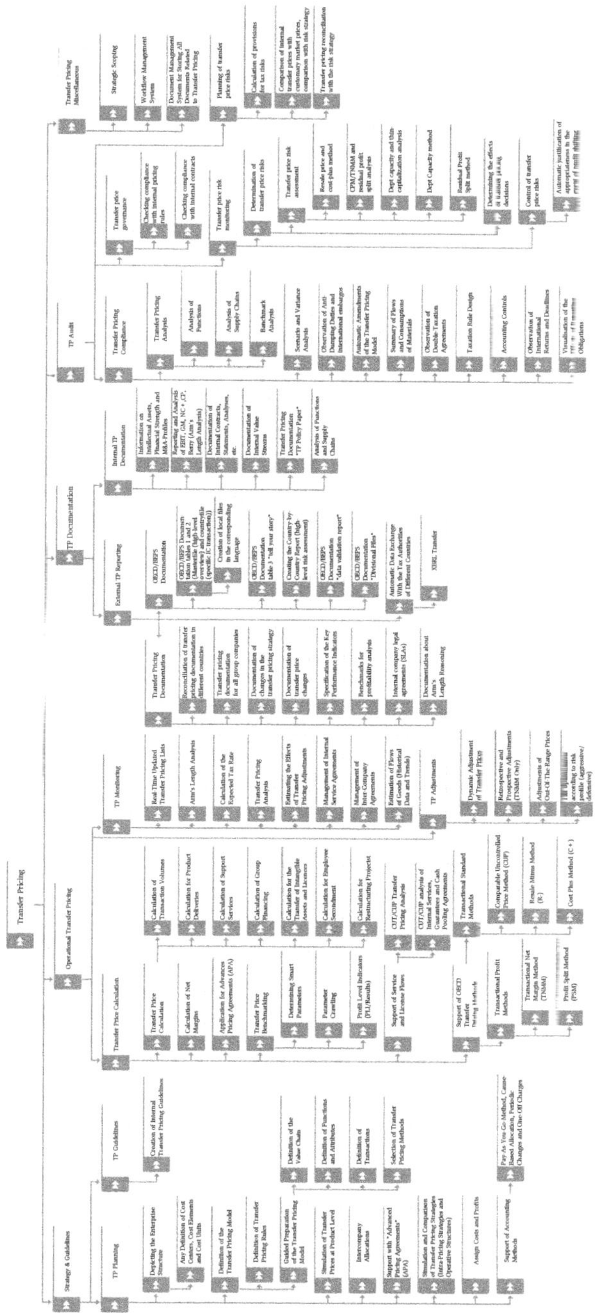

Source: Authors' own research.

4.4 Key Findings by Technology

Figure 1.11 shows the distribution of technologies: sixty-six out of seventy-nine tools can be assigned to at least one technology (*see* section 3.3 for a detailed list and description of the technologies considered, although the authors are aware that this list may not be completely comprehensive). The area most addressed is the area of information retrieval with forty-four tools (67%), followed by knowledge management and big data, each of which are addressed by twenty-nine tools (37%) respectively.

Figure 1.11 Distribution of Technologies

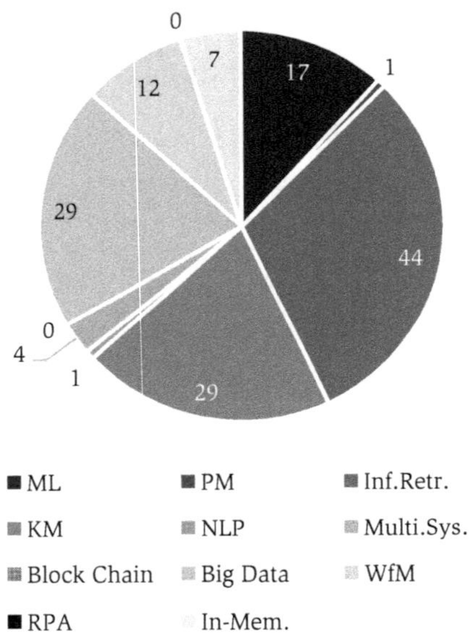

Source: Authors' own research.

It is not entirely surprising that information extraction, knowledge management, and big data are the technologies that are most addressed by the tax tech tools studied. This finding corresponds to the current situation tax departments find themselves in: as data from different corporate departments increasingly converge on tax departments, they are increasingly required to act as data hubs. Thus, tax departments serve more and more as data suppliers for both strategic and operational management within a company. Therefore, technologies that address data storage and processing - and currently trending topics such as data lakes - are in demand.

The next most common technologies addressed by the tools are machine learning with seventeen tools (26%), and workflow management with twelve tools (18%). Technologies such as in-memory computing seven tools (11%), multimodal systems four tools (2%), process mining one tool (1%), NLP one tool (1%), blockchain zero tools (0%), and RPA 0 tools (0%) do not feature as highly amongst the tools studied. However, many of these areas could well be classed as 'future trends', as is the case of 'automation', for example, combining RPA and workflow management (*see* section 4.5).

Information retrieval and data integration functionalities addresses problems of data transfer between different information systems and tax tools. The main application areas are mapping data in two systems, providing additional (external) information for decision-making, and transferring data between different stakeholders using standardized transfer protocols. Advanced document management also belongs to this topic. Modern technology enriches documents with many collaboration features and knowledge management. However, currently most tools provide self-managed, standalone systems rather than globally connected central document databases. Progressive approaches often use cloud technologies as outsourcing tools, where raw data is transferred to tax consultants to support the outsourcing process.

Many tools provide some kind of workflow support. Typically, these implementations allow – based on predefined workflow templates – the execution of tasks, responsibilities, and resources. Such functionality can be compared to an 'advanced' to-do list.

Machine learning is used in modern tax tech solutions for advanced analytics. Most applications are classification problems in different forms, and application fields. However, due to the hype of machine learning, qualitative statements regarding implementations of concrete algorithms cannot be made at the time of analysis.

The assessment of technologies in standard applications is a challenging topic and cannot always be clarified beyond any doubt. The technical appraisal has been conducted by knowledge and belief. However, marketing materials often do not describe the technical aspects of a product in detail.

4.5 Key Findings by Trends

Figure 1.12 shows the distribution of trends. With trends, the authors subsume upcoming technology and application developments that emerge from current applications. In order to draw conclusions about future developments, an attempt has been made to map the tools to the predefined trends: Seventy-eight out of seventy-nine tools can be assigned to at least one trend. The area most addressed by the tools is automation with sixty tools (77%). Automation goes hand-in-hand with standardization, an area into which thirty-eight tools (48%) fall. The second most addressed area by the tools is connectivity, with forty-one tools (52%) addressing this area. Big data tools are less common with twenty-one of the tools identified (27%) addressing this trend, as are cloud computing tools with twenty (25%), AI tools with nineteen (24%), and real-time analytics tools with sixteen (20%). There were very few instances, or none at all, of tools which addressed the areas of IoT – just one tool (1%) – and blockchain – 0 tools (0%).

Figure 1.12 Distribution of Trends

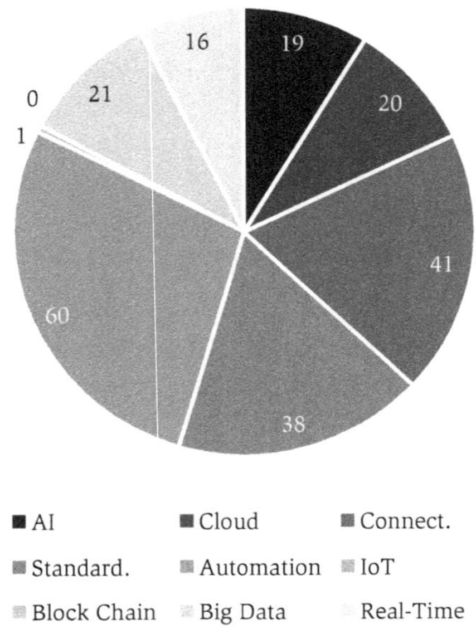

Source: Authors' own research.

Standardization and automation capabilities are important features of modern tools. Almost every tool addresses at least one aspect of these areas. While these trends seem to be relevant for tax departments, the authors have observed that many tools focus on special tax issues; often, this leads to an isolated operational use. In parallel, standardization is becoming more relevant and enables greater end-to-end process support. However, there are not yet many tools that provide this specifically in the field of taxation.

Connectivity features also occur quite often. The aim of this feature is to assist collaboration within businesses, and communication between clients and consultants. Connectivity capabilities include features such as structured and maintained document exchange, topic-related chat possibilities, structured and unstructured data exchange, and company-wide integration of information systems and processes.

Cloud computing is another significant trend. It can be used, for example, as an interface to enable an entire tax department to be outsourced, for data and document sharing for collaboration purposes, and to facilitate externally maintained information centres for tax-relevant information. AI is certainly an upcoming trend and is mostly used for advanced analysis tasks, such as for information extraction, analysis, and operational data analytics, amongst other things. AI for information extraction maps facts to requirements and enables a more flexible connection between systems. The trends of IoT and blockchain are not currently widely addressed by tax tech tools.

5 COMBINED VIEWS

By providing combined views of the various criteria used in this study, the authors have attempted to derive new insights. The following combinations have been used and are elaborated on in sections 5.1-5.4: technology and tax type; technology and application area; application area and tax type; trend and tax type.

5.1 Technology and Tax Type

Figure 1.13 shows the investigated technologies in its rows and the tax types in its columns. The technologies used in the tools for (the various) aspects of transfer pricing are worth highlighting; these tools use machine learning, information retrieval, and knowledge management to assist in the assessment of complex transfer pricing cases. This includes, first, advanced data and information storage, and, second, an adaptive and flexible ecosystem for making and documenting international transfer prices. Another remarkable number exists for machine learning, information retrieval, knowledge management, and big data technologies in the field of tax compliance systems. In this area, anomaly detection and pattern recognition in particular have a broad field of application. It is also interesting to observe that some emerging technologies, such as blockchain and RPA, do not play a role in modern tax tech solutions. Further, the investigated tools do not primarily support process-based analytics and workflows. There are some stand-alone and next-level applications that do use these technologies, but these are currently under development and not yet market-ready. NLP and multimodal system technologies are more present than the aforementioned emerging technologies, but they are still rare and only occur in very specific situations. Another point worthy of note in this combined view of technology and tax type is how many machine learning use cases there are in tax compliance, such as detecting anomalies in transactional tax data, or analytics capabilities like tax code prediction, tax forecasts, and questioning and answer systems. Due to the analytical nature of these tools, machine learning can have huge benefits, as using this technology can lead to greater instances of detecting anomalies and recognizing suspicious patterns in data, and it can also assist in processing huge amounts of data. However, explainability and traceability are wide issues in these technologies, that become more critical in future from a technological as well as a business perspective. Solutions for these issues are addressed under the term 'explainable artificial intelligence' (XAI). XAI describes a new research field that deals with different approaches and techniques to explain the behaviour of developed AI models. With its focus to provide transparency and trust concerns, decisions made by algorithms are made traceable for the users. [29]

29. Amina Adadi & Mohammed Berrada, *Peeking Inside the Black Box: A Survey on Explainable Artificial Intelligence (XAI)* 52138-52160 (IEEE Access 2018).

Figure 1.13 Technology and Tax Types

	VAT	TP	Customs	Tax Compliance	Reporting	Other
Machine Learning	3	4	1	12	2	5
Process Mining	0	0	0	0	0	0
Information Retrieval	5	4	1	14	2	7
Knowledge Management	4	3	1	10	0	3
NLP	1	0	0	2	1	1
Multimodal Systems	1	0	0	1	1	0
Blockchain	0	0	0	0	0	0
Big Data	12	6	5	24	5	7
WFM	2	4	1	7	0	2
RPA	0	0	0	0	0	0
Real-Time Analytics	0	1	0	3	1	1

Source: Authors' own research.

5.2 Technology and Application Area

Figure 1.14 shows the investigated technologies in its rows and the application areas in its columns. The diagram shows that document management is enriched by information-related technologies like information retrieval, knowledge management, and big data. This shows the development from simple document management towards smart document repositories with lots of additional features like document recognition and information extraction to allow forecasts and diligence. This effort is highlighted by the high number of workflow management technologies in this field, which further allow an intelligent processing of documents with document sharing, status tracking, and task processing. In particular, workflow management also includes collaboration features. The number of data analytics tools that use machine learning technologies is particularly interesting, as is the number of machine learning technologies used for decision management. Both application areas – data analytics and decision management – are closely related, as analytics forms the basis for decision-making. Further, there is a (weak) relation between machine learning and NLP. Some of the advanced analytics capabilities for decision-making use NLP, for example for the analysis of texts or other unstructured data. However, the number of data analytics tools that use machine learning is almost four times higher than in real-time analytics tools. Most current tools are more retrograde or real-time oriented, which implies further analysis of the past instead of proactive analysis.

Figure 1.14 Technology and Application Area

	Declaration Management	Document Management	Data Analytics	Process Support	Decision Management	Platform/ Infrastructure
Machine Learning	3	5	15	8	1[illegible]	7
Process Mining	0	0	0	0	0	0
Information Retrieval	2	8	17	8	10	6
Knowledge Management	2	8	11	9	8	6
NLP	0	1	2	1	2	0
Multimodal Systems	0	0	1	1	1	0
Blockchain	0	0	0	0	0	0
Big Data	7	11	30	19	17	12
WFM	6	8	8	10	[illegible]	5
RPA	0	0	0	0	0	0
Real-Time Analytics	0	2	4	1	2	4

Source: Authors' own research.

5.3 Application Area and Tax Types

Figure 1.15 shows the investigated application areas in its rows and the tax types in its columns. The most found application area is data analytics: it plays a major role in all tools and application areas. Analytics are strengthened by new technologies to make analysis more precise and predictions more reliable. As data and knowledge is traded as the 'new gold', it is obvious why analytics plays a major role in modern tools. Especially in the taxation field, the most precise knowledge about business events results in the most benefits. Another universal application present in all taxation areas is process support. Process support allows to manage, maintain, and monitor workflows: workflows can be automated by tools, and these technologies therefore allow end-to-end process support. The individual setting up of task-specific workflow templates is also possible, such as for the orchestration of dedicated services using more complex tools like business process management suites. Unexpectedly, low numbers are found for declaration management. One possible reason could be the focus of this market overview being on new, highly sophisticated tools, only in the field of taxation; tools for filing are often not as sophisticated or as technologically supported as other areas of application.

Figure 1.15 Application Area and Tax Types

	VAT	TP	Customs	Tax Compliance	Reporting	Others
Declaration Management	4	3	1	6	1	1
Document Management	5	5	1	12	1	5
Data Analytics	14	7	4	29	5	10
Process Support	11	7	2	18	4	5
Decision Management	8	3	3	19	3	6
Platform/Infrastructure	7	3	3	11	1	3

Source: Authors' own research.

5.4 Trends and Tax Types

Figure 1.16 shows the aforementioned trends in its rows and the tax types in its columns. As previously mentioned in section 5.1, tax compliance is an interface topic and addresses VAT, transfer pricing, and customs equally. Thus, these numbers are higher, and remarkably so. Big data, information retrieval, and knowledge management have applications in all tax types. As the buzzword 'tax data lake' illustrates, tax tech is highly influenced by big data. All of these technologies should streamline the data flow and the information gathering that is necessary every time information is available in order to process tax-relevant tasks and make reliable tax decisions. There is a high number of customs tools that use connectivity technologies. One reason is that customs brings many national and international stakeholders together. Customs tools provide several interfaces to several portals of these stakeholders. Another high number can be identified between VAT and automation. These are tools that automate the invoicing process via standardized interfaces with seller platforms, such as Amazon or eBay.

Figure 1.16 Trends and Tax Types

	VAT	TP	Customs	Tax Compliance	Reporting	Others
AI	5	2	1	14	3	5
Connectivity	5	2	4	14	1	7
Cloud	4	5	1	8	0	2
Standardization	5	6	3	13	2	5
Automation	15	7	4	26	5	9
Internet of Things	0	0	0	1	0	0
Blockchain	0	0	0	0	0	0
Big Data	10	6	4	25	5	8
In-Memory	4	2	2	12	[illegible]	4
Outsourcing	1	0	0	1	[illegible]	0

Source: Authors' own research.

6 HOT TOPIC – TAX PLATFORMS

During this market overview, the authors have identified a shift towards tax platforms. A result of the increasing process orientation within tax departments, a tax platform is a framework that consists of a set of functions that support tax departments in an end-to-end manner. Implementing a tax platform requires both standardizations and a reorganization of IT and the tax department within a company. However, the terms 'design' and 'scope' regarding tax platforms do not have precise definitions and can mean different things to different stakeholders, as can the term 'platform'. Stakeholders of such platforms include tax departments, tax consultancies, and tax authorities. The different interpretations of these terms result from their vagueness, not to mention the different expectations of the different stakeholders. The end users also all have their own individual needs and requirements. For tax departments, for example, these can include the monitoring and status tracking of documents and workflows in relation to deadlines. Tax consultancies focus more on the provision and orchestration of services related to the needs of the customer. On the other side are tax authorities, whose needs, requirements, and expectations, and therefore interpretations of these terms, deviate significantly: for tax authorities, a 'platform' is a collection of component technologies that forms a reliable infrastructure from which authorities operate and monitor their online tax services. In general, the terms 'tax platform', 'tax centre', 'tax engine', 'tax portal', and 'tax suite' are often used synonymously. In this context, the terms 'tax manager', 'global', 'one', or 'source' within the tool's name often suggest that it could be a tax platform. What all these various terms imply is that they all address issues that are made accessible at a central location (e.g., through a web portal). Such issues are, for example, the provision of dedicated functions and services, but also an IT infrastructure required for the development of new services (e.g., by linkage of data and business departments). In the following, an overview of the characteristics pertains to tax platforms and how they enable stakeholders to fulfil their tax-related tasks is provided. They are often realized by different components and are provided as microservices (modularity). They:

- allow for global cooperation and exchange of information between stakeholders;
- provide intra and inter-company process support;
- allow for the integration of internal resources (data, people, functions); and
- facilitate service orchestration (e.g., workflow management systems).

Figure 1.17 Capabilities of a Tax Platform

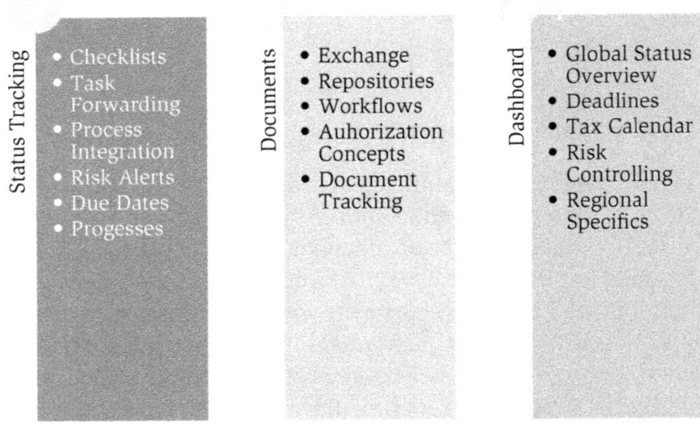

Source: Authors' own research.

Based on the market overview, the authors derived typical characteristics and requirements a tax platform should address. An overview is provided in Figure 1.17. While this was done from a functional-oriented perspective (tax department's view), a more detailed list of potential functions and features from a technological perspective is provided in Table 1.1. In this context, functions describe tasks that belong together, while features describe special technical possibilities provided to the user by the platform. Table 1.1 is neither complete nor covers all functions, as it relies on publicly available information and subjective understanding. However, it does provide a broad overview of a tax platform's potential functionalities.

By means of summary, tax platform designs range from technical, simple, and isolated 'Excel-based' tools, to dedicated tools – referred to as 'smart helpers' – right up to complex tax platforms. While Excel-based tools refer to simple data transformation and monitoring tasks that are used in an ad-hoc manner, 'smart helpers' offer more, but very specific, functionalities for particular tax-related tasks. For example, this could be a simple workflow for capturing information (like questionnaires) or collaboration features. Tax platforms refer to all kinds of information systems that not only address the prior connectivity function but also logical functions, such as tax calculation, monitoring, or the validation of information. As tax platforms provide a set of dedicated tax services, processes within tax departments should thus be supported end to end.

Table 1.1 Overview of Tax Platform Functions and Features

Category	*Functions and Features*
Workflow management	Definition of compliance and consulting tasks Tracking of compliance and consulting tasks Hierarchization (via sub-tasks) Progress tracking (via checked sub-tasks) Audit management Rule-driven workflow management Cross-process and cross-department collaboration Interactive to-do lists Workflow visualizations
Questionnaires	Gather or exchange semi-structured information with clients
Document management and exchange/shared data pool	Cloud computing (e.g., Microsoft Azure) Document status and (proposed) next actions Tagging of files and documents Assignment of metadata (region, entity, due date, status, period, compliance type) Sorting and filtering (direct tax, indirect tax, other) Multimedia storage Folders and data rooms/drawer principle Change report tracker Role and user concept Report/document generation
Knowledge management	Capturing, organization, storage, and sharing of relevant information Providing links to company policies, intranet, etc. 'App store' for extensions
Connectivity/ collaboration	Allocation of responsibilities Correspondence module (communication with the tax authorities) Historization of correspondence and document management Workspaces for collaboration with colleagues and advisers
Real-time notifications	New content alerts Timely messages

Category	*Functions and Features*
Data visualization and analytics	Filtering by jurisdiction, process, and year Online analytical processing (OLAP) capabilities (e.g., PowerBI) Tailorable interface to preference and usage parameters Functional and regional groupings and segregation Multi-year comparisons for variance and trend analysis Analysis of the profit effects of risks Assessment of risks according to probability of occurrence and impact on earnings
Status tracking	Different statuses (draft, in progress, review, completed, overdue) Flags for immediate review Tax codes
Location-based calendar	Gathering of travel information Allocation of time spent on projects
Due tracking/deadline checking	Automatic population of various compliance due dates for every entity Automatic sync of due dates Generation of workflows from due dates Urgency flags for documents Milestone concepts
Process integration	Determination and completion of the required forms for transactions Within collaboration platforms, completion and review of various input fields in the form by stakeholders Automatic data storage and reuse
Secure online access	Server-based access Mobile apps Web apps
Tax rule engine	Calculation of deferred taxes Report generator Mapping between key figures and form fields Transparency related to data origin in tax forms Account-specific mapping of the tax data to the taxonomy Automatic filling of master data Automated data transfer from different external modules (e.g., SAP MM/FI/CO or consolidation feeder systems) Data validation

Source: Authors' own research.

7 CONCLUSION AND OUTLOOK

The willingness of companies to invest in information technologies depends in general on the return on invest. Today, no organization is effective or efficient without information systems. The efficient and effective implementation of processes is taking on an increasingly important role, even for tax departments. The thesis that successful business processes require the use of such modern tax tech tools forms the foundation of this chapter. At the same time, it was the reason for creating an overview about the current tools on the market and their functionalities. As this market overview has shown, there are many heterogenous tools and solution providers. In the past, IT solutions were derived based on individual needs and were implemented independently from the other business areas. Investment in individual tools as stand-alone solutions was standard. Nowadays, as a result of the increasing complexity in taxation as well as increasing data volumes, a change of thinking from a functional-oriented view towards an integrated process-oriented view can be observed. This trend is also reflected in the market's shift towards tax platforms.

The increasing digitalization of the tax area, as well as economization and globalization, will create new kinds of demands on systems that are currently only in their initial stages. The tax platforms currently provided by companies indicate that there will be a breakthrough in communication between the stakeholders. The most important thing is to use well thought-out concepts and not to immediately find a solution to a problem that becomes obsolete when another problem of the same kind arises. Modern tax tech tools make a valuable contribution to companies and address both challenges of profitability and of knowledge accessibility.

CHAPTER 2

Digital Tax Administration 4.0: Towards a Distributed Tax System

Dennis Post

1 INTRODUCTION

The digital revolution has impacted many individuals, countries, and regions, as well as sectors and industries. Where paper forms, faxes, and manual processes were common practice in most business processes up until two decades ago, it is exciting to see the enormous progress that has been made in, for example, supply chain and logistic processes, e-commerce, financial services, and the automotive sector by using and implementing advanced technologies. Although the world of tax law and tax economics is not necessarily well known for its innovative nature and can, in most instances, be considered as quite conservative, the tax domain has been catching up rapidly over the last couple of years when it comes not only to using and implementing technologies such as robotic process automation (RPA) and artificial intelligence (AI) – including machine learning – but also statistical sampling and data analytics. And more importantly, these technologies have been used and further developed by both tax authorities and taxpayers. The use of technology to create more robust tax processes and, in some instances, even more robust tax systems is not only contributing to more efficiency and effectivity, but it has also led to an entire new academic field of play which can be caught under the umbrella of 'tax technology'. Over the course of the last years, new specialists have emerged in this very broad and yet specific field of play, and lots of opportunities for academic research have emerged and are in progress. Notwithstanding the tremendous opportunities that technologies like AI and RPA as well as data analytics and statistical analysis may bring to the field of taxation, personally this author is most passionate about the opportunities that blockchain and distributed ledger technology (DLT)[1] may bring for the tax practice. This chapter therefore explores and highlights the opportunities that this nascent technology may bring in several areas of taxation (including customs and trade). However, identifying the potential opportunities is most likely the easiest part. Looking at the general aspects and benefits of DLT, like tamper-proof transactions, coding tax legislation into smart contracts, transparency, and trust, it is obvious from the outset that the DLT and tax jointly make a compelling case for more robustness when it comes to developing tax systems and processes. The complexity kicks in when a deeper look is being taken at some of the other aspects of DLT, like the governance framework, the approval mechanisms surrounding blockchains, privacy preserving aspects as well as the nature of the ecosystem (e.g., private versus public). And let us not forget unbiased, transparent algorithms, and smart contracts and identity management. Further, the taxation of crypto-assets or 'virtual currencies'[2] has become so increasingly complex, from both a (tax) technical perspective and a tax policy perspective, it can be considered as a specialism on its own. With several disparities between countries occurring in terms of terminology and nomenclature, the unclarity around the tax treatment of certain transactions like 'hard forks' and 'air drops' as well as the tax treatment surrounding the taxation of, for example, utility tokens versus payment tokens versus security tokens provide for a cocktail of complexity which by default is of an interdisciplinary nature. This implies that tax professionals need to understand how the underlying technology works in order to understand the potential nuances when it comes to taxation of these virtual currencies. Lastly, we should also keep in mind that there is a clear trend emerging where not only countries but also supranational organizations like the European Union (EU) have expressed interest in implementing a digital currency, typically referenced as a central bank digital currency (CBDC). This is a trend that seems to be driven by and can be regarded as a response to the ambitious initiative from the Diem Association to implement such a digital currency.[3] CBDCs seem to have some great potential when it comes to 'programmable tax', i.e., the programming of tax aspects into the code base of these digital currencies. Does anybody still think that tax is boring?

This chapter contains the following items. Section 2 briefly discusses the current state of tax technology, the recently published report from the Organisation for Economic Co-operation and Development (OECD) on Tax Administration 3.0, and the potential impact this may have on tax administrations and taxpayers. From that point on, it is a nice pivot into looking at the future potential of blockchain and DLT for the world of tax. After a brief explanation of the key aspects of blockchain and DLT, the

1. A blockchain is a form of distributed ledger, but not all distributed ledgers are blockchains. For the sake of simplicity, the terms 'blockchain' and 'distributed ledger technology' (DLT) will be used interchangeably in this chapter.
2. The term 'virtual currencies' is also used by the OECD in its report on taxing virtual currencies, which will be discussed in section 5. For the sake of consistency, this chapter will also use this terminology. However, in some instances, reference is also made to crypto-currencies, (utility and security) tokens as well as to digital assets or digital tokens.
3. The Diem Association was previously named the Libra Association and is an initiative from Facebook, albeit one that seems to operate (somewhat) independently from Facebook currently.

potential areas of attention when it comes to tax will be discussed in section 3. Section 4 will then address how DLT can contribute to creating more robust tax systems and some of the potential use cases that we will likely see emerge in the world of tax will be discussed, including the potential emergence of 'programmable tax' into CBDCs. This section cannot ignore addressing some of the key challenges when it comes to developing these distributed tax networks, such as governance, quality and privacy of data, transparency, and the role of governments and supranational organizations in setting up these networks. Section 5 will go into some of the aspects of taxing virtual currencies. This chapter ends with some closing remarks in section 6 on the future direction of where this author believes these interesting developments may go. As indicated, the topics discussed are by default interdisciplinary in their nature. This brings both limitations and opportunities. There are limitations, as it would be difficult to understand the potential tax implications around DLT if one does not grasp (at least to a certain extent) what the underlying technology entails. It is therefore necessary to briefly discuss some of these (technical) features of the technology before diving into the potential tax aspects thereof. And there are opportunities, as those who are able to understand the features of the underlying technology will also be able to understand and explore the opportunities that the technology can bring. The interdisciplinary nature of this chapter also has the unavoidable consequence that it is by no means meant to be exhaustive; rather, it aims to serve as a good point for future reference and academic research when it comes to the tax aspects of blockchain and DLT.

2 THE CURRENT STATE OF TAX TECHNOLOGY IN VIEW OF (DIGITAL) TAX ADMINISTRATION 3.0[4]

As indicated in section 1, it is exciting to see that more and more tax professionals, in both the private and public sectors, are using technology to improve and enhance tax processes. Whether it is data analytics, statistical sampling, visualization by means of dashboards, or advanced machine learning to potentially detect anomalies or tax fraud, generally the last couple of years have demonstrated that advanced technologies are also disrupting the tax function. Generally speaking, tax processes are becoming more and more integrated with the business processes (as they should be), and tax has also become a boardroom topic. Suffice to say that the OECD's Base Erosion and Profit Shifting (BEPS) Project has largely contributed to this. In addition, the challenges around the taxation of the digital economy have proven to be some of the most complex issues to solve not only in terms of trying to obtain consensus within the OECD, but also in terms of the technical aspects of the taxation itself. It seems that the OECD is set to reach an agreement in this important area later this year with its initiative around Pillar One: Tax Challenges Arising from Digitalisation.[5] Undoubtedly, this will lead to

4. The term 'Digital' is added here considering that this author believes this is better reflecting the actual content of the document which is clearly focussed around the digitalization of tax processes.
5. *See*, for example, the Blueprint document on Pillar One, published on 14 October 2020, https://www.oecd.org/tax/beps/tax-challenges-arising-from-digitalisation-report-on-pillar-one blueprint-beba0634-en.htm.

new legislation in this area. For tax professionals, this also requires the obtention of more insights into understanding the underlying business models of the digital economy.

However, there is more happening in the world of digital tax. On 8 December 2020, the Forum on Tax Administration published its report *Tax Administration 3.0: The Digital Transformation of Tax Administration.*[6] The document contains truly valuable insights into tax authorities' perspectives on the future of tax administration. It also highlights the changes occurring in the world through the increasing digitalization of the economy and of society in general.[7] This calls for a new model of tax administration which is called Tax Administration 3.0. In this model, tax administration processes are increasingly built into the natural systems used by taxpayers in their daily lives and businesses, which allows for the automation of many aspects of tax administration not only to (ultimately) reduce the administrative burden of taxation, but also to acknowledge and adhere to an ever-changing society built around digitization. It is this author's view that the report correctly states that an important precursor to wider connectivity between the private and public sectors will be reinforcing trust in the use of data and in the security of national systems.

It is therefore surprising and also a bit disappointing to see that the report only makes implicit reference to the use of blockchain technology to create more robust tax systems. This could imply that either tax authorities are not yet ready to start thinking about the opportunities that blockchain technology can bring, or that that they fail to understand the potential benefits. In this author's opinion, both arguments are not necessarily convincing. Governments in general are starting to not only experiment but also implement blockchain technology in several of their underlying processes, so there is no particular reason why this could not be expanded to (some) tax processes as well. Furthermore, even though not everybody may be capable of grasping all potential benefits of blockchain technology, it is quite obvious that increased trust in the data, reduction of administrative costs, tamper-proof transactions, and increased transparency provide for a compelling case (if not a no-brainer) for the combination of blockchain technology and tax.

The implicit reference to the use of blockchain technology in the report can, in this author's view, be read in the key chapter of the report, Chapter 4. Chapter 4 contains the building blocks of Tax Administration 3.0 that have been identified. The building blocks are the following:

- Building Block 1: Digital identity;
- Building Block 2: Taxpayer touchpoints;
- Building Block 3: Data management and standards;
- Building Block 4: Tax rule management and application;
- Building Block 5: New skill sets; and
- Building Block 6: Governance frameworks.

6. OECD (2020), Tax Administration 3.0: The Digital Transformation of Tax Administration, OECD, Paris, http://www.oecd.org/tax/forum-on-tax-administration/publications-and-products/tax-administration-3-0-the-digital-transformation-of-tax-administration.htm.
7. *See* p. 3 of the report.

One could say that some, if not all, of these building blocks are also relevant when it comes to implementing a blockchain system for tax. And in this author's view they are. Therefore, it is even more surprising that no direct reference is made to DLT or blockchain technology. This is even more striking when a further look is taken at Annex B of the report, which is called 'Technology Trends in the Digital Era'. There is no reference at all to DLT or blockchain technology as a technology trend.[8]

In view of the above, and notwithstanding some of the great conclusions of the report, this author believes the time is right to also bring blockchain technology and DLT into the tax equation. This author would like to call this: Digital Tax Administration 4.0 with a clear emphasis on the word 'Digital'. And for this author, there is no question that Digital Tax Administration 4.0 is just a matter of time.

3 KEY ASPECTS OF BLOCKCHAIN AND DLT AND THE RELEVANCE FOR TAX

3.1 Blockchain as a General-Purpose Technology

It is far beyond the scope of this chapter to dive extensively into all relevant aspects of blockchain technology.[9] Nevertheless, it is helpful to briefly touch upon some of the key aspects of the technology to understand the relevance for tax. Blockchain technology can generally be described as a decentralized ledger or a special kind of database where all transactions in an ecosystem are being recorded. As a consequence, a decentralized exchange of trusted data can occur. Every participant in the blockchain ecosystem holds its own copy of all transactions, whereby these transactions are 'hashed', i.e., cryptographically secured to prevent fraud. After that, these transactions need to be approved on the blockchain based on a so-called consensus mechanism. Currently, the most commonly known consensus mechanisms are proof-of-work and proof-of-stake, but other mechanisms are also used and explored.[10] Proof-of-work can be described as a consensus mechanism whereby the participants on the blockchain have to solve a complex puzzle. If they manage to do so, the party that solves the puzzle gets a reward (e.g., a bitcoin). The proof-of-stake consensus mechanism is more focussed around the actual 'stake' a party holds in the particular blockchain. Generally, it can be stated that the more stake, the more influence such a party can influence in

8. One may explain this by stating that the trends mentioned in this Annex are not necessarily focussed on the technology itself. The trends identified came from the 2019 OECD report Measuring the Digital Transformation: A roadmap for the Future (OECD, 2019).
9. There are several good books on blockchain basics and the potential of the technology. This author recommends: D. Shrier, Basic Blockchain, Robinson Publishers, 2020; A. Davis / M. Le Merle, Blockchain Competitive Advantage, Fifth Era Media, 2019 and D. Furlonger / C. Uzureau, The Real Business of Blockchain, Harvard Business Review Press, 2019, for further reading. *See also* P. De Filippi / A. Wright, Blockchain and the Law, Harvard University Press, 2018, on the coherence between blockchain and law.
10. For further reference, *see*, for example, the whitepaper from A. Baliga, Understanding Blockchain Consensus Models, Persisent Systems Ltd., April 2017.

approving transactions.[11] Similar to, for example, electricity and the internet, blockchain technology is considered a general-purpose technology. This implies it has many potential use cases and can be applied in several ways.

In a so-called permissioned blockchain, only certain users may be able to approve a transaction, while in a 'permissionless blockchain' (like bitcoin) in principle anybody can approve a transaction, although for bitcoin currently only a selected group of parties is actually able to approve these transactions, given the significant computer power (and thus energy consumption) it takes to actually solve the complex underlying puzzles. A group of (proposed) transactions is included in a block which is connected to the previous block via a cryptographic code. As a consequence, an unbreakable[12] chain of transactions will arise: the blockchain.

In view of the relevance for tax, a very specific element of blockchain is most interesting: smart contracts. Smart contracts can be described as small, programmable lines of code or algorithms that can determine if, when, and how transactions are being processed. Therefore, to the extent that a particular tax process can be translated into an algorithm (along the lines of a so-called IF-THEN-ELSE-statement), there is also potential that this particular process may make up a good blockchain use case.

Considering the above, the key characteristics of blockchain can be summarized as follows:

- it is a safe peer-to-peer network;
- it is based on a shared network;
- it contains secure and verifiable transactions;
- cryptography is used to validate transactions;
- transactions are grouped in a block;
- cryptographic hashes connect the blocks, which leads to an unbreakable chain: the blockchain; and
- smart contracts may provide the specific conditions under which a transaction can be processed.

Consequently, the application of blockchain technology can provide benefits in one or more of the following situations, when:

- data that has to be stored centrally is only available on a fragmented basis;
- there are multiple parties in a complex ecosystem;
- there are multiple versions of the 'truth' (e.g., paper, PDF, fax, email);
- there is a lack of trust between parties transacting with each other; and/or
- there is a lack of security in transacting with each other.

11. It is expected that Ethereum 2.0 will be shifting from a proof-of-work consensus mechanism to a proof-of-work mechanism.
12. The cryptographic code used to connect blocks to each other is, in principle, considered to be practically unbreakable. However, this is not entirely certain. Potentially, with the expected rise of quantum computing in the next decade, it may very well be that cryptographic code becomes more vulnerable.

In a business environment, blockchain can typically address several of the typical business-process symptoms. For example, with blockchain, it is no longer necessary to use multiple databases for the same information. Also, there is less or no reconciliation necessary, and manual and paper processes are being reduced to a minimum. Operational and counterparty risks can be eliminated via algorithms built into smart contracts (e.g., tax can be paid directly, at the moment at which the debtor pays to the creditor). So considering the aforementioned points, it is very clear that connecting the benefits of blockchain technology with some of the typical and recurring elements in a tax process makes a compelling use case to be explored further.[13]

3.2 The Gartner Hype Cycle

In order to understand the potential that blockchain technology evidently has, it is imperative to understand a little bit more about the typical development process of nascent technology. This can best be explained by means of the so-called Gartner Hype Cycle.[14] The Gartner Hype Cycle is a graphic depiction of the expected development of new technologies, as shown in Figure 2.1.

Figure 2.1 Gartner Hype Cycle

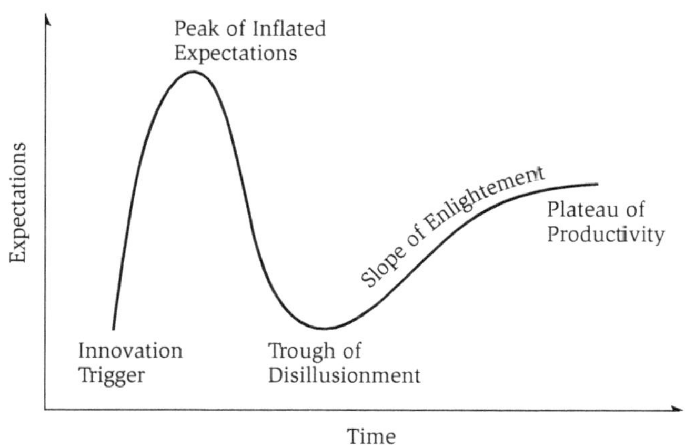

Source: Jackie Fenn & Mark Raskino, *Mastering the Hype Cycle: How to Choose the Right Innovation at the Right Time* (Boston Harvard Business Review Press, 2008).

13. It is fair to state that not everybody is necessarily convinced about the benefits of blockchain technology. Nouriel Roubini, a Professor of Economics from New York University's Stern School of Business, is one of the most profound critics of blockchain technology. *See*, for example, N. Roubini, The Big Blockchain Lie, 15 October 2018, available at, https://nourielroubini.com/the-big-blockchain-lie/. *See also*, on his strong scepticism towards crypto-currencies: N. Roubini, The Great Crypto-Heist, 16 July 2019, available at, https://nourielroubini.com/the-great-crypto-heist.
14. *See* https://www.gartner.com/en/research/methodologies/gartner-hype-cycle.

As follows from the depiction in Figure 2.1, the Gartner Hype Cycle distinguishes the following five phases:

(1) Innovation Trigger.
(2) Peak of inflated expectations.
(3) Trough of disillusionment.
(4) Slope of enlightenment.
(5) Plateau of productivity.

It is this author's estimation that the development of blockchain technology is currently somewhere between Phase Three (the trough of disillusionment, or perhaps more aptly referred to as the 'blockchain winter') and Phase Four. It is a crucial stage of the development, and a stage in which the technology (or better said: the blockchain community) will have to demonstrate that it can live up to its (extremely) high expectations. In this author's view, the technology and its underlying benefits are too promising not to make it through this crucial stage. Separately, the emerging economy around crypto-currencies and trade finance (decentralized finance, 'DeFi'), as well as around CBDCs, have become simply too large already to ignore. This does not mean, however, that there is not a long way to go, in particular as advancements pertains to technological and governance challenges surrounding the building of a blockchain ecosystem. This is even more important when it relates to tax (*see also* section 4).

The development and success of blockchain technology also relates – to a large extent – to the debate around private (permissioned) versus public (permissionless) blockchains. Clearly, private blockchains have a lot of limitations, one of them being that they typically have scaling issues. Parties may typically be hesitant to join ecosystems that are started and/or dominated by others. In some instances they do not seem to have a choice, for example, where a dominant supplier or market player is mandating parties to join their blockchain ecosystem. Also, the actual benefits of blockchains as described earlier in this section typically do not come to full fruition when parties have to join multiple ecosystems, let alone if they are all built on different underlying technologies (i.e., interoperability may be an issue) or business logic. Conversely, public blockchains in the world of tax also have some challenges; in the world of tax, it is imperative to understand and know who the counterparties in the ecosystem are. Therefore, a fully permissionless blockchain does not seem to be suitable to capture a tax process. This applies also in a broader enterprise business process leading towards a somewhat hybrid blockchain (characteristics of a public blockchain supported by proper identity management and governance). Section 4 will also touch on this topic.

4 DISTRIBUTED TAX NETWORKS: DIGITAL TAX ADMINISTRATION 4.0

4.1 Another Way of Approaching a Tax Problem

Section 3 highlighted the upside potential with respect to the convergence between blockchain and tax. Where tax processes are typically – and to a very large extent – still paper driven and often manual as well, they are very clearly also prone to errors. Combine that with the lack of trust between taxpayers and tax administrations and you almost have your business case for a blockchain solution right there. However, there is more to this. In this author's opinion, fundamentally it has to do with how a tax problem is being addressed. Two elements will come into play here:

(1) Can you convert the underlying tax into code (i.e., an IF-THEN-ELSE-statement)?
(2) Are you trying to solve an individual's or a single enterprise's problem, or an ecosystem problem?

With respect to the first element, the fundamental question to be addressed is whether a tax process can be converted into code. This may imply that the actual process is being broken down into smaller pieces. For example, in order to determine whether a company may recover value added tax (VAT), the first question to be addressed is whether the company is considered an entrepreneur for VAT purposes. Subsequently, questions of whether the company is registered for VAT, and whether it can actually reclaim VAT, etc., have to be addressed. Not all processes, however, can be broken down into smaller processes. It may also be that the underlying response to a question cannot simply be answered with a yes or a no. As tax law professionals, we can all appreciate that the response to a tax query has multiple shades of grey to it, depending on the facts and circumstances of the specific situation of the taxpayer. This author is yet to see this being programmed into an IF-THEN-ELSE-statement. More forward looking, it would be helpful if tax legislators would start to think more about how newly applicable tax rules can be converted into tax code. This way, tax code can be more easily embedded into technology-driven solutions, which can contribute to more efficient, robust, and effective tax systems.

With respect to the second element, it may be that a fundamental rethinking is required in terms how tax problems are being addressed. As mentioned in section 2 of this chapter, the convergence around using technology to support tax problems is clearly focussed on point-to-point tax processes. What is meant by this is that, typically, a problem is being considered as engagement from a taxpayer that leads to a tax obligation towards a tax authority. Where in the past and in some instances this was a paper and/or manual process, the shift is being made towards using technology-driven solutions, starting with the electronic submission of tax data and forms to tax authorities and slowly but gradually moving towards real-time data collection and verification, in some instances supported by AI and data analysis. Of course this can lead to significant improvements in the underlying process. However, such a point-to-point approach will not help address the problem in a proper way in all instances, in particular as business processes and the way taxpayers interact with each other are becoming increasingly complex. In some instances, it is therefore worthwhile – if not necessary – to address the underlying problem as an ecosystem issue. A typical example is the VAT gap problem, that is the amount that tax administrations are missing out on every year due tax fraud (e.g., Missing Trader Intra-Community fraud). This is typically an ecosystem problem that may be properly addressed when looking at all the relevant parties in the ecosystem rather than simply a ringfenced number of taxpayers.[15] Similarly, withholding taxes, custom duties and origin declarations, transfer prices as well property taxes, or social security benefits and wage taxes may be approached by means of looking at this from an ecosystem perspective. And for the avoidance of doubt, tax administrations (including customs where applicable) play a fundamental and indispensable role in that ecosystem. But this does not mean that it is only their problem to solve.

4.2 Potential Use Cases

In section 3.1, some of the potential use cases of blockchain in the world of tax and global trade were already briefly highlighted. Examples are:

- VAT, Goods and Services Tax, and other types of sales taxes;
- withholding taxes on dividends, royalties, and interest;
- customs declarations (including origin declarations, electronic transport documents like e-bills of lading/e-CMR);[16]
- property taxes;
- carbon taxes and emission rights;
- exchange of information on rulings and country-by-country reporting;
- social security and wage taxes;
- transfer pricing.[17]

This chapter will not go into detail as to the specific merits of the above-mentioned potential use cases. Setting aside some existing business initiatives around blockchain and tax or trade, it seems that the most advanced countries in terms of exploring its potential benefits are China,[18] Dubai,[19] Estonia,[20] and Brazil,[21] although it

15. This does not mean that blockchain technology may solve all VAT fraud problems as several publications in tax literature (e.g., by Richard Ainsworth) have demonstrated. It is a hugely complex problem to solve.
16. CMR stands for Convention Relative au Contrat de Transport International de Marchandises par Route. It is an international Convention for the transport of goods over the road.
17. This author is not completely convinced about the transfer pricing use case for blockchain in the near future, although it has been mentioned on several occasions in tax literature. *See*, for example, A. Kosyan / L. von Grambusch, Blockchain's Relevance for Tax and Transfer Pricing Purposes, Bloomberg Tax, Tax Management Transfer Pricing Report, 7 December 2018. Transfer pricing is closely connected to the underlying services and/or goods that are being transferred. This implies that those transactions may also need to take place via a supply chain blockchain which requires a fundamental disruption to the entire supply chain process. With some of the other use cases mentioned, this seems less necessary.
18. *See*, for example, https://www.coindesk.com/tencent-partners-with-city-authority-to-combat-tax-evasion-with-blockchain.
19. *See*, for example, https://mag.wcoomd.org/magazine/wco-news-91-february-2020/dubai-customs-introduces-blockchain-based-platform-to-facilitate-cross-border-e-commerce/.
20. *See*, for example, https://e-estonia.com/solutions/business-and-finance/e-tax/. Estonia has a completely digitally organized public service framework.
21. *See*, for example, http://lawsofbrazil.com/2018/11/29/blockchain-adopted-by-brazils-tax-authority/.

is not always clear how advanced these systems are and whether they have actually been fully implemented.

Generally speaking, the author thinks that given the nature of blockchain (i.e., transactions occurring on a distributed ledger), a blockchain and tax use case should be predominantly focussed on transactional taxes and customs duties; income tax transactions and/or journal entries may therefore not be directly suitable for a blockchain, also given the volume of transactions that would be required.

A separate 'use case' concerns the opportunity that the implementation of CBDCs may bring when it comes to building 'programmable tax language' into the underlying code base of these digital currencies – think about automating the withholding of wage taxes and social security contributions when salary payments are being made, or directly transferring VAT to the tax authorities when a purchase is made.[22] Further academic research is necessary into the possibilities of programmable tax into CBDCs, provided countries will also start implementing these digital currencies (beyond a wholesale (i.e., intra-financial institutions) model). China currently seems to be most advanced in terms of developing and implementing a digital renminbi.[23]

4.3 Potential Challenges When Implementing a Blockchain and Tax Use Case

This section briefly addresses what the author believes are some of the key challenges when it comes to implementing a blockchain use case. The starting point would be that tax administrations start embracing the upside potential of the technology when it comes to tax and global trade. As indicated in section 2 and based on the OECD's report on Tax Administration 3.0, education and creating awareness of blockchain's potential are still necessary. However, assuming that this will eventually happen, several other challenges remain, which include, but are not limited to:

- *Identity management:* There needs to be a safe and transparent system around identity management for taxpayers transacting on blockchains. This identity management needs to be accessible for everybody. In this author's view, this means that the initial focus on blockchain and tax/customs use cases should be around enterprise business tax/customs processes as opposed to individual taxation matters.
- *Consensus mechanism*: Evidently, proof-of-work consensus mechanisms are – in the opinion of this author – not per se viewed as being the most optimal mechanism for the approval of tax processes. The same may go for proof-of-stake mechanisms. This may imply that a more federated model is required with a larger role for tax administrations. Potentially, tax administrations may

22. In some countries, this is addressed via other technologies whereby 'split payments' are being made.
23. Although it seems that in the first instance the Chinese CBDC may not necessarily involve blockchain. *See*, for example, https://cryptodaily.co.uk/2020/02/blockchain-involved-china-cbdc.

not need to approve all underlying transactions, but rather have a role as a 'tax node' on the blockchain that can audit the data and transactions.

- *Governance*: As indicated earlier there are several issues with private blockchains that become more immanent when it comes to tax processes, a public-private process by default. It is this author's view that tax administrations need to start thinking about the role they envision playing when it comes to blockchains for tax and global trade. This holds even more true in an international context when one looks at cross-border tax and/or customs transactions. It seems there is currently not a (supranational) body that may be willing to host/govern a blockchain platform, although one would expect that organizations like the OECD and/or the World Customs Organization would play a role here. Further thought and research in necessary as to the role of public and private stakeholders in relation to the problem at hand, and which an international platform may ultimately solve.
- *Privacy*: Tax processes by default concern sensitive (business or personal) data. This means that privacy is a key topic, closely connected to identity management. Privacy regulations like the General Data Protection Regulation (GDPR) therefore also come into play. To some extent, a lot – if not all – privacy matters may be solved with technologies such as zero-knowledge-proof technology.[24] Also, sensitive business data should not be put on the blockchain per se, but rather hashes of data. Therefore, to some extent, privacy issues related to blockchains may be somewhat overstated. However, it is yet to be seen whether zero-knowledge-proof technology is considered to be fully compliant with the GDPR and other privacy laws; it would not be a surprise if new legislation needs to be enacted to facilitate this use of the technology in a tax environment.
- *Standards*: When setting blockchain systems for tax and/or global trade, not only is the governance relevant, but standards also need to be taken into consideration, such as standards around participating, the rules of engagement (including dispute resolution), and the use of data. In every sector where blockchain is being considered, standard setting is being considered as a top priority.
- *Transparency*: Transparency about the proper use of algorithms to avoid biased and inclusive decision-making, or discrimination, among other things, is a fundamental aspect of creating a fair and balanced system where the rights of all participants (from both the private and public sector) are being properly balanced and addressed.

It is suffice to say that the aforementioned list may not be complete, and potentially other aspects should be added to it. Further research is also required with respect to all of the aforementioned items.

24. In essence, zero-knowledge-proof technology can be described as 'cryptographic alchemy', whose value lies in the seemingly paradoxical property of proving a statement without revealing anything about it.

5 TAXING VIRTUAL CURRENCIES

5.1 The Relevance of Taxing Virtual Currencies from a Policy Perspective

In mid-March 2021, the website coinmarketcap.com, which is well known among holders of virtual currencies, reported over 8,700 virtual currencies with a total market capitalization of almost USD 1,600 billion, with Bitcoin and Ethereum dominating the market with a market share of roughly 60% and 13% respectively.[25] These are huge numbers which, not surprisingly, have also led to increasing interest from policymakers and tax authorities, as well as fiscal intelligence units and financial crime police. It is fair to state that governments have faced extreme issues in attempting to properly tax these virtual currencies, as well as trying to combat money laundering via virtual currencies and prevent illicit trade via the dark web and other forms of (cyber) crime.[26] The world of virtual currencies started as a largely unregulated market space that has not only led to uncertainty and unclarity, but has also led people to believe that any income pertaining to these virtual currencies would go unnoticed and could therefore potentially remain untaxed. Although some blockchain purists may still think that virtual currencies should remain unregulated, it is this author's personal opinion that it is more a matter of 'which regulation' rather than 'no regulation'. In an EU context, initial steps have been taken with the introduction of 'AMLD5', the EU's Fifth Anti-Money Laundering Directive[27] of 30 May 2018, in terms of further regulation of this market. This Directive provides for further regulation and registration of companies that allow the exchange of virtual currencies into fiat currency and of custodian wallet service providers. It also provides for additional customer due diligence requirements. Unless registered these providers are not allowed to provide any of those services anymore. As a next step in the EU, the draft of an EU regulation on Markets in Crypto-Assets (MiCA) is relevant.[28] The objective of MiCA is to harmonize the European framework for the issuance and trading of various types of virtual currencies as part of the EU's Digital Finance Strategy. It provides for a draft legal framework for assets, markets, and service providers that are currently not yet regulated. If adopted, it will open the possibility to provide licensed services across the EU.

25. The value of the currencies in mid-March 2021 was around USD 51,000 for Bitcoin and USD 1,800 for Ethereum.
26. Reference is also made to the report from Financial Action Task Force (FATF) from June 2019 in which the so-called Travel Rule was introduced for Virtual Asset Service Providers (VASPs) and virtual currencies. Under this (proposed) rule, VASPs are required to share identification details of users transacting virtual currencies worth USD 1,000 or more. *See* FATF (2019), Guidance for a Risk-Based Approach to Virtual Assets and Virtual Asset Service Providers, FATF, Paris, www.fatf-gafi.org/publications/fatfrecommendations/documents/Guidance-RBA-virtual-assets.html. In the EU, the Travel Rule has not yet been adopted into legislation.
27. Directive 2018/843 (AMLD V) on anti-money laundering and terrorist financing came into effect on 9 July 2018 and mandated EU Member States to implement this Directive before 10 January 2020.
28. Proposal for a Regulation of the Markets in Crypto-assets and amending Directive (EU) 2019/1937, COM 2020) 593, 24 September 2020, https://ec.europa.eu/transparency/regdoc/rep/1/2020/EN/COM-2020-593-F1-EN-MAIN-PART-1.PDF.

From a taxation perspective, the case of a large United States (US) exchange for virtual currencies is very illustrative.[29] In 2017, after a long legal battle, this exchange had to provide the data of over 14,000 taxpayers to the US tax authorities (Internal Revenue Service or IRS) after it appeared that many US taxpayers did not include their taxable transactions on virtual currencies in their income tax return. Not surprisingly, this was a trend also happening in several other countries. From a policy perspective, the taxation of virtual currencies has therefore become a key priority, in particular in view of the surge in prices of virtual currencies in 2016 and 2017 (and more recently in 2020 and 2021).

5.2 The OECD Report

5.2.1 The Report at a Glance

It goes beyond the scope of this chapter to extensively dive into all (tax) technical aspects of the taxation of virtual currencies.[30] Therefore, the focus will be on some of the key aspects and challenges of taxing virtual currencies. On 12 October 2020, the OECD/G20 Inclusive Framework on BEPS released a report called *Taxing Virtual Currencies: An Overview of Tax Treatments and Emerging Tax Policy Issues* (hereinafter, 'the Report').[31] It is the first report from the OECD on this important topic, and it provides a cross-jurisdictional overview of tax treatments and emerging tax policy issues in relation to virtual currencies, in particular in relation to income tax, property tax and VAT. In terms of the scope of the Report, it clearly states that the policy considerations are not intended as recommendations or best practices, but rather as observations that domestic legislators and policymakers may take into consideration when strengthening their regulatory framework for taxing virtual currencies. That said, the Report provides some valuable insights as to the directional roadmap the taxing of virtual currencies may take. As mentioned in section 1, the interdisciplinary nature of virtual currencies, as well as of blockchain and DLT in general, requires that policymakers as well as tax authorities become familiar with several technical terms related to them, such as airdrops, staking, and hard forks. Also, they must have a common understanding of some of the key distinctions between virtual currencies that serve as actual currencies versus those that serve as so-called utility tokens and security tokens. This is highly relevant for the potential tax treatment thereof.

The Report was prepared for presentation to the meeting of G20 Finance Ministers and Central Bank Governors on 14 October 2020, and covered three main discussion items:

29. *See* https://techcrunch.com/2017/11/29/coinbase-internal-revenue-service-taxation/.
30. For a country survey on the taxation of virtual currencies, reference is, for example, made to N. Schmidt et al., Taxation of Crypto Assets, Wolters Kluwer International, 2021. In the book, several taxes are addressed, including income tax, value added tax, real estate transfer tax, and wage taxes.
31. OECD (2020), Taxing Virtual Currencies: An Overview of Tax Treatments and Emerging Tax Policy Issues, OECD, Paris, available at, https://www.oecd.org/tax/tax-policy/taxing-virtual-currencies-an-overview-of-tax-treatments-and-emerging-tax-policy-issues.htm.

(1) key concepts and definitions of blockchain and crypto-assets, looking at the characterization, legality, and valuation of virtual currencies, and analysing the tax consequences across the different stages of their lifecycle, from creation to disposal;
(2) tax policy implications of several emerging issues related to the taxation of virtual currencies, including the rise of stablecoins (e.g., Libra/Diem, Tether) and CBDCs, as well as the evolution of the consensus mechanisms used to maintain blockchain networks (e.g., the increasing use of proof-of-stake rather than proof-of-work), and the rise of DeFi; and
(3) identifying key tax policy considerations based on a comparative overview across some fifty countries of the tax treatment of virtual currencies from the perspective of income, consumption, and property taxation.[32]

The differences in regulatory approaches highlight the need for policymakers to balance competing goals and perspectives in order to safeguard a coherent and robust regulatory regime for virtual currencies. For the time being, domestic differences create a tension where regulatory arbitrage may take place without sufficient disclosure mechanisms in place. Such a hypothesis is counter to the BEPS Project's Action Plan on reducing legal hybrid regimes for tax purposes and should be considered within this larger context.

5.2.2 *Key Concepts and Definitions*

Not surprisingly, the Report states that there is no uniform definition of the various features of virtual currencies. The common features, however, are related to financial assets based on DLT (e.g., blockchain) and cryptography as an inherent part of the perceived value of the assets. The Financial Action Task Force (FATF) in its report in June 2019 defined a 'virtual asset' as 'a digital representation of value that can be digitally traded or transferred, and can be used for payment or investment purposes'.[33] Such a definition is clearly too broad to be utilized for taxation purposes. More generally, a threefolded subdivision of virtual currencies is typically being made between:

(1) *Payment tokens*: These tokens represent an asset that can be used for the exchange of goods and services. Payment tokens are commonly referred to as virtual currencies.
(2) *Utility tokens*: These tokens are primarily used for accessing certain services or an infrastructure, where the tokens can represent pre-payments, vouchers, or the licensing of specific rights.

32. It is this author's view that the aforementioned book from Niklas Schmidt et al. contains a more detailed review on the current state of taxation of virtual currencies in several countries. It also discusses some additional taxes, like wage taxes and inheritance tax. *See* n. 29.
33. FATF Report, 'Virtual Assets and Virtual Asset Service Providers' – Guidance for a risk-based approach, June 2019. The report can be found here, https://www.fatf-gafi.org/media/fatf/documents/recommendations/RBA-VA-VASPs.pdf.

(3) *Security tokens*: These tokens are tradable in nature and are often held for investment purposes.

Given the specific nature of these various types of tokens, it is clear that from a taxation perspective one cannot simply state that all of these tokens should be treated the same from a tax perspective. Also, within these three categories, varieties exist in addition to the fact that some tokens may hold 'hybrid' features covering more than one category. Further, tokens may change over time due to their multilayered nature, which resembles multilayered derivatives contracts. Virtual currencies or payment tokens are predominantly discussed in the jurisdictions covered by the Report. By contrast, less information is currently issued by policymakers on utility and security tokens. Typically, it is expected that these types of tokens follow the same treatment as payment tokens. In this author's view, the Report is somewhat oversimplifying the potential differences and nuances that may arise based on the nature and features of these tokens that may also allow for a different tax treatment. An example may be the timing of taxation: the sale of a payment token leads to a taxable event (e.g., a capital gain) at the moment of its disposal, whereas utility tokens may only create a taxable event at the moment that the underlying service or utility is being consumed or used. Also, the value of utility tokens may be harder to determine based on the underlying 'utility' built in the token. Security tokens, for that matter, may in some instances be more similar to payment tokens when it comes to taxation, although one may also expect an option to defer a capital gain if this gain would, for example, be reinvested.

5.2.3 *Brief Overview of Tax Considerations*

5.2.3.1 *Income Tax*

In most countries covered by the Report, virtual currencies are to be considered as a form of property, and most often as intangible assets other than goodwill. Income tax is common upon the disposal or exchange of a virtual currency, even though some jurisdictions allow individuals to exchange virtual currencies for fiat currency without the transaction representing a taxable event. Also, the exchange of virtual currencies for services, goods, or wages would qualify as a taxable event. There may be differences in the tax treatment of transactions in virtual currencies depending on the status of the parties involved. For instance, occasional traders may be subjected to capital gains tax liabilities which can be reduced based on losses. Companies that are trading virtual currencies as part of the business generate business or capital income, which will be subjected to business tax rates and potentially deductible losses.

5.2.3.2 *Property Tax*

As indicated, virtual currencies qualify as property for tax purposes in most of the jurisdictions covered in the Report, subjecting the value of virtual currencies to inheritance, gift, and wealth taxes in countries where these taxes exist. There may be different property taxation for resident and non-resident companies affecting the tax rate or method of calculation. In some countries, such as Switzerland, a regime applies where virtual currencies must be converted to Swiss francs for tax assessments, provided by the Federal Tax Administration.

5.2.3.3 Value Added Tax

The trading and handling of virtual currencies, including the creation process of mining, may all have VAT consequences. Generally, the VAT treatment of virtual currencies is more consistent than in the area of income tax. The main reason for this seems to be a Court of Justice of the European Union case from 22 October 2015, *Skatteverket v. Hedqvist* (C-264-14), which ruled that transactions including the exchange of fiat currency for virtual currencies and vice versa are transactions exempt from VAT. Hence, most EU countries have a joint consensus that the exchange to or from virtual currencies is not subject to VAT. The same applies for using virtual currencies to buy goods or services. Hence, no VAT should in principle be charged on the use of virtual currencies itself. However, on the opposite side of the same transaction, the supply of taxable goods and services that are paid with virtual currencies are considered subject to VAT. As for the act of receiving new virtual currencies due to a reward from the mining process of the creation of the tokens, most countries - with exemptions for, for example, Italy and France -consider this a non-VAT-liable event. However, not all types of virtual currency services are aligned among EU Member States or other countries; online wallet services and virtual currency exchanges are two examples of such.

5.2.4 Tax Policy Considerations

Although the Report explicitly does not make any recommendations, it does provide a number of general insights that policymakers may wish to consider in the taxation of virtual currencies, namely:

(1) Ensuring that their country has clear guidance and a clear legislative framework, for example, by:
   - Providing guidance on how virtual currencies fit within the existing framework and determining if and to what extent the existing laws are unclear or not adapted to virtual currencies given their special characteristics (e.g., price volatility, hybrid nature, type and number of transactions, creation protocols). Similarly, providing a definition of virtual currencies for tax purposes would be helpful.
   - Addressing comprehensive guidance on major taxable events and income forms associated with virtual currencies. Major taxable events may include: the creation of virtual currencies (via mining/forging, initial token offerings, and airdrops); exchange with other virtual currencies and/or fiat currency, and for goods and services (including valuation); disposal via gift or inheritance; loss or theft; emerging developments

(hard forks, stablecoins, CBDCs, interest-bearing tokens); and related services (e.g., exchange services and wallets).
- Providing guidance that usefully indicates how other forms of crypto-assets (including security and utility tokens) are to be treated for tax purposes, including official guidance on the boundaries between different types of crypto-assets, and on how other forms of these assets are treated for tax purposes.
- Frequently reviewing and adapting guidance to ensure that it remains relevant and current in the face of technological and market developments.

(2) Communicating the rationale behind the adopted tax treatment to provide more transparency and flexibility.
(3) Considering whether the taxation of virtual currencies is consistent with the taxation of other assets in order to secure tax system neutrality.
(4) Facilitating a coherent regulatory framework for virtual currencies where the tax treatment is included and competing interests are avoided as much as possible.
(5) Supporting improved compliance in terms of disclosure and the taxation of virtual currencies. This is particularly challenging due to volatility, various exchange rates for the same virtual currency, lack of a one-to-one relation between the value of virtual currencies and fiat currency, and keeping records of transactions. This may include considering whether intermediaries such as crypto exchanges and custodians of private keys could be included in a broader disclosure regime for tax purposes (*see also* hereafter section 5.3).
(6) Considering a simplified taxation regime for occasional or non-professional small traders that can exempt capital gains tax for completed transactions, or alternatively introducing a 'de minimis exemption' for small traders.
(7) Considering how the tax treatment of virtual currencies could align with or undermine other policy objectives. For example, a decline in cash use has led some governments to look into how to support electronic payments, including the development of CBDCs. In addition, environmental challenges concerning energy aspects with regard to the costly computing power required to generate and mine virtual currencies could also be taken into consideration in terms of (their) tax treatment.

The aforementioned items are clearly on the priority list in terms of recommendations for policymakers. What is interesting is that, to a large extent, the focus seems to be on providing a framework for countries in the national context. Equally, the importance of agreeing on a global characterization of virtual currencies for tax purposes should, in this author's view, be on this list. Failure to do so can likely lead to international mismatches between countries and thus potentially lead to double (non-)taxation. In an ecosystem that is mostly active in a digital environment, tax policymakers should strive to avoid this. This is even more important when considering that most countries do not have clear definitions and nomenclature for virtual currencies, nor have they established their tax treatments. Tax policymakers, therefore, have a great opportunity to arrange this properly by means of international standard setting straight from the outset.

5.2.5 *Future Regulatory Challenges*

The Report also focussed on some trends and emerging developments within the field of virtual currencies where policymakers can pay particular attention to the tax treatment. Areas where separate (or updated) guidance may be needed are:

(1) The tax treatment of new assets received when a hard fork occurs: this is a topic only addressed by a handful of countries. One of the main challenges is when the taxpayer is deemed to have received the assets for tax purposes. Exercising dominion and the time of first disposal can be considered against a basis of zero. In addition, the receipt of new tokens can raise questions of liquidity concerns for the taxpayer based on the timing of when the tokens can be accessed. Hence, volatility issues such as how losses are to be treated if the value of the token falls after it is received and taxed should be considered.

(2) Stablecoins and CBDCs represent new forms of virtual currencies: these new asset types have unique characteristics to be considered further and more specifically. Stablecoins and CBDCs are often backed by other assets or fiat currencies. Hence, their characteristics can be key for tax purposes, and policymakers should determine whether existing rules are appropriate.

(3) Other new token types and characteristics are also emerging for which no tax treatment guidance has been issued (e.g., proof-of-stake generated tokens or virtual currencies as an interest-bearing asset): in some instances, similarities with traditional capital or financial assets can be drawn. Hence, consideration should be given to whether a tax treatment akin to capital income is more appropriate than capital gains income. Tax guidance on such issues can provide certainty for taxpayers and prevent tax planning opportunities.

5.3 Introduction of a Common Reporting Standard for Virtual Currencies?

As indicated in section 5.2.1, the Report is the first formal report of the OECD and its Inclusive Framework on BEPS that is specific to taxing virtual currencies and emerging tax policy issues. It is very likely (and in this author's view, also necessary) that more will follow on this relevant topic. Countries can certainly benefit from an international and common approach on the tax treatment of virtual currencies to avoid both double taxation and potential mismatches. The Report also stated that the OECD is currently developing technical proposals in order to ensure an adequate and effective level of reporting and exchange of information with respect to crypto-assets. At this stage, it is not yet clear what these technical proposals will entail. Similar to the increasing regulatory requirements that are being proposed and implemented for Virtual Asset

Service Providers (VASPs), it may be that additional measures will be proposed to improve tax transparency. This may include what information tax administrations need to know about transactions for purposes of compliance and enforcement.

It is very likely that countries will adopt the Common Reporting Standard (CRS) for VASPs so that information about holders of virtual currencies can be automatically exchanged with tax authorities to combat tax evasion. In an EU context, the Commission has already started taking initial steps with respect to the exchange of tax-relevant data for alternative means of payment (including crypto-assets and e-money). On 23 November 2020, the Commission released a roadmap for the proposal of the DAC8 Directive,[34] expected in the second half of 2021.

Suffice to say that the exchange of information would be a first step towards more consistency, transparency, and clarity around the taxing of virtual currencies. However, it does not necessarily mean that this will not give rise to additional challenges and queries around the scope of the exchange of information. These challenges may include, but are not limited to, the following questions:

(1) Are the current standards of CRS directly applicable to virtual currencies or is it necessary to introduce new rules that are more closely connected to the specific characteristics of these currencies and the way transactions occur?
(2) What definitions for the various virtual currencies and tokens are being used?
(3) Is there (some) consensus on how income is determined, including:
    - the cost price for tax purposes of a virtual currency?
    - which country may levy on the capital gain?
    - how are 'hard forks', 'air drops', and 'staking' treated for tax purposes?
(4) For which platforms would the exchange of information be applicable? It may make sense to follow the AMLD5 Directive, but perhaps a broader or narrower approach is desired.
(5) What if a transaction is occurring via an exchange but the underlying virtual currencies is located in a so-called hard wallet?
(6) Is it desirable to have exemptions from taxation and/or the exchange of information mechanisms in relation to certain virtual currencies?

Obviously, the list of practical and technical questions can get much longer, and it may be hard to get overall consensus on an approach, not only within the context of the EU but also for OECD member countries. The complexity and interdisciplinary nature of the subject at hand surely does not help to achieve the relevant level of transparency and consensus. This may lead to underkill or overkill in legislation in an international context. However, what is also clear is that virtual currencies, despite debates surrounding the lack of underlying value, are clearly here to stay. Consequently, it is imperative for countries to have clear and transparent legislation in place with respect to the taxation of these virtual currencies. That said, there is still a long way to go before this will actually be achieved.

34. DAC stands for Directive on Administrative Cooperation. DAC8 will be the 8th Directive on administrative cooperation.

6 CLOSING REMARKS

This chapter has attempted to address some of the key aspects in terms of the challenges and opportunities concerning blockchain, tax, and global trade. It is a rapidly developing field of play with lots of exciting, complex, and new aspects for academic research as well as for practical experimentation and implementation. For the parties involved, it requires knowledge of all interdisciplinary aspects that come together; it is a new and very specific area of expertise, whether about the challenging aspects of taxing virtual currencies or about setting up and developing blockchain systems for tax or global trade. To fully exploit the potential of these new technologies and to minimize the risks, it will require close cooperation between government, business and academia. Jointly, they have the unique opportunity to come up with a comprehensive framework from the outset. One could therefore state that they are better positioned for this than they have been for any other international tax topic before.

CHAPTER 3

Blockchain in Tax and Customs Processes

Matthias Gries, Karl Gürges & Michael Tobai

1 BLOCKCHAIN: A NEW WAY TO 'TRANSPORT' DATA IN A SECURED ENVIRONMENT

The taXchain is a network initiative of the tax departments of Henkel and Siemens to leverage blockchain technology for the data exchange of tax and customs information across companies and authorities. Blockchain was selected as the technological backbone of the network due to its unique combination of features, such as the immutability of data, encryption, and decentralization. The technology is appealing to the cause of taXchain because it provides:

- improved compliance and control for companies and authorities; and
- streamlined operative procedures.

The first application of the taXchain network focusses on long-term suppliers' declarations (LTSDs), a largely paper-based process to exchange customs master data information between companies. This process was selected as it is harmonized across the European Union (EU) and is essential for every company that engages in international trade.

Currently, taXchain is about to conclude the incubation phase of the project during which the LTSD solution is implemented in Henkel's and Siemens' procedures, while onboarding the first partners for a soft launch. Besides the LTSD application as a first use case of the taXchain network, further applications are envisioned, for example proof of delivery, excise taxes, value added tax (VAT) registrations, energy taxes, and others.

2 CHALLENGES: WHAT WAS THE INITIAL PROBLEM?

Rules in international trade require companies to provide customs-specific master data when goods should be moved across a boarder, namely:

- the commodity code, an international nomenclature number that clusters similar materials in a comparable category; and
- the country of origin, that indicates where, for example, the last substantial production step was undertaken.

This information functions as a 'passport' for the shipped good. It provides a nexus to both the importing and exporting country to levy duties, or to enforce international trade compliance requirements.

A manufacturing company in the EU currently faces the challenge that it can only issue this 'passport' information for its manufactured goods in an optimized way once it has also collected the 'passports' of the raw materials it utilizes in its production process. Hence, it relies on its suppliers to provide this information (*see* Figure 3.1). In the EU, so-called LTSDs have simplified and standardized this master data exchange between suppliers and customers, as LTSDs are valid for a maximum period of two years.

Figure 3.1 Simplified LTSD Process

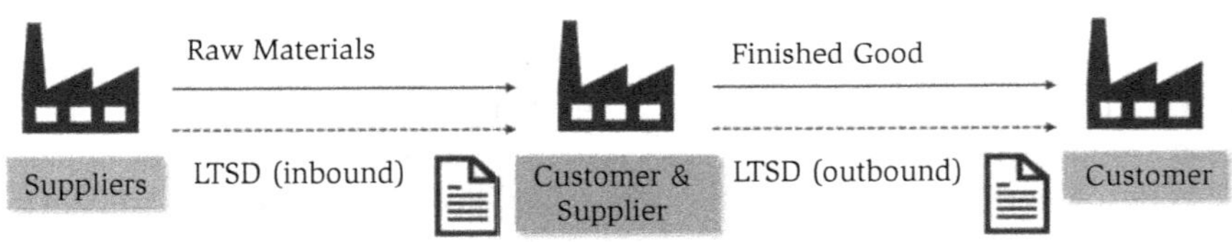

As helpful as the LTSD is for operational trade procedures, in practice, it still leads to a generally complex and time-consuming process. Imagine you are a producer of chemicals that contain raw materials such as fragrances, alcohols, fatty acids, and other chemicals that are all sourced from different suppliers. First, an LTSD must be requested from every single supplier, which can take from one day to several weeks based on the responsiveness and process know-how of your suppliers. Second, the information needs to be manually transferred into an enterprise resource planning (ERP) system once the documents are collected via electronic, or even physical, mail. Only once both of these steps have been completed can you issue your own respective LTSD to your customer in the best possible manner.

As a manufacturer, you now face multiple procedural issues that make the assessment of the 'passport' information – in the form of an LTSD – of your produced good challenging: the process of requesting the information from each supplier is time-consuming due to the sheer multitude and timing of the individual communication flows. Another challenge is the heterogeneous media formats that you receive the inbound LTSD in (i.e., differently formatted paper or electronic documents), as they typically must be manually entered into your ERP system. Lastly, the data transparency is limited, as the end-to-end tracking of the information flow is only sporadically possible at best.

In summary, the LTSD process is a standardized framework that is helpful and essential for trade procedures in the EU. However, due to the above-mentioned operational and transparency (i.e., audit-readiness) issues, the overall processes of LTSD collection from suppliers and LTSD issuance to customers have huge potential for operational standardization and automation.

3 IMPLEMENTATION OF TAXCHAIN/LTSD USE CASE

In 2019 the tax departments of the German companies Henkel and Siemens joined forces to lay the foundations for an industry-driven initiative to take LTSD data exchange to the next level: taXchain. The reason for taXchain was the potential to improve the robustness of LTSDs and potentially other tax processes by utilizing blockchain technology. The goal was to build a technological platform with an open technological and governance framework that is driven by industry requirements. The LTSD use case would function as a technological pilot of the blockchain framework and could potentially be followed by the technology being applied to proof of delivery, excise tax, or VAT compliance and registrations.

Early on it became immanent that blockchain would be used as the technological backbone of the platform due to its unique set of characteristics, such as traceability, immutability, and efficiency. Due to the novelty of blockchain technology and the overall challenge to set up a technological platform, Microsoft supported the industrial team as a technology partner to provide its expertise from similar set-ups. During the first workshop, an initial rough timeline was designed.

Figure 3.2 Conceptual Phases of Implementation

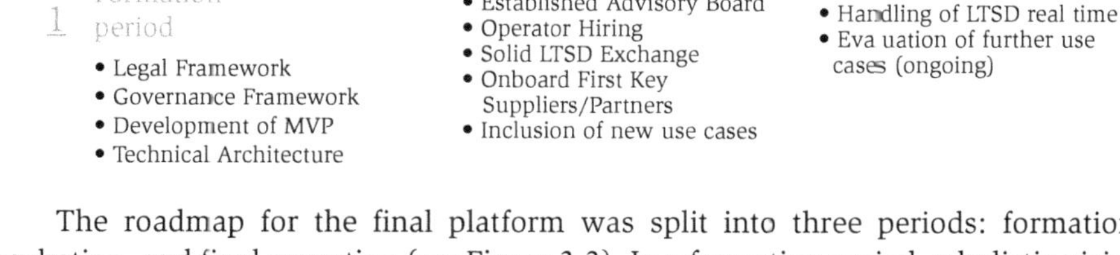

The roadmap for the final platform was split into three periods: formation, incubation, and final operation (*see* Figure 3.2). In a formation period, a holistic vision of the platform and a minimal viable product of the technology were designed. Individual working groups in ecosystem governance, business solution, and technology infrastructure were thereby incrementally developing a first outline of all aspects of the taXchain platform. Based on the successful results of the formation period, all initiators decided that they would move to the incubation period in which a stronger focus would be put on connecting the platform with Henkel's and Siemens' IT systems, implementing a sustainable legal structure, and onboarding the platform's first partner companies in the form of a soft launch. Both the formation and incubation periods were solely driven by the 'taXchain founders' Henkel and Siemens. This centralized set-up ensured secured funding, and streamlined organizational structure while developing the platform. Once taXchain goes live to the public, it is intended that the operational period will begin, and that the overall set-up will reflect a robust governance structure with an elected board, and a technology platform that will be hosted and maintained by an operator.

4 IMPACT: WHICH MEASURABLE RESULTS HAVE BEEN ACHIEVED?

Eighty-three per cent of all European companies issue LTSDs in paper form.[1] Currently, the issuance of LTSDs involves relevant administrative and personnel costs. In addition, an effective compliance management system is required which needs to be reviewed regularly. In 2019, Henkel and Siemens together processed 11,916 LTSD documents.[2] This indicates the enormous administrative and manual effort required to enter the necessary data into their respective systems.

The foremost result of taXchain is that a technological platform has been launched that makes the benefit of blockchain technology tangible and accessible to EU companies that apply the LTSD process. It was specifically considered that access to the platform must be inclusive to cover small, medium, and large companies alike. This was achieved by designing a web-based access to the platform and a back-end solution that can be connected to a participant's IT system via an application programming interface (API). The latter is intended to be used by large companies such as Henkel and Siemens.

This platform allows Henkel and Siemens alone to automate the processing of their combined 8,000-12,000 LTSDs per annum in principle. The previously document-based process between the parties involved is being digitalized using blockchain technology. Media disruptions are thereby eliminated. The query, data exchange, validation, and storage of the LTSDs shall now take place via the blockchain solution.

The LTSD is an important information and verification document for the direct or indirect claiming of customs benefits. Next to the streamlined operation, blockchain technology also enables a certified and immutable single source of truth, which makes the overall process more robust.

Lastly, the LTSD use case has the potential to prove the unique benefits of applying blockchain when exchanging tax and trade-relevant information in a distributed network (*see* Figure 3.3). These proven benefits have also triggered ideas of its broader application (e.g., to other taxes such as VAT/sales and use tax, transfer pricing or excise taxes). This, of course, would require two key elements, as follows:

1. Cf. Björn Helmke, *Warum sind die Kosten für Langzeit-Lieferantenerklärungen gestiegen?* (12 May 2021), https://www.aeb.com/de-de/magazin/artikel/lieferantenerklaerungen-werden-teurer.php.
2. Cf. *Risse/Gries*, beck.digitax 2020. 392.

(1) a substantial number of companies would need to use the blockchain-based platform, as the benefit per company is based on its respective suppliers and customers participating; and

(2) participation and involvement of local, national and supranational authorities would be crucial to play out the encompassing compliance and audit benefits for both the public and private sectors.

Figure 3.3 Associated Benefits of Blockchain Technology[3]

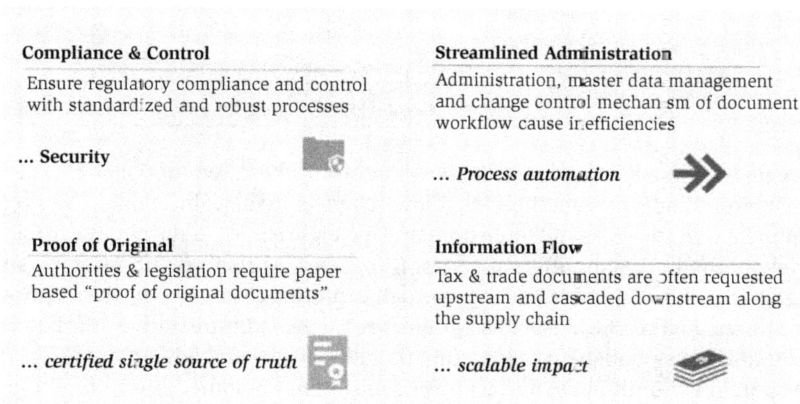

5 TECHNOLOGY: HOW WAS TECHNOLOGY USED FOR BOTH THE FRONT END AND THE BACK END?

Before we have a look at the IT architecture of taXchain, it is important to point out that the blockchain platform follows the thought model that, from an economic perspective, such a solution can only work if everyone (small, medium and large companies as well as authorities) benefits from it and can participate. In this respect, it is important to underline that the blockchain system is embedded in a platform that provides benefits to all stakeholders, creates positive network effects, and offers easy access.

In this respect, there are two different possibilities for a new company to connect to the blockchain system: option one is that the connection to the blockchain system is managed by an IT partner (as Siemens intends to do); option two is that the company itself manages the connection to the blockchain (as Henkel intends to do; *see* Figure 3.4). While the latter offers maximum control and allows access to reusable components/infrastructure, the first option enables easy onboarding and is cost-efficient.

3. Cf. *Risse/Gries*, beck.gigitax 2020, 392.

Figure 3.4 Generic Options and Potential Scenarios to Connect to LTSD taXchain

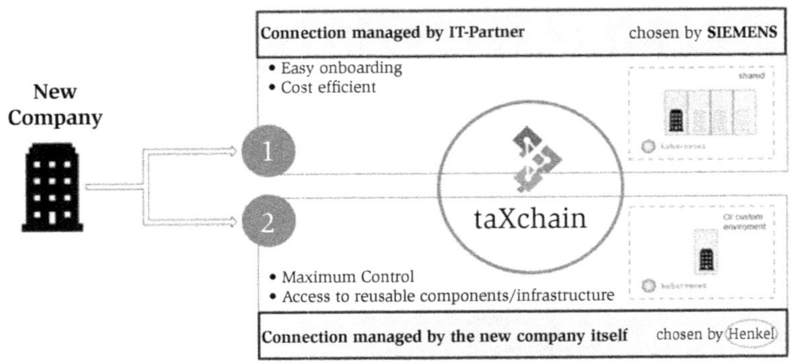

A new company can choose between either of these two options.

The front-end solution, thereby, allows users to manage both the LTSDs received by suppliers and those issued to customers (*see* Figure 3.5). A dashboard provides an overview of the LTSDs in different states. If the user wants to request that its supplier issue an LTSD, it can simply do so by manually entering the respective key-information required (*see* Figure 3.6). As this would mean the administrative burden is only partially lifted, a spreadsheet upload functionality is also embedded into the platform, as the sourcing of multiple materials from one supplier is something common to many companies. The same is, of course, also feasible when issuing LTSDs to customers, either upon proactive issuance or upon request. Each interaction per LTSD is logged in a dedicated and immutable block on the chain, which can be mapped based on a unique identification number (i.e., a unique hash key).

Figure 3.5 Front-End Interface of LTSD taXchain (Example)

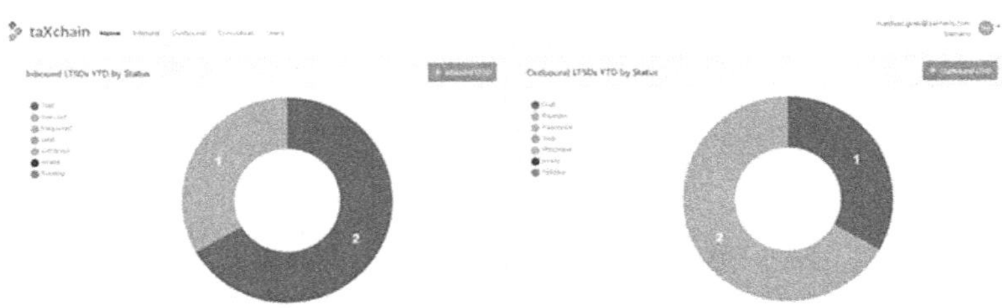

Figure 3.6 Request Supplier LTSD via Front-End Interface (Example)

The second connection point to the taXchain LTSD platform is an API connection that participants can use to directly connect their international IT systems to the blockchain. Based on the unique hash key of the transaction, two information exchanging companies can jointly access the LTSD data fields of this specific transaction stored on the blockchain (e.g., validity period, country of origin, or preference status). The information can thereby be directly pushed and pulled in the respective IT systems. This enables a frictionless integration of the platform into each company's respective process, thereby automating cumbersome communication flows (*see* Figure 3.7).

Figure 3.7 Schematic IT Architecture and Potential Modes of Participation (taXchain)

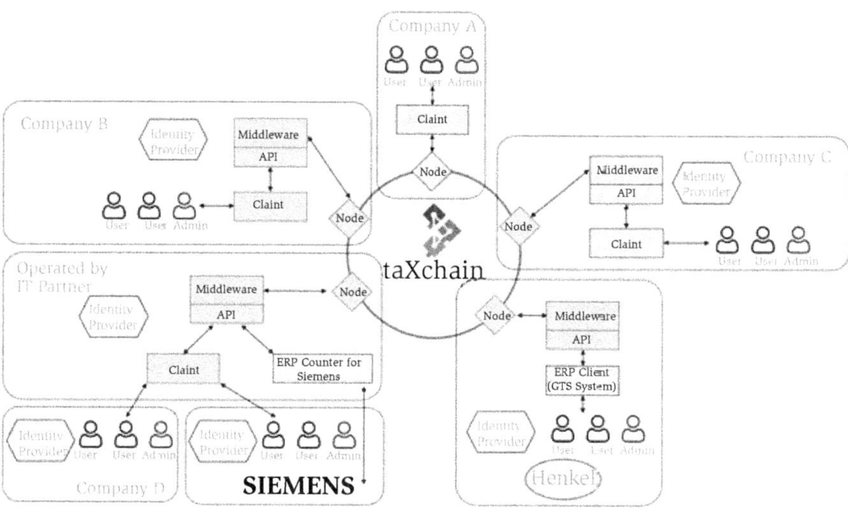

6 LESSONS LEARNT: WHAT WENT WELL AND WHAT FAILED? WHAT CAN OTHERS LEARN FROM THE EXPERIENCES?

From the point of view of these authors, there are several things that contribute to our current perception of blockchain technology in the tax and customs area.

The blockchain hype began a few years ago, and Henkel's and Siemens' tax departments intend to demonstrate that a blockchain solution such as taXchain has the potential to drive cross-company processes in tax and customs to the next level.

While blockchain is not the solution for everything, it can be an essential part of a digital business infrastructure for companies to operate tax. But what does 'digital business infrastructure' mean? Let us take a practical example: in the past, we had to create business infrastructure through highways to make the economy more efficient. We are, once again, at such a point where we have to start rethinking our infrastructure, but this time from a digital perspective, and, in times of digitalization, prepare our systems for the next steps in creating a more efficient economy, on this occasion through developing our 'digital business infrastructure'.

This requires a common digital tax ecosystem in which public authorities, research, companies, and technology providers jointly set standards and provide broad engagement (whether directly or via inter-operational models). In such a scenario, collaboration and alignment among the stakeholders is considered key for success.

For the future, it will be important that companies and authorities work together to create technological standards in the tax and customs area. Otherwise (national) economies may not see any progress in digitization, as everyone will once again be working individually on isolated solutions without data and technical standards.

From an economic point of view, this would counteract the opportunities that the digitization of tax and customs processes would offer, and would result in cost and international competitive disadvantages. Companies are typically not competing on tax and customs issues but have the common interest to lower administrative burdens. For this reason, the digitization of tax and customs processes should be economically efficient, since companies, as well as authorities, are seeking not only greater compliance in the tax and customs process, but also greater efficiency of processes and, ultimately, a cost reduction in tax allocation and declaration.

It is likely that taXchain will not be the only blockchain solution. One important point to consider for the future will therefore be the interoperability of different blockchain platforms.

There are several ways to connect blockchain systems. On the one hand, one blockchain system can, of course, be taken over by the other blockchain system, which means that the various solutions in the tax and customs area would run on one single blockchain solution – the classic scenario of digitalization: the winner takes it all. On the other hand, there is a smarter opportunity, one that would allow different blockchains to communicate with each other. This approach is called 'Fediverse', whereby the individual blockchain solutions can communicate with each other by using certain communication protocols. Thus, differently designed blockchain solutions (independent of the chosen blockchain) can interact with each other. In this variant, one solution is not taken over by the other; instead, both solutions remain in place. This sophisticated solution becomes increasingly interesting as more unified data models are taken care of in the tax and customs area (technological standards), for example whether an address always consists of city, postal code and street or of coordinates.

7 OUTLOOK: PERSPECTIVE AND EXPECTATIONS FOR THE FUTURE OF THE DIGITALIZATION OF TAX LAW?

In order to fulfil their tax and customs duties, companies have to perform an ever-increasing number of compliance tasks, which also cause a high administrative burden. Documentation obligations in particular prove to be resource-intensive for two reasons: on the one hand, the administration works largely on the basis of paper-based documents, and, on the other hand, the procurement of information is dependent on numerous internal and external stakeholders. In this context, this administrative burden can be reduced for both companies and authorities through current technological applications such as blockchain. However, the main reason is not only the potential time and cost savings; it is also hidden in the improvement of data transparency and process robustness, and its benefits for all stakeholders.

In this context, the blockchain technology has the potential to drive cross-company processes in tax and customs to the next level. Besides the aforementioned use of blockchain technology in the tax and customs function, other potential use cases can be identified. Those possible use cases within the tax and customs area are illustrated in Figure 3.8.

Graphically, the (potential) use cases are shown separately by area of law/topic (VAT, customs, transfer pricing, capital gains tax and tax audit) and arranged according to the expected development period (one to two years or three to five years, with the development time within the individual time zones being specified by the distance from the centre point). Against this background, it becomes apparent that the use of blockchain technology is particularly suitable for tax types with mass cases that take place at the transactional level. Consequently, the legal areas of VAT and customs law as well as the topic area of transfer pricing are particularly predestined for the use of blockchain technology. Figure 3.8 shows only one selection of possible uses cases for blockchain technology in the tax and customs area. The possible uses of blockchain technology presented are then explained in summary by area of law/topic. Due to the scope, only individual use cases for the application of blockchain technology in the tax and customs function are highlighted here and presented in a highly abbreviated form.

Figure 3.8 Possible Uses of Blockchain Technology in the Tax and Customs Function[4]

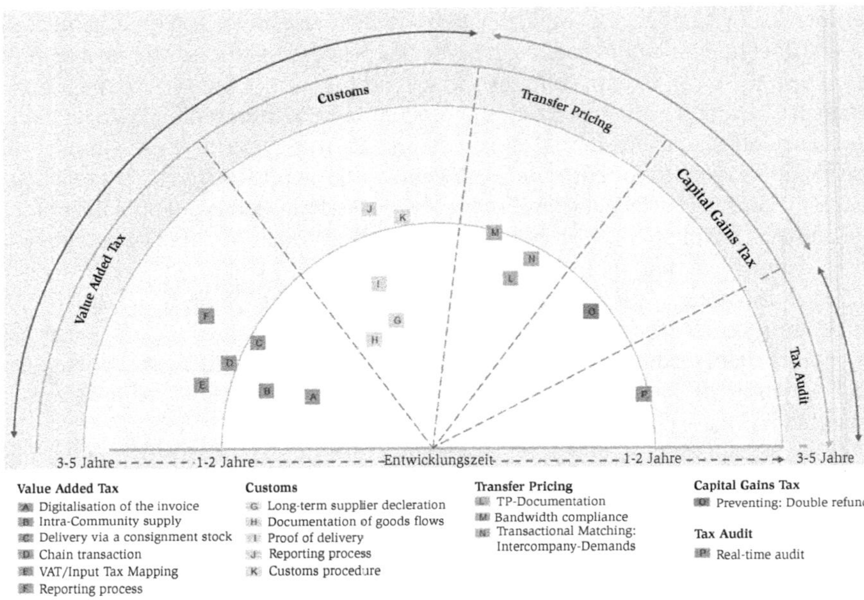

7.1 Value Added Tax

Blockchain technology offers a variety of different use cases in the area of VAT. For example, and as shown in Figure 3.8, it is possible to map individual VAT facts, such as the intra-Community supply (B), the delivery via a consignment stock (C), and the chain transaction (D) via the blockchain. The spectrum here ranges from providing proof of the tax exemption of the intra-Community supply via the blockchain (e.g., confirmation of arrival), the digital exchange of documents and the monitoring of the transaction between the companies (in accordance with the requirements of Article 45a MwStVO)[5] to the digital processing of chain transactions with the possibility of digitally recording the goods, and thus their localization.[6]

4. Cf. *Risse/Gries*, beck.digitax 2020, 394.
5. This use case is currently being investigated by another cooperation between BASF, BOSCH, HILTI and SAP. The two research cooperations exchange knowledge and, together with the BDI, are pursuing the idea of a platform for setting standards in the digitalization of the tax and customs function; Durchführungsverordnung (EU) 2018/1912 DES RATES vom 4. Dezember 2018 zur Änderung der Durchführungsverordnung (EU) Nr. 282/2011 hinsichtlich bestimmter Befreiungen bei innergemeinschaftlichen Umsätzen.
6. Cf. *Dietsch*, Umsatzsteuer 4.0 – wie Blockchain grenzüberschreitende Reihengeschäfte transparenter machen könnte, MwStR 2018, 813.

According to the current estimates by the EU Commission, the EU states lost almost EUR 140 billion in VAT revenue in 2018.[7] One of the causes of this deficit is the so-called carousel transactions, in which one of the parties involved (the so-called missing trader) disappears with the VAT while his transaction partner has the input tax refunded. Using blockchain technology, a technical allocation between VAT liability and input tax refund (the so-called VAT/input tax mapping (E)) could take place. This could eliminate the susceptibility to fraud of the current VAT system, in that a corresponding input tax refund would only be made automatically on the blockchain after payment of the VAT debt.

On the other hand, the current VAT reporting process (F) could be reformed. Instead of up to forty-nine notifications[8] annually for an entrepreneur participating in cross-border trade in goods, blockchain technology makes it possible to replace the (active and bureaucratic) notification procedure with a (passive) data retrieval system[9] in real time that can be accessed by the authorities. In terms of the process, every outgoing invoice is recorded on the blockchain. If congruent information is available from the transaction partners on the provision and receipt of services, it is bundled on the blockchain. Payments (e.g., VAT liability) can be made automatically, and a mapping between VAT liability and input tax refund would also be applicable in this context.

7.2 Customs, Transfer Prices, Capital Gains Tax and Tax Audit

The LTSD (G) serves as proof of the various components/raw materials in the goods supplied. Depending on the tariff classification under customs law, special customs procedures, such as the use of a free trade agreement, can lead to exemption or reduction of the customs duty. Customs duties arise from transaction-related operations across state borders. Customs clearance and the customs clearance of goods at borders are characterized by the documentation of goods flows (H). The individual transactions and their documentation can be recorded in a blockchain and made available to the contracting parties and the authorities. The same applies to the reporting and customs procedures (J and K), for the other information, such as the country of origin certificates, where-used lists, and other documents.

The transfer prices are maintained and documented in the ERP systems. In addition, a wealth of further information and documentation is required to determine

7. Cf. *Press Release of the European Commission* of 10.9.2020, doc. no. IP/20/1579. The so-called VAT gap is the difference between the VAT expected and the actual tax revenue in the EU. Although the validity of the estimates is questionable, the sheer size of the gap calls for a critical examination of the current VAT system in the EU. Cf., in this respect, also on combatting the VAT gap: *Gries*, Umsatzsteuerliche und statistische Untersuchung der Meldeverpflichtungen im innergemeinschaftlichen Warenverkehr – Eine normative und quantitative Analyse zum Bürokratieabbau in den Unternehmungen am Beispiel der Siemens AG, 2019, 255.
8. These forty-nine notifications comprise: 12 × advance VAT returns, 12 × recapitulative statements, 1 × annual VAT return, 12 × dispatch returns and 12 × receipt returns (Intrastat).
9. Cf. *Gries*, Umsatzsteuerliche und statistische Untersuchung der Meldeverpflichtungen im innergemeinschaftlichen Warenverkehr – Eine normative und quantitative Analyse zum Bürokratieabbau in den Unternehmungen am Beispiel der Siemens AG, 2019, 265 ff.

the 'correct' transfer price in terms of the arm's length principle (L). The selection of the transfer pricing methodology as well as the determination of the so-called ranges in which comparable arm's length transactions are priced could be documented by means of the blockchain and made available to the tax authorities. According to the Organisation for Economic Co-operation and Development Base Erosion and Profit Shifting Action Plans from 2015, the existing documentation and the extended documentation, such as country-by-country reporting, will have to be prepared regularly by the companies concerned. The blockchain platforms could provide not only the evidence required for tax purposes (M) but also a reconciliation within a group of companies in the sense of as a verification of the correct implementation of the intercompany transactions. Such reconciliations become necessary if a group of companies does not have a uniform ERP system in which the group reconciliation of receivables and payables can take place automatically (N).

The multiple refunds of capital gains taxes in cum-ex transactions, which are currently in the spotlight, could have been avoided with the use of blockchain technology (O). Proof of capital gains and withholding tax must be verified regularly as part of a tax audit. If the issuers of a withholding tax certificate confirm the transaction triggering the tax in a blockchain, the certificate in the conventional sense can be dispensed with, because it is stored electronically in the blockchain in a way that cannot be changed and is available to the contractual partner as well as to the authorities.

In the verification of tax returns as part of a tax audit, standard audit actions on the various topics could be automated, documented and shared with the tax authorities (P). Examples are manifold, such as the documentation of travel expenses and non-deductible expenses, donation receipts, and so on.

The transaction-related tax processes from excise duty, such as for the proof of use, the use of raw materials subject to excise duty, and so on, are currently being examined for further possible uses of blockchain technology.

8 OUTLOOK

In order to fulfil their duties under tax and customs law, companies have to perform a steadily increasing number of compliance tasks, which also generate a high administrative burden. Documentation obligations in particular prove to be resource-intensive for two reasons: on the one hand, the administration works largely on the basis of paper files, and, on the other hand, the procurement of information is dependent on numerous internal and external stakeholders. Yet, this administrative burden can be reduced for both companies and government agencies through current technological applications such as blockchain. However, the main reason is not only the potential time and cost savings but also the improvement of data transparency and regulatory compliance for all stakeholders.

In this context, every new technology first goes through a test phase until it is potentially deployed. In the area of tax processes, customs, and excise, digitization will significantly change these 'fields of work' in the coming years. The various types of taxes follow legal mandates or compliance requirements that must be met. These prescribed sets of rules make the related tax processes particularly suitable for digitization. Blockchain technology is not a 'triple-entry bookkeeping', but a technology that ensures a completely secure transfer of data. Moreover, blockchain only requires several acting persons/parties to share this information among themselves. This new form of communication leads to a significant reduction in the administrative effort required to fulfil tax obligations. This, in turn, results in the widely demanded positive business cases for the use of the new technologies. In addition, blockchain can be combined with artificial intelligence, if the acting persons connected on the blockchain platform make available, for example, data for transactions that an algorithm uses for an automation of a tax process for the benefit of all partners. This gives rise to more advanced combinations of tax types, such as the linking of customs, European VAT, and transfer pricing.

Transfer pricing and customs charges are closely intertwined. For excise processes, the customs tariff number is determinative for calculating the tax burden. One-to-one information via blockchain could bring about optimization across tax types.

As a result, blockchain technology can be a solution that meets compliance and documentation requirements, is auditable by authorities, and streamlines – as well as automates – the standardized flow of information between the parties involved. However, as a success factor for the digital transformation in the tax and customs sector, collaboration in the development of technological standards between companies and authorities is required, most likely starting with common data models. By means of an interdisciplinary platform for digitization in tax law, traditional substitute solutions of individual companies, which are ultimately associated with international competitive disadvantages, could be avoided and investment risks for technological developments in the tax and customs area minimized.

CHAPTER 4

Process Mining in VAT

André Flottmann

1 INTRODUCTION

The value added tax (VAT) is a transaction-driven tax with global relevance. It is applied in accordance with the Organisation for Economic Co-operation and Development's International VAT/Goods and Services Tax Guidelines in 165 states worldwide.[1] Depending on the specific scenario, up to 27% VAT needs to be invoiced to and paid by the customer for an outgoing transaction. Input VAT, which is invoiced by suppliers, can be refunded by the tax authorities under certain conditions. But not all types of transactions require the application of VAT. Cross-border transactions are usually exempt from VAT but trigger special reporting obligations. That is why the VAT determination of a transaction, whether done manually or automated, must be an integral part of almost every purchasing (purchase-to-pay, PTP) or sales (order-to-cash, OTC) business process. The information entered and the decisions made during these processes are likely to be VAT-relevant.

However, it is usually a non-VAT-experienced person who enters what is considered to be the VAT-relevant information of a business case, such as which legal entity invoices the customer, from which country to which country goods are delivered, and under which conditions goods are shipped or services are rendered. Rules also need to be considered during the maintenance of this master data. Materials, customers, or vendors can be VAT-relevant or exempt from VAT for instance. Therefore, VAT departments are an important part of a company's finance functions for most companies engaging in cross-border transactions, and the main responsibility

1. OECD (2017), *International VAT/GST Guidelines*, https://www.oecd-ilibrary.org/docserver/9789264271401-en.pdf?expires=1609360323&id=id&accname=guest&checksum=75AF7E9D54367C1DDDCB67831DB8A7D1.

of a VAT department is to ensure correct and VAT-compliant reporting to the tax authorities.

The reporting requirements vary per country. While some countries still require a relatively simple and cumulative monthly reporting without any information about the transactions, the global trend is clearly steering towards a more complex transaction-based live form of VAT reporting.[2] In such a scenario, the taxpayer no longer has the chance to review and correct transactions before they are reported to the tax authorities. It has therefore become even more relevant for companies to ensure a VAT-compliant business process.

In that vein, providing advice and training within a company are part of the daily business of a VAT specialist; a basic understanding of business processes and enterprise resource planning (ERP) functions is fundamental to providing successful and substantial training and advice. The current trend for reporting obligations and ever-increasing business relations mean that VAT departments need to be involved in the business process design and modelling: a correct business process from a VAT perspective is key to compliant VAT reporting. While it is relatively easy to check the VAT aspects of transactions, the monitoring of a business process from a VAT perspective is complex, especially as a process stakeholder; missing knowledge of the process functions is likely to result in errors from a VAT perspective.

This chapter evaluates the relevance of the process mining technique for VAT compliance within a business organization. As a technique to check both the conformance and the performance of a process,[3] process mining is promising to allow VAT functions a successful review of business processes, the idea being that VAT-relevant changes and violations of a business process can be identified and tackled. This chapter aims to describe the pillars of a successful process mining project in VAT, as well as the future possibilities for using the technology.

2 PROCESS MINING TECHNOLOGY

Process mining technology allows the user to analyse running processes based on the actual data in a system, and – drilling down even further – based on a certain data set. The idea of how a process must be run within an organization – a 'To-Be' process – can be compared with the actual process – an 'As-Is' process. Despite technical restrictions and requirements (which do not fall under the scope of this chapter), a defined and aligned To-Be process is a fundamental precondition for applying process mining technology. ERP-based business processes (like the incoming PTP process or the outgoing OTC process) are usually defined and aligned within an organization. As previously mentioned, both of these business-owned processes are also of great relevance from a VAT perspective. Process mining technology allows a comparison to be made between the To-Be process and the As-Is process: potential process changes in

2. Cf. OECD (2017), *Mechanisms for the Effective Collection of VAT/GST*, https://www.oecd.org/tax/tax-policy/mechanisms-for-the-effective-collection-of-VAT-GST.pdf.
3. Marlon Dumas, Marcello La Rosa, Jan Mendling, Hajo A. Reijers (2017), *Fundamentals of Business Process Management*, 419-420.

these senses of not aligned process steps or changes to relevant VAT information in transactions can be uncovered using this technology. Such changes can mean not only violations and a risk of incompliance but also missed benefits such as a lack of input VAT deduction.

Process mining technology offers one big advantage over analysing change logs using other technologies, such as business intelligence (BI): it allows the user to see the bigger picture. Whereas the change log on a transactional level only shows a single change in a single transaction, process mining allows the user to see the impact of a change on the overall process.

3 VAT PROCESS MINING PROJECT

Process mining is complex. To obtain accurate and compelling results from a VAT point of view, it is recommended that a process mining project is initiated between the VAT department, the organization's IT department, and the process owner. The IT department must set up the process mining technology and drive both the tool's maintenance and its ongoing improvement, while the process owner must contribute and share process knowledge and customized settings as well as commit to performing follow-up actions – another important part of the process (*see also* sections 3.2 and 3.3). Practically speaking, with three different departments involved in one project, questions of financing and the project leadership should be settled beforehand.

The role of the VAT department in a process mining project can be either as the project leader or as a project participant. However, a VAT department's role is defined; its ultimate task is to identify non-VAT-conformant changes to the process. Process violations also need to be highlighted. The identification of VAT-relevant changes and violations is challenging; business processes can include hundreds of single activities from the process start to the process end.

If the project is led by the VAT department, it is recommended that specific VAT use cases are created. The idea is that non-VAT-conformant process changes and violations are anticipated by the VAT specialist before the process is mined. The specific VAT use cases can limit the scope of data to be considered for the project in the first place. Deeper knowledge of the ERP process that is subject to the process mining is – of course – essential. The project's goal is therefore to confirm already anticipated deviation from a VAT perspective. The process mining tool can be designed according to the VAT specialist's needs for better detection of process changes and violations. Dashboards inside the process mining tool showing details of transactions can be created, which allows the VAT department to find changes more easily and make a link from a process to a single transaction that needs to be corrected. For the tool design, strong collaboration with the IT department is required.

Another scenario could be that the VAT department acts as a participant in the process mining project. In such a case, it has less influence on the design of the tool and on project management, but the benefit of its involvement can still be significant. Process owners can identify changes or delays within the process, which are linked to VAT-related steps (e.g., a high number of invoice reversals or required manual changes of tax codes). VAT departments are required to identify root causes and elaborate on solutions to avoid those delays.

The rest of this section provides examples of potential process mining projects initiated and led by a company's VAT department. By means of use case examples, section 3.1 intends to provide inspiration on how VAT process mining use cases in the area of PTP are created and implemented. A similar methodology can be applied in the area of OTC of course.

3.1 Determining Appropriate Use Cases

To determine appropriate use cases, possible changes to VAT-relevant information in PTP process elements need to be checked. Relevant information could be Incoterms (or International Commercial Terms), the departure and destination country, and the nature of the service. The VAT specialist must understand (with the help of the process owner and the IT department in most cases), where and how this information is considered in the company's ERP process. The more complex an organization, the more customized and complex the logics in the ERP system might be. These customizations need to be reflected in the process model within the process mining tool.

The central element of the PTP process containing most of the VAT-relevant information can be the purchase order. Goods and invoices received based on a purchase order are posted to accounting. Therefore, changes to an Incoterm, departure or destination country, or material information may impact the final accounting posting that is reported to the tax authorities.

Figure 4.1 Simplified Visualization of an Exemplary PTP ERP Process

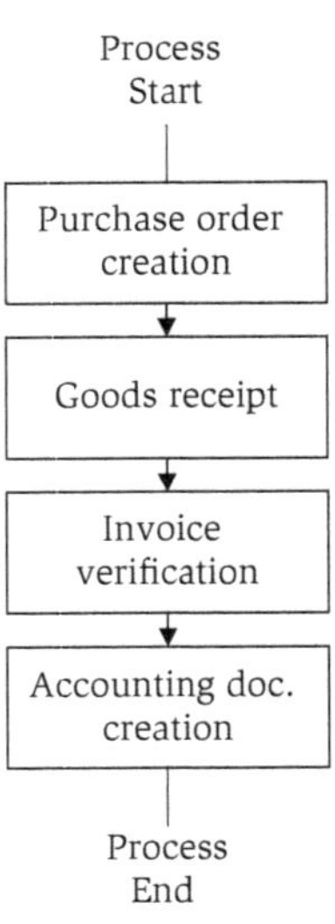

Source: Author's own illustration.

Figure 4.1 shows a very simplified possible PTP process inside an ERP system. It is assumed that goods are delivered. The purchase order contains most of the VAT-relevant data, and it is therefore also the key element in the PTP process from VAT perspective. Information that impacts logistics and finance is combined with PTP-relevant data. The purchase order is usually sent to the supplier, and the supplier then delivers goods based on the agreed terms. Among other things, the purchase order can contain the delivery address, the quantity, the pricing, and the delivering and ordering legal entities. An indication of the VAT treatment might also be given. As shown in Figure 4.1, the goods receipt is posted once the delivery arrives at the destination address.

Goods and invoices are verified and mapped. In theory, the verification activity may lead to further VAT-relevant decisions. Depending on whether a manual or automated tax code determination is implemented in the ERP system, this activity serves as 'pre' step for the final accounting posting. The accounting document posting is definite and is reported to the tax authorities.

Therefore, the aim of VAT use cases is to analyse changes, especially at the level of the purchase order, and to highlight the corresponding VAT impact on the activities that follow. Sections 3.2-3.3 give examples of VAT use cases in order to provide ideas and inspiration about how process mining technology may be used. The same approach can also be applied to the OTC process.

3.2 Use Case: Incoterm Changes

Incoterms define the risks, costs, and insurance transferred from the seller to the buyer, and can be divided into four groups. There are the Incoterm groups E and F, which shift most of the risks, costs, and insurance obligations to the buyer – a relevant Incoterm in these groups is Free Carrier (FCA). The Incoterm groups C and D shift most of the risks, costs, and insurance to the supplier. Incoterm Delivered Duty Paid (DDP) bears all responsibilities to the seller.[4] Incoterms are a good indicator to determine at which point in time the right to dispose of the goods is transferred from the seller to the buyer. The transfer could happen at the start of the delivery or at the end of the delivery. The place where the right to dispose of the goods is located is the key to determining if a transaction is subject to VAT in the departure or in the destination country.[5] For that reason, a change of Incoterm may have an impact on the VAT treatment of a transaction.

From a PTP perspective, the agreed Incoterm can be maintained at purchase order level, so established before the actual delivery happens. Otherwise, the responsibilities concerning the delivery would not be clear. But changes to the Incoterm may still be possible, even after the purchase order has been shared with the supplier. Logical reasons for a change could be: rush deliveries, pricing topics, or a lack of

4. International Chamber of Commerce (2020), *Incoterms 2020* (Incoterms® 2020 - ICC - International Chamber of Commerce (iccwbo.org)).
5. Cf. Article 14 Council Directive 2006/112/EC of 28 November 2006 on the common system of value added tax (EU VAT Directive).

capacity on the freight forwarder side. This type of change can become VAT-relevant in the case of cross-border supplies that trigger export and import responsibilities. The impact of this will be shown using the following exemplary business case.[6]

This business case assumes the Incoterm field in the purchase order changes from Incoterm Delivered At Place (DAP) to DDP. The flow of goods is cross-border from a non-EU (European Union) country into an EU Member State. The definition of the Incoterm DAP means that the supplier bears most of the risks and costs of the delivery but not the import responsibility, as Figure 4.2 shows. The goods are assumed to be delivered when the goods are placed at the disposal of the buyer on the arriving means of transport, ready for unloading at the named destination. The export responsibility is with the supplier, but import formalities are with the buyer. The buyer is the importer of records in the EU Member State.

Figure 4.2 Illustration of Incoterm DAP

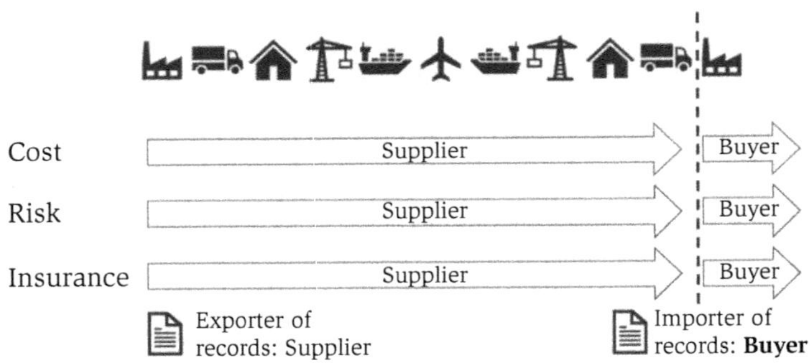

Source: Author's own illustration.

With Incoterm DAP, the transaction is assumed to be a cross-border supply and exempt from VAT in most of the cases, since the power to dispose of the goods is transferred before the goods arrive in the destination country. The transaction is assumed to take place in the country where the delivery starts. Most non-EU countries applying the VAT regime exempt such transactions from VAT according to the destination principle.[7] Therefore, the buyer expects to receive an invoice from the supplier showing no VAT, as this transaction is neither subject to VAT in the departure country nor in the destination country according to the destination principle. The import VAT paid to the authority during the import clearance in the destination country can be deducted by the buyer under certain conditions in most scenarios.

6. The use case description in section 3.2 is a simplified explanation of a transaction's VAT treatment. The final VAT treatment requires a case-specific review considering the exact legal requirements of the relevant departure and destination country.
7. Cf. OECD (2011), *International VAT/GST Guidelines on Neutrality*, http:////search.oecd.org/ctp/consumption/guidelinesneutrality2011.pdf.

Incoterm DDP per definition means that the supplier bears all responsibilities, including the import clearance in the destination country, as Figure 4.3 shows. The goods are assumed to be delivered when the goods are placed at the disposal of the buyer, are cleared for import on the arriving means of transport and are ready for unloading at the named destination.

Figure 4.3 Illustration of Incoterm DDP

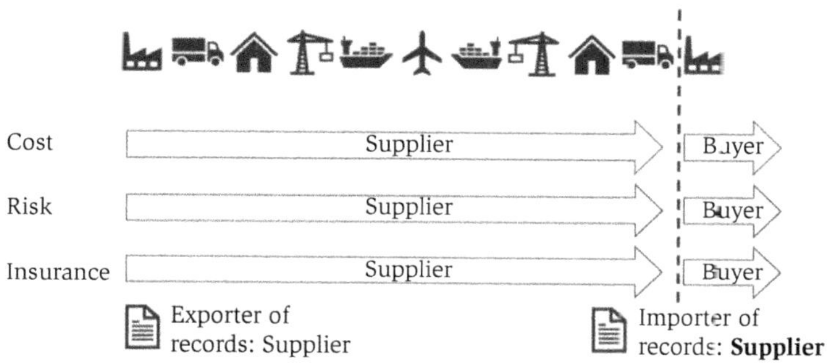

Source: Author's own illustration.

The export and import responsibilities are with the supplier. The buyer receives the right to dispose of the goods in the country of destination. The place of supply is shifted from the departure country to the destination country, which may trigger VAT obligations for the supplier in the destination country. Therefore, the buyer expects a VAT-compliant invoice showing – in most cases – the VAT rate of the destination country.[8] The import VAT paid during the import clearance in the destination country can be deducted by the supplier under certain conditions in most scenarios.

This business case shows why a change of Incoterm from DAP to DDP can be relevant from a VAT perspective, and it also proves that a change of Incoterm acts as a root cause for further amendments in the ensuing purchasing process. A change of Incoterm can, and in some scenarios must, be followed by an action that reflects the change of VAT treatment also. Usually, the VAT treatment of a transaction is reflected in an ERP system by a tax code.[9] Therefore, a change to the tax code in the purchase order or during invoice verification would be required to comply with the Incoterm change from DAP to DDP in the given example.

But further changes during the purchasing process can also be expected based on the above. With Incoterm DAP, the buyer as the importer of records is allowed to deduct the import VAT paid on the import in certain scenarios. In such a case, the assigned broker may pre-finance the import VAT at the time of importation and

8. The VAT treatment and the description are simplified in order to highlight the potential impact of an Incoterm change on a VAT treatment of a single transaction. The final VAT treatment of a transaction should be checked based on the specific business scenario.
9. A tax code is an unique indicator in an ERP system, which can reflect the VAT treatment of a transaction and thus how a transaction is reported.

invoices it along with the import documents to the buyer in a second step. The PTP process, therefore, must include an activity reflecting the deduction of the import VAT from the broker's invoice. The process flow will likely include a second loop of invoice verification and accounting document posting in this PTP case. This time, the accounting posting would not be to the supplier account of the goods, but to the supplier account of the broker.

So, overall, the expected process flow for a supply of goods from a non-EU country into an EU Member State under Incoterm DAP is that there are at least two invoice postings within one business case: one is most likely showing no VAT (goods invoice) and the other may show VAT (import VAT). With Incoterm DDP, a correct process would not show an invoice issued by the broker and referring to import VAT. The goods supplier must account for it according to the Incoterm. For this reason, the change of Incoterm from DAP to DDP can force two VAT-relevant changes: the first one is related to the VAT treatment of the supply of goods, and the second one is concerning the posting of the broker's invoice.

This example gives an idea of how process mining technology can be used to detect process deviations and violations. While it is comparatively easy to track the impact of an Incoterm change in a single business case, it is very complex to retain an overview of VAT-relevant Incoterm changes occurring in millions of business cases. Process mining technology offers this type of transparency on big data processes, but the use case design is important. The best approach is to pre-filter the data pool on use-case-relevant changes to filter out business cases and activities that are not of interest to the user. Taking the use case 'Incoterm changes' as an example, it is recommendable to focus specifically on export and import transactions with an Incoterm change from any Incoterm to DDP, or from DDP to any Incoterm due to the details given above. This will reduce the number of transactions in scope and make it easier to run further deep-dive analysis. Another key to success is to have a link between process analysis and transactional analysis within the process mining tool, and dashboards allowing to filter for a specific flow of goods, certain tax codes, or suppliers will add significant benefit. The transactional details allow targeted follow-up actions, since purchase order numbers or specific vendors, for which this process violation happens the most, can be communicated better to the process owner. Furthermore, it is recommendable to also think about key performance indicators (KPIs) within a VAT process mining use case to highlight the most important figures, such as VAT volume or transaction volume. The dashboard must be designed in such a way that a non-project member is able to easily understand the relevance of the findings. A good communication and information sharing platform can be achieved through the design.

Besides identifying relevant business cases and how to present them in the tool, the follow-up actions are also of utmost relevance for a use case to be successful, and project members need to be aware of the efforts connected to the follow-up action, as illustrated in the following example.

One hundred changes of the Incoterm DAP to DDP for export- and import-relevant supplies are identified in the use case. Eighty of these changes were followed by a change of tax code. Twenty did not have their tax code changed. It is the VAT specialist's task to confirm the plausibility of the eighty tax code changes. The meaning of the 'new' tax code needs to be in line with the fact that 'new' Incoterm DDP may trigger VAT obligations for the supplier in the destination country. In the course of this, it must be confirmed whether the supplier invoice and the supplier master data (e.g., VAT registration number) are in accordance with the new tax code and new Incoterm. So, a detailed check of the single transaction is required. Furthermore, the twenty cases that did not have their tax codes changed need to be checked case by case and assessed as to whether input VAT was maybe missed (i.e., a financial opportunity or a compliance issue), or if the documents – such as supplier invoices – actually show the DAP Incoterm (i.e., a data quality issue) but the ERP data has Incoterm DDP. Both scenarios necessitate further actions:

(1) If a missed financial opportunity is identified, the VAT specialist could initiate trainings with the company's accountants to ensure accurate posting in the future. Potential errors in the ERP logic leading to the incorrect postings could also be checked with the process owner.
(2) If a data quality issue is identified, a side project could be initiated with the process owners and stakeholders. Buyers may also need to be trained on the relevance of Incoterms for cross-border transactions, and the Incoterm changes could be continuously monitored from a VAT perspective to ensure future data quality.

Process mining projects, thus, require time and effort, and do not end with the identification of deviations.

3.3 Use Case: Invoice Reversals

Another possible use case, among others, could be to specifically filter process flows including an invoice reversal. Depending on which ERP system is used in a company, a reversal could be identified on a specific document type, for instance. However, it can be difficult to understand the context of an invoice reversal, and especially difficult to verify if the reversal was VAT conformant or not. The holistic expectation from a VAT point of view is that a reversal has the same VAT treatment as the initial invoice. From an ERP perspective, this could mean that the reversal is posted with the same tax code as the initial invoice.[10]

10. The use case description in section 3.3 is a simplified explanation of a transaction's VAT treatment. The final VAT treatment requires a case specific review considering the exact legal requirements of the relevant departure and destination country.

Figure 4.4 Illustration of the Invoice Reversals Use Case: Posting of the Initial Invoice

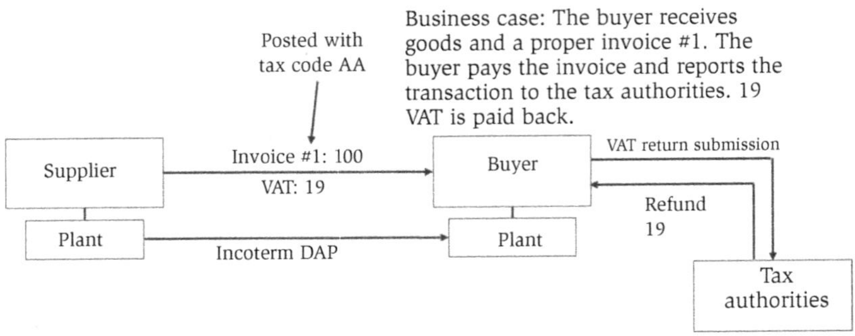

Source: Author's own illustration.

Figure 4.4 illustrates a simplified way that an incoming invoice could be processed. Assuming, a VAT-compliant gross invoice with a net value of 100 and VAT of 19 was initially received, 19 can be deducted as input VAT by using a certain input VAT tax code (here: AA). The amount of 19 would be reported to the tax authorities as input VAT, and the tax authorities can refund 19 under certain conditions (*see* Figure 4.4). To offset the input VAT deduction, the reversal of this invoice should have the same tax code.

Figure 4.5 Illustration of the Use Case: Incorrect Posting of the Invoice Reversal

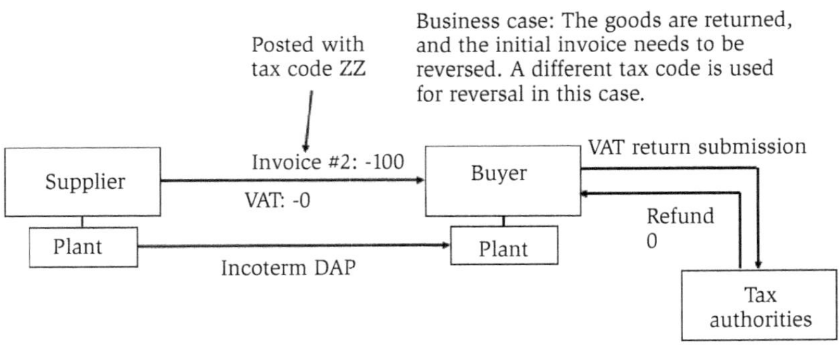

Source: Author's own illustration.

Figure 4.5 underlines the impact of a non-conformant process. If a different tax code is used for the reversal than that used for the initial invoice, the taxpayer may miss a requirement to pay back input VAT to the tax authorities. It could also result in a VAT overpayment if a net invoice is reversed with an input VAT tax code, relating to an input VAT deduction. Process mining technology can help to link the initial invoice with the invoice reversal and to unveil overlaps. One overlap could be that invoice reversals happen more often for a specific vendor and that an invoice following the invoice reversal could have a different tax code. This could be an indication for checking this supplier in more detail from a VAT point of view. A specific dashboard could be created in the process mining tool to compare transactional details, such as the invoice number, VAT amount, and supplier name on the initial invoice and on the invoice reversal. A logic check function in the tool's dashboard would be helpful, as this allows the user to directly filter according to cases with different tax codes.

Besides the transactional comparison, the temporal component also could be included in the use case design. The expectation from a VAT point of view is that the time between posting the initial invoice and reversing the posting is reasonable. Process mining technology can give information about how long it takes to get from one activity to another activity. It also uncovers activities in between.

Let us assume that an invoice is posted in December 2019, and the goods are returned in February 2020; it may not be plausible to have an invoice reversal in December 2020. The reason for the late reversal should therefore be checked from a VAT perspective. Other process mining techniques, as described in section 4, can be used for this purpose.

This use case offers several benefits for VAT departments and shows other possible benefits of using process mining technology. If the initial invoice and the according reversal are identified to have the same tax code, this is documented and this confirms that the process is essentially running in a VAT-compliant way. If cases with different tax codes are identified, corrections and immediate follow-up actions with the process owner are required to prevent any future mistakes. The temporal component gives further indications of whether the business process is running according to expectations from a VAT perspective; a lot of cases displaying an 'unreasonable' time discrepancy between invoice posting and invoice reversal may indicate VAT-relevant problems in the purchasing process that need to be checked with the process owner. Root causes and further process violations can also be identified through alternative process mining techniques.

4 PROCESS MINING TECHNIQUES

The utilization of a specific process mining technique depends on the user's needs and aims. Section 3 introduced the process mining 'technique' of creating use cases and designing use-case-specific dashboards, which is likely the best and most effective way to learn how to work with process mining technology. The creation of use cases allows a non-process expert to focus on relevant changes via the sorting of all irrelevant activities within a complex process. Use cases also allow specific dashboards to be used to highlight relevant information.

However, three further process mining techniques exist,[11] all of which have added value for VAT specialists during process mining projects. The most common of these techniques is the process discover function. This function is also a significant part

11. Marlon Dumas, Marcello La Rosa, Jan Mendling, Hajo A. Reijers (2017), *Fundamentals of Business Process Management*, 419 ff.

of the use cases detailed in sections 3.2-3.3, and gives a detailed overview of process flows and changes to these.

4.1 Process Discovery

The process discovery (or exploring) technique can allow the user to see the full business process with all its changes and activities. The user can understand the number of cases that are in accordance with the intended To-Be process model. But with the full process view, it is also possible to identify all the changes made within a process. If the process is more complex, more changes and deviations can be expected, and - especially in complex process models - the process explorer function appears overwhelming (*see* Figure 4.6, which shows what a process flow may look like).

Figure 4.6 Process Discovery: Illustration of a Business Process

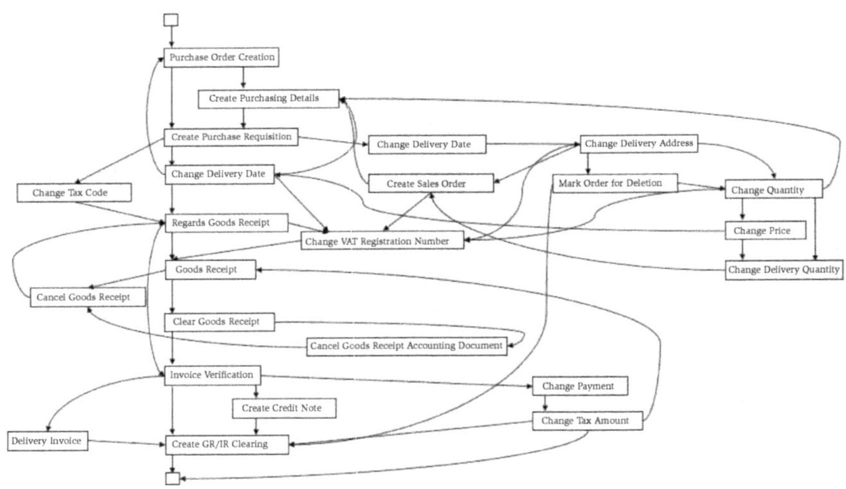

Source: Author's exemplary illustration.

One option would be to start a process mining project simply by investigating the unfiltered business process and searching for non-compliant cases. This technique requires a basic understanding of the process; but the approach is helpful in the case that process owners initiate a process mining project and want to get an overall picture of the process. Focus areas for the project can be detected in this way. This is also valid for stakeholders of the process. A VAT specialist could search for changes and analyse such changes according to their relevance. So, the process exploring approach has added value for both the process owner and the process stakeholder. Depending on the project's approach, the process discover function can, therefore, either serve as starting point or as a support method to search for the root causes of process deviations that have already been identified (e.g., through use cases).

4.2 Variant Exploring

The variant explorer illustrates the different variants, how a process flows from the process start to the process end (*see* Figure 4.7).

Figure 4.7 Variant Exploring

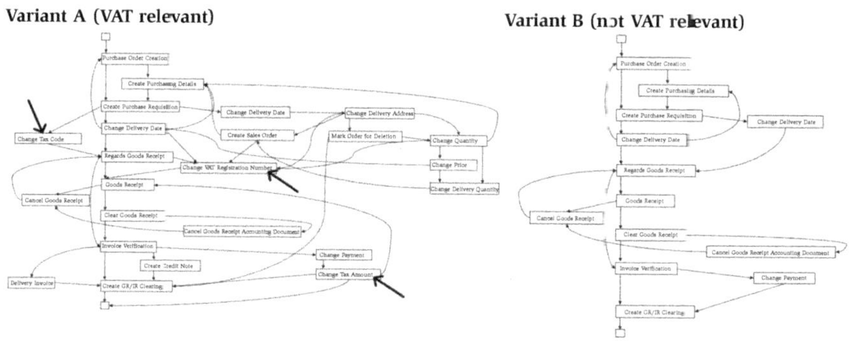

Source: Author's exemplary illustration.

A business case running completely in accordance with the To-Be process (without any change) is the 'best' scenario and represents one possible variant (*see* Figure 4.1). Another variant of how a process can get to the process end could be a scenario with a change of tax code or a change of the tax amount for invoice posting as illustrated in Figure 4.7 (Variant A). This variant is a VAT-relevant possibility of how a process can flow as it is including a possible change of the VAT treatment of transactions. Variant B in Figure 4.7 has no VAT-relevant process step and would therefore not be of interest in the process analysis from a VAT perspective. The process variant comparison can give the user an idea of which process variant, the process mining project should focus on and can thus limit the scope.

In more general terms, the variant explorer gives an indication of the process' complexity. The more variants a process has, the more complex a process seems to be. This type of analysis has added value explicitly for the process owner. Information about how fast a process variant runs from the process start to the process end and how many process variants there are in the ERP system help to improve business processes. From a VAT point of view, the variant analysis of a business process can lead to several different types of recommendation: the more relevant a process variant with VAT-relevant changes to the overall business process is, the more VAT trainings should be given to the business. Continuous checks need to be implemented to decrease the changes in VAT-relevant process steps. Furthermore, the process owner may identify that the business process requires adjustments, for example to increase the process efficiency. The enhancement of the process can also have an impact on the VAT department. If the process owner of the OTC process would decide to automate the invoice posting to increase the efficiency, it must be ensured that tax code determination is accurate.

4.3 Conformance Check

The conformance check allows the user to visualize the comparison between the process model (To-Be process) and the actual ERP data (As-Is process). Each change to the process model is a violation per definition. The goal of the conformance check is comparable to the approach described in section 4.1, the process discovery analysis. A single violation is checked and classified as acceptable or not acceptable. The 'not acceptable' violations need to be tackled. KPIs (e.g., the VAT amount in a case with a non-conformant process change) could give a good indication of the prioritization. This technique can be beneficial for both the process owner and the stakeholder.

All of the four techniques described in this section can be a part of a process mining project. If a first-time process mining project is initiated by a VAT team to evaluate a business-owned process, it is best to start with the creation of use cases. If detailed process knowledge is available, it is also possible to start a project with the exploration of a process and trigger appropriate actions, like trainings, process enhancements with the process owners, and possible correction of invoice postings.

5 EVALUATION OF PROCESS MINING IN VAT

Process mining projects in VAT offer a comprehensive analysis that cannot be achieved with other technologies such as BI or advanced VAT reporting tools. Complex business processes leading to VAT-relevant transactions are visualized in an easy-to-understand manner so that process violations and deviations as a root cause for incorrect transactions can be uncovered. This helps to tackle non-VAT-compliant changes in a business process and avoid them in future. A decrease in incorrect transactions and an increase in data quality can be expected as a result. Further, a process mining project between the VAT department and process owners promotes process thinking within a VAT department as well as the understanding of VAT relevance on the process owner side. It can boost the collaboration between a VAT department and the business functions (e.g., PTP or OTC) inside a company. It helps both sides to better understand one another's requirements and, in turn, also has the effect of tearing down barriers.

Thinking in processes is becoming more and more important for VAT specialists, as audit techniques and the implementation of a risk control matrix focus on 'incorrect processes' as opposed to 'incorrect transactions'. Process mining appears to be the best technology to prepare for this scenario. Moreover, process mining technology can also prove useful for internal VAT processes such as VAT reporting: on the condition that the reporting process is documented accurately and is technically correct, process mining of complex VAT return preparations can be beneficial, as this type of analysis will unveil potential for optimization in the VAT compliance process.

However, there are also some downsides to applying process mining technology in VAT: project members will experience a high workload; a strategy must be in place to tackle all identified problems; there must be dedication to doing this; and detailed resource planning is required to ensure that process problems and incorrect postings are corrected – this can become difficult, especially in the case of cross-functional process mining projects like those described in the use case examples given in sections 3.2-3.3.

6 PROCESS MINING AND FUTURE-ORIENTATED VAT

The strongest positive aspect of process mining is the future-orientated approach. Identifying incorrect processes of course triggers the cleaning of past transactions. But process analysis especially highlights how things need to work in future. Moreover, process mining in VAT can prepare for a higher level of automation concerning the VAT determination in the PTP and the OTC processes. A successful project will confirm the conformance of process parts, will lead to an amendment and optimization of incorrect processes, can enhance the quality of the master data, and will underline areas for improvement. Such outcomes could allow for the implementation of both artificial intelligence and process mining to monitor and positively influence VAT-relevant decisions (e.g., tax code changes) when they occur.

Take the first use case as detailed in section 3.2 as an example of this: if an Incoterm is changed from DAP to DDP, but no tax code change follows this activity, a notification could be sent to the user containing a specific recommendation or asking the user to contact the VAT department for further advice.

Such a real-time check from a VAT perspective can only work if the business process is behaving in accordance with the VAT expectations, but, if successful, incorrect postings could be avoided before they happen. For this to be achieved, strong collaboration between the business functions and the VAT department is required. In light of the demanding live reporting requirements that are coming into force in more and more countries, the application of process mining technology should be among the list of priorities for future-orientated VAT departments.

CHAPTER 5

Using New Technologies to Improve Existing VAT/GST Systems

Raul Zambrano

1 INTRODUCTION

In the first half of the 2010s, the Chilean tax administration (*Servicio de Impuestos Internos*, SII) started a project that focussed on the implementation of a national electronic invoicing system. At that time, there was already an application of electronic documents within value added networks, and this was followed by a proposal for an invoice standard format a couple of years later from the United Nations Centre for Trade Facilitation and Electronic Business. This proposal was mostly directed towards international commerce at first, and then at government purchases. The Chilean initiative focussed on domestic transactions.

Currently, we can see solid and steady implementations of national electronic invoicing systems in Argentina, Brazil, Colombia, Chile, Costa Rica, Ecuador, Mexico, Peru, and Uruguay. Other countries like Bolivia, the Dominican Republic, Panama, and Paraguay have successful pilot projects and have started the massification process. Still more countries are developing, or are considering starting, a project.

Figure 5.1 Date of Adoption of Current Operational Models of Electronic Invoices in Latin America

Source: Author's own illustration.

1.1 Operational Models

Although no two systems are identical, there are several common elements to all electronic invoicing systems that have been implemented in the Latin American countries depicted in Figure 5.1. Some of these elements are fundamental to the operational models chosen, as detailed below.[1]

– *The tax administration receives all original electronic documents*

Traditional paper invoices were regulated by the tax administration on aspects such as the information detailed, the numbering mechanism used, the printing businesses where the forms could be printed, the range of documents required for a specific period, and so on. Taxpayers were required to send tax-related information about their value added tax (VAT) operations, either summarized or on transaction-by-transaction basis in some cases. The actual documents were only accessible to the tax administration in an audit or when a tax lottery had been put in place. The introduction

1. Barreix, A. & Zambrano, R. (2018). Factura Electrónica en América Latina. Washington – Panama City: IADB – CIAT.

of electronic invoicing systems changed that paradigm, not only because the tax administration now receives these documents automatically, but also because the documents are validated in terms of format and business rules – in some countries, there may be a hundred or more business rules implemented.

– The document format is standard and mandatory for all operations and all taxpayers within a country

With the exception of El Salvador, which is currently developing its national invoicing system and will use the JavaScript Object Notation (JSON) file format, all formats are XML-based.

In general, there are two possibilities: designing a local format or using a standard. Most countries have designed their own format in naming the fields according to the local standard, taking into consideration both language and local traditions and customs. For instance, instead of using a general tax identification number (TIN) label for the tax identifier, the formats use local names (RUC in Ecuador, NIT in Colombia, the CNPJ in Brazil, etc.). Colombia and Peru are exceptions to this: both countries use adapted versions of the OASIS Universal Business Language (UBL) standard.

There are pros and cons to both approaches: on the one hand, using the UBL standard facilitates international commerce and speeds up the adoption of the system by multinationals working in the country;[2] on the other hand, using a local format facilitates the implementation of the format by local businesses and developers that would not have to deal with labels in different languages, complex namespaces, and fields that would never be used. Despite possible further analysis of the pros and cons of the two approaches, we see that both work and that the majority of taxpayers have adapted and are using the chosen standard as intended.

The chosen standard is complemented with catalogues to describe units of measurement, types of packaging, currency, geographic location, means of payment, and other elements. In recent years, some countries have introduced a classification code for goods or services.

While the document format is standard and mandatory, there may be specialized sections for some specific kinds of operations (exports of goods, business-to-consumer (B2C) transactions, occasional operations), or for some economic sectors or industries that would require particular fields and business rules.

– With minor exceptions, documents are digitally signed using certificates supported by a public key infrastructure

In some countries, the root authority is the tax administration itself and the certificates are used for specific purposes only. The use of digital signatures also ensures that the document is valid, that it has been prepared and signed by the issuer, that it cannot be tampered with, and that the document is fully digital – a printout of the document or a PDF view are only representations of the document. The signed electronic document has executive merit.

2. OASIS (1993-2021). *UBL Resources*. Retrieved from ubl.xml.org, http://ubl.xml.org/wiki/ubl-resources.

- The projects are led by the tax administrations

The projects to implement national electronic invoicing systems require the involvement of various actors, including government agencies and representatives of the private sector, but the projects are led by the tax administrations: the tax administration leads the design process, prepares the documentation and guidelines for implementing the system, supports the testing process, and, depending on the operational model adopted, facilitates the involvement of third parties either as solution providers or as delegates to act on behalf of the tax administration when validating documents.

- The massification of the system requires low-cost solutions targeted at small and medium-sized taxpayers

To facilitate the massification of the system, low-cost solutions targeted at small and medium-sized taxpayers have been put in place. The solutions vary from online applications hosted by the tax administration that would allow to prepare and produce invoices online to stand-alone applications that can be installed by taxpayers on their local computers, and, more recently, mobile apps that can be used for B2C operations. In Mexico, third parties that act on behalf of the tax administration - *Proveedores Autorizados de Certificación* - need to offer free alternatives for small issuers.

- Supported documents

The supported documents include electronic invoices, but the system extends to debit and credit notes, and could also include other documents such as transport manifests or withholding certificates.

- Scheduled mandatory adoption

The adoption of such electronic invoicing systems is mandatory for taxpayers in the country and is scheduled over a relatively wide time range. The schedule used in each country has different criteria, focussing either on economic activity or taxpayer size to determine when taxpayers should start using the system.

There are also differences that exist between the models implemented in each country. These differences respond to various factors, but the two most significant differences come from: (i) the tax system and (ii) the operational model adopted. In some countries, different documents are used in B2C transactions, as opposed to in business-to-business (B2B) and business-to-government (B2G) transactions: documents used in B2C transactions do not give tax credits in purchases, while invoices are used for B2B and B2G transactions. In other countries, the same documents are used regardless of the type of transaction. In countries like Argentina, Brazil, and Chile where different documents are used, the inclusion of electronic documents to support transactions with final consumers (i.e., in B2C transactions) has only occurred after the massification of electronic invoices for B2B transactions.

The operational models vary per country, particularly in terms of the moment at which the tax administration receives and validates a document. There are three different models possible:

(1) The document is prepared, signed, and delivered to the buyer. It is then sent to the tax administration within a defined time interval after the transaction has taken place. The tax administration later sends a confirmation of the validation process.
(2) The document is prepared, signed, and delivered to the buyer and the tax administration simultaneously. The tax administration sends a confirmation of the validation process after confirmation has occurred.
(3) The document is prepared and signed by the issuer, and is sent for validation and approval by the tax administration. Only after confirmation by the tax administration is the document sent to the buyer.

The first model is a post-audit model where tax administrations do not require real-time or near real-time control of the transactions, yet documents need to be in the tax administration's systems at the end of the defined period for them to be considered as valid. This model can be used for B2C transactions where immediate validation may not be required.

In the second model, in practice, since the response time of the tax administration is very short, taxpayers could wait for a response from the tax administration before delivering the invoice to the buyer. In this instance, the system works in near real time, in a similar way as the third option mentioned, with a clearance model in most cases.

Another significant difference is how the services that receive and validate the electronic documents have been implemented. In most cases, the services are hosted by the tax administration. In Mexico and Guatemala, there are third parties – regulated by the respective tax administrations – that act on behalf of the tax administration to provide the certification service. Brazil, where ICMS (*Imposto Sobre Operações Relativas à Circulação de Mercadorias e Serviços de Transporte Interestadual de Intermunicipal e de Comunicações*) is at state level, has an alternative mechanism hosted either by the individual state, the so-called national environment hosted by the state-owned IT company SERPRO, or the so-called virtual SEFAZ (*Secretaria de Fazenda*) to process transactions.[3]

In all cases, contingency mechanisms are a must to ensure that failures would not disrupt the economy at large. Contingency mechanisms are also distinct between models.

The underlying technology used to run a system as well as that used to process information for control purposes also varies per model. In some cases, to meet the demanding requirements in terms of storage and processing capacity, tax administrations may use cloud services.

1.2 Electronic Invoicing in Latin America: A Few Stats to Clarify How Widespread It Is

In a country where an e-invoicing system has been implemented and all invoices are sent to the tax administration, the total number of documents that needs to be received,

3. de Freitas, V. & Maldonado, N. (2020). *Invoices and Electronic Documents*. In CIAT (ed.), ITC as Strategic Tool to Leapfrog the Efficiency of Tax Administrations. Panama City: CIAT.

validated, stored, and processed is larger than any previous type of information processed. Currently, countries like Argentina, Brazil, Chile, or Mexico that are – in practical terms – issue 100% of B2B documents and a large percentage of B2C documents in electronic format, while other countries are expanding the number of issuers in the system but already cover a large portion of documents since taxpayers that issue a large number of invoices are already part of the system.

Currently there are more than 160 billion electronic documents stored by the tax administrations of Latin America. While this is a large number, we may not be able to fully grasp its real significance. Therefore, some individual figures may help to give us a better idea. In Mexico, for example, over 6 billion documents per year are stored by the tax administration, that is an average of 200 documents per second. In Brazil, there are 1.8 million issuers with more than 27 billion B2B documents[4] and 1 million issuers with 52 billion documents of B2C invoices.[5] In Colombia, where the massification of the system has taken place over the last couple of years, more than 360,000 taxpayers are already issuing electronic documents.[6]

The online services provided by tax administrations are quite significant. What is more, the volumes of information that need to be processed are huge, and it is a truly permanent operation. Figures 5.2 and 5.3 show public statistics provided by two tax administrations: Ecuador (population of 17.6 million) and Costa Rica (population of 5 million).

Figure 5.2 shows that 4.4 million electronic invoices were issued in Ecuador on 13 December 2020, which was a Sunday. This number is substantially lower than on the other days detailed, when the numbers reached over 6 million electronic invoices per day. Figure 5.3 shows that the majority of electronic invoices received by the Costa Rican tax administration (*Dirección General de Tributación*, DGT) were processed during regular working hours. We see that over 100,000 documents were processed per hour during the peak times, and that numbers were still high in the evening with a few thousand documents still being processed between 1 am and 5 am.

Figure 5.2 Statistics on Electronic Invoices Received by the Ecuadorian Tax Administration (Servicio de Rentas Internas, SRI): Number of Invoices in the Last Five Sates (9-13 December 2020)

Últimos 5 días	
Día	No. Comprobantes
13 December 2020	4.405.023
12 December 2020	6.235.009
11 December 2020	6.410.168
10 December 2020	6.521.402
9 December 2020	6.139.919

Source: SRI website, 13 December 2020.

4. Receita Federal do Brasil (2021). Retrieved from Portal da NF-e, https://www.nfe.fazenda.gov.br/portal/principal.aspx.
5. ENCAT (2021). *Estatísticas. Nota Fiscal de Consumidor Eletrônica*. Retrieved from Nota Fiscal de Consumidor Eletrônica, nfce.encat.org/estatisticas.
6. Márquez, M. (2020). *La factura electrónica llegó para quedarse*. In DIAN (ed.), Transformación DIAN. Por una Colombia más honesta. Bogota.

Figure 5.3 Graphic Showing the Number of Invoices Received Each Hour by the DGT

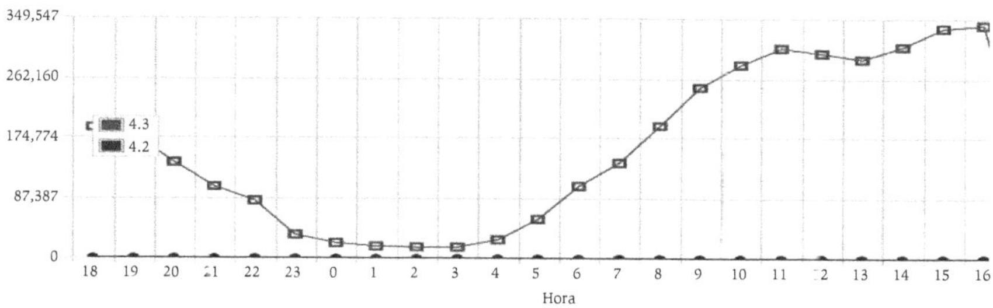

Source: DGT website 13 December 2020.

Within the space of just a couple of days, tax administrations now receive more information than they used to receive over the course of a year just a decade ago. Of course, these volumes put pressure on the systems not only in terms of response times – below one second on average – but also in terms of supporting taxpayers with their operations via the associated resource websites, guidelines, contact centres, and through providing new services, for example, services that allow taxpayers to query invoices or download documents.

2 USING ELECTRONIC INVOICING INFORMATION FOR CONTROL PURPOSES

The use of electronic invoices, once the tax administration has the complete documents, with all their elements and fields, should – naturally – support control objectives. The potential reach that comes from the implementation of an electronic invoicing system depends on the proportion of taxpayers using the system, both as issuers and as recipients of documents. In the initial phases of rolling out such a system when only a small number of taxpayers are using it, this 'potential reach' is limited to the taxpayers actually using the system at that moment and, to some extent, those taxpayers that buy from them. However, once the massification process is underway, a larger proportion of taxpayers are covered and the potential reach also grows.

2.1 Cross-Matching with Tax Returns and Third-Party Information

The first thing a tax administration can do with electronic invoices is straightforward: it can verify the total value a taxpayer has according to their invoices in terms of sales and debits documented in issued invoices, and purchases and credits documented in invoices issued by other taxpayers in which they are identified as a buyer. These total amounts are compared with the corresponding figures presented in VAT tax returns to identify any differences, allowing the tax administration to take action when these differences are significant.

The cross-matching of information can occur at any time after tax returns are filed, that is if no statute of limitations has been reached for a particular period.

However, the sooner the action is taken by the tax authority the better, including the possibility of making this comparison at the moment that a taxpayer files a return, and issuing an immediate note to the taxpayer informing them of any discrepancies that may later be reviewed.

What is more, the tax administration could show - or send via email - to the taxpayer a summary of the invoices issued, total sales, debits, purchases, and credits that the tax administration already knows about before the taxpayer prepares their tax return.

2.2 Electronic Audits

A more comprehensive approach is to conduct electronic audits using all the information contained in electronic invoices in addition to the other information that the tax administration may have concerning the taxpayer, including tax returns (VAT or income tax), current and previous third-party information reported by other actors (including banks and credit-card operators), withholding reports, and so on.

One significant example of this comes from Mexico, where the process of electronic auditing includes more than seventy audit working papers and ends with proposed reassessments that can cover several periods. This new process, that has changed the tradition in terms of auditing, has had a significant impact in terms of the audit outcomes, as depicted in Figure 5.4,[7] which shows a direct return from audit interventions in terms of revenue.

Figure 5.4 Collected MXN over a Hundred Invested MXN

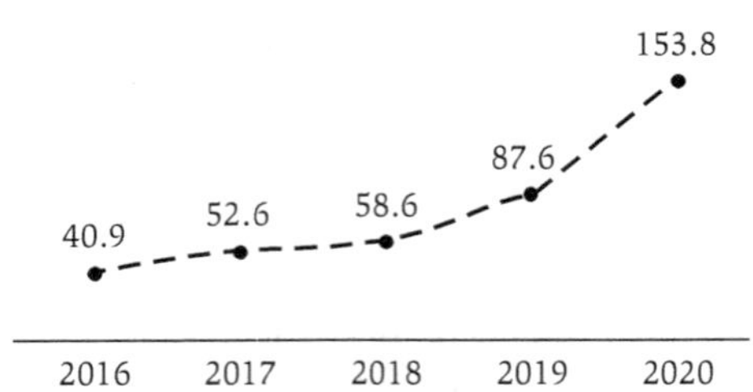

Source: Mexican Tax Administration (*Servicio de Administración Tributaria*, SAT), 2020.

2.3 Pre-filled Tax Returns

Electronic invoice information can be used to pre-fill tax returns. In some cases, such information has been used to support or verify claims related to deductions of education or health expenses in personal income tax returns when the taxpayer has been identified in the invoice; in such a case, the expenses that the taxpayer claims must be reflected in the invoices that the tax administration already has.

7. Servicio de Administración Tributaria - SAT (2020). *Informe Tributario de Gestión*. México.

In September 2017, the SII launched a new service offering a pre-filled tax return to VAT taxpayers under the general regime. As a necessary prior step, the tax administration kept detailed registries of all purchases and sales documented in electronic invoices.[8] This registry has functionalities that allow taxpayers to query and download all purchases and sales details stored by the tax administration. The registry contains four pieces of information: (1) the sum of purchases and the nature of operations; (2) pending documents (i.e., the invoices that have been sent to the tax administration but have not yet been confirmed by the buyers); (3) disputed documents (including transactions that have been disputed or rejected by the buyer); and (4) values in purchases that the taxpayer is not claiming as credits (because such expenses are not related to business activity).

With the information from this registry, the tax administration prepares a pre-filled VAT return that is offered to all taxpayers. Over 93% of VAT taxpayers use the pre-filled return, and this accounts for 92% of all VAT collected in the country. Taxpayers have reported through surveys that filing the VAT return, which now involves a review and confirmation process in the registry, is 60% faster than the traditional method.

The system not only simplifies compliance by not requiring purchasing and selling books, but it also expedites the process, reducing the cost of compliance. In addition, this service acts as a control measure; taxpayers know that the tax administration already has information about them, making it futile to hide information. It also helps to reduce disputes, since inconsistencies and errors are handled before the return is prepared within the mechanisms implemented in the registry of sales and purchases. Other countries are also pursuing pre-filled VAT returns. Ecuador, for example, is already populating fields.

2.4 Identifying Fraudulent Invoices

One recurrent problem that tax administrations face related to VAT is the existence of fraudulent invoices that have been issued to support inexistent or simulated operations to justify claims of VAT credits or expenses in order to reduce the taxes that a taxpayer must pay. These schemes are supported in general by 'ghost' companies that are created exclusively to conduct these operations. The introduction of electronic invoices makes this type of fraudulent operation more difficult, but, unfortunately, it does not eliminate the problem.

There are different approaches to dealing with the problem. However, in most cases it starts with identifying the documents that likely correspond to simulated operations. This process could make use of advanced analytics or machine learning to classify invoices that show problematic patterns or anomalies. In this respect, there are three main options:

8. Barraza, F. (2020). *Tax Returns, Payments and Refunds Processing: The Chilean Experience with Pre-filled VAT Tax Returns*. In Borja, D. et al. (eds), ICT as a Strategic Tool to Leapfrog the Efficiency of Tax Administrations. Panama: CIAT.

(1) The first option – used in many countries – is to create a criminal case with all parties involved, including the issuer, the recipients of the invoices, and any third parties that might have been facilitators in the scheme.
(2) The second option – used in Mexico – comes when the tax administration identifies documents that are likely related to legal entities simulating operations and rejects them for all purposes, including claiming VAT credits or supporting expenses. Subsequently, the involved taxpayers are published in lists which in Mexico are called EFOS (companies invoicing simulated operations) and EDOS (companies deducting simulated operations), but are granted the opportunity to prove that the operations concerned are, in fact, real. If the taxpayers fail to prove this, they are then included in the list that indicates that the documents in question do not have any fiscal consequences, and that the taxpayer may be subject to prosecution.[9]
(3) The third option – used in Argentina – is to implement a withholding of VAT on invoices issued by high-risk taxpayers. Such invoices are referred to as '*Factura M*'.

2.5 Using Artificial Intelligence with Electronic Invoices

One difficult task for tax administrations is to validate that all credits claimed by a taxpayer in VAT operations correspond to their line of business. This would require an analysis of the content of each invoice to see if the products or services described could really be claimed. In practice, finding this type of situation would happen only as part of an audit process when the auditor reviews the invoices or – more commonly – a sample of the invoices.

Once the tax administration has all the details of every VAT-related transaction in the country, the tax administration could, in theory, use Artificial Intelligence (AI) mechanisms, in particular machine learning algorithms, to facilitate such a process. In this vein, the SII is running a project that analyses the different items detailed on invoices and assigns each item a code in catalogue of goods and services. It then segments taxpayers according to their economic activity and later assigns risk to taxpayers that might be claiming disputable credits. This process is illustrated in Figure 5.5.

Figure 5.5 Using AI to Identify Risk

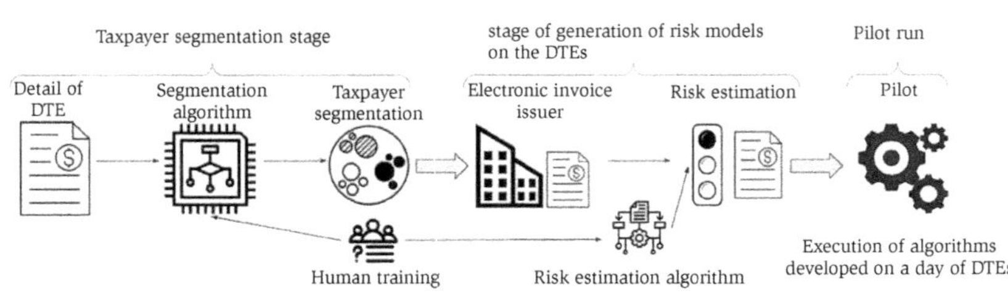

Source: Erick Marinkovic, SII, 2020.

9. Diario Oficial, M. (2018). https://www.dof.gob.mx/nota_detalle.php?codigo = 5528960&fecha = 25/06/2018. Retrieved from Diario Oficial de México.

3 ELECTRONIC INVOICING AND THE PROVISION OF SERVICES

The aggregated information about electronic invoices could be valuable to the provision of services by the tax administration. Some such services have already been mentioned in this chapter. For instance, taxpayers could visualize all documents in which they appear as buyers, either in the purchase and sales registry, as in Chile (*see* section 2.3), or directly in their taxpayer inbox, as in Mexico (*see* section 2.2). Some tax administrations also provide applications, either online or through mobile apps, where invoices can be completed and sent to their customers; some tax administrations provide a query service on their websites to check recognized service providers for electronic invoice-related services; and all tax administrations provide the means for taxpayers and individuals to verify that an invoice they have received has been validated or authorized by the tax administration.

In addition to the services related to electronic invoicing systems, there are other uses of electronic invoices that have been improved as a result. Some of these applications even go beyond the scope of tax administration processes.

3.1 Purchases and Prices

In some Brazilian states, databases containing the fair prices of items frequently bought by the government have been built with data taken from electronic invoices related to purchases that have been made by the government. These databases contain the actual prices of specific items that can later be used as reference values in the public procurement of common items. The databases allow potential suppliers to be identified and actual prices that the government paid in previous purchases to be published. With this data, and the implementation of automated processes for procurement, these processes have been improved: the manager who is in charge of the purchasing processes instead of using quotes and offers can base analysis on actual market values.[10]

Some Brazilian states have also deployed applications that can be used by citizens to search for the lowest price of a specific product in stores near the user's location. Capturing the barcode with the app, the user receives a list of the actual prices of previous purchases in different stores. The data is updated frequently based on recent transactions.[11] Figure 5.6 illustrates the interface and the main menu of the application – an appropriate recent addition to the app is a direct link to search for cleaning and health-related items that can prove useful during the COVID-19 pandemic.

10. Correa, G., Dezolt, A. & Muñoz, A. (2020). BID Mejorando Vidas. Retrieved from Innovación digital para una contratación pública más eficiente en Salud: La Factura Electrónica como parámetro de precios, https://blogs.iadb.org/gestion-fiscal/es/innovacion-digital-contratacion-publica-eficiente-salud-factura-electronica-parametro-precios/.
11. Lowest Price Application (2020). Google Play, https://play.google.com/store/apps/details?id=br.gov.pr.celepar.sefa.mp&hl=pt_PT&gl=US Apple Store, https://apps.apple.com/br/app/menor-pre%C3%A7o/id1164088000.

Figure 5.6 Screen Shot of an Application Used in Brazil to Query for Lowest Prices of Articles Within a Geographic Area[a]

Source: Menor preço application.

a It Includes a Section Specifically Related with Items to Fight the COVID-19 Pandemic.

3.2 Statistics and Economic Studies

The data of all electronic invoices can be used to conduct economic analysis. As a result, it is possible to monitor how the economy, excluding informality, is performing, and identify disruptions that could impact revenue collection. During the COVID-19 pandemic, this is precisely what some tax administrations have done. Using data from electronic invoices, tax administrations have been able to analyse the impact of COVID-19 on sales according to economic activity, geographic location, or taxpayer size.[12] These analyses have helped to design policies that will help affected taxpayers, while still pursuing the tax contribution of taxpayers that continued to do well during the pandemic. Figure 5.7 shows examples of how the Brazilian economy, in one of its states, has been impacted during the COVID-19 pandemic in specific economic sectors.

12. Zambrano, R. & Díaz de Sarralde, S. (14 April 2020). Electronic Invoicing in Times of Pandemic. Retrieved from CIAT, https://www.ciat.org/electronic-invoicing-in-times-of-pandemic/?lang=en.

Figure 5.7 Evolution of Sales of Retail Products by Category, Showing the Daily Average During the 2020 Period Compared with 2019[a]

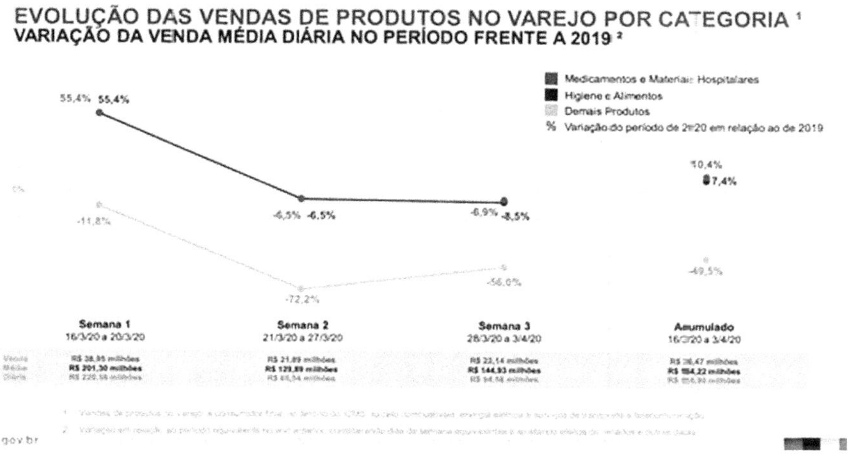

Source: *Secretaria da Fazenda* (SEFAZ) – Rio Grande do Sul, Brazil.

a Black text: medicines and hospital materials; soft black text: hygiene and food light grey text: other products. B. Each instance refers to a week (semana) in March 2020.

Electronic invoice data can be used to conduct studies that might go beyond the sphere of tax-related matters. One interesting example of such an application is Ecuador, where such data were used to identify the percentage of local goods and services involved in production chains. Instead of just comparing a taxpayer's local purchases against imports to determine the local and imported components of its inputs, the process determined the same information via the taxpayer's suppliers. The suppliers were identified via electronic invoices. Even if a company buys everything in the local market, its suppliers could well be importing a lot, so the local component in the value chain would be smaller. The objectives of the study were to support the design of public policy identifying local production nodes, and to target public investment or incentives aimed at strengthening local industries. Figure 5.8 illustrates a single step of the process.

Figure 5.8 Illustration of Local Value-Added Component Determination

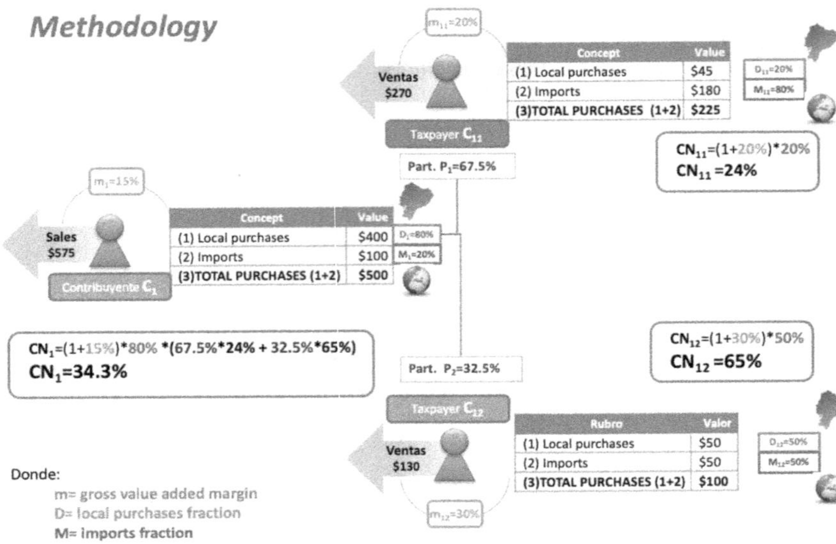

Source: SRI, 2017.

The elaboration of economic studies using electronic invoices has a lot of potential. It is feasible to think of applications to measure inflation rates, consumption trends, and estimations of gross national product. However, the tax administration needs to ensure the confidentiality of data and that only aggregated information is used for statistical purposes.

3.3 Factoring

In Chile, invoices have executive merit and invoice factoring allows for the assignment of accounts receivable to third parties at a discount. In the 'paper world', this process required the endorsement of a third copy of the invoice using the reverse of the document to stamp and write down the details of the operation. However, with the introduction of electronic invoices, this process has been replaced by an electronic assignment document that needs to be annotated in a public registry of transfer of credits.[13] In addition, in 2016, a newly enacted law established an eight-day period to confirm or reject an invoice creating the necessary conditions so all parties know the documents will not be cancelled or rejected.

This infrastructure has allowed factoring to significantly expand in the country. The growth rate of factoring has increased up to 50% year-on-year. The total value of

13. Barraza, F. (2018). Influencia de la Facturación Electrónica en el desarrollo del Factoring en Chile. In Barreix, A. & Zambrano, R. (eds), *La Factura Electrónica en América Latina.* Washington - Panamá: BID - CIAT.

negotiated documents has reached 8% of the gross domestic product (GDP) in 2016,[14] extending financing alternatives to small and medium-sized taxpayers also. Figures 5.9 and 5.10 show the statistics related to invoice factoring in Chile.

Figure 5.9 Factoring in Chile: Number of Electronic Documents Assigned

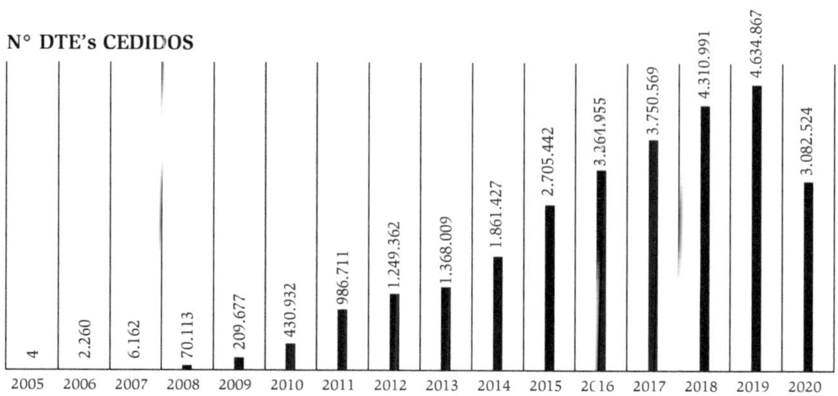

Source: SII, 2020. (Data as of September 2020)

Figure 5.10 Factoring in Chile: Total Negotiated Amounts in Millions of USD

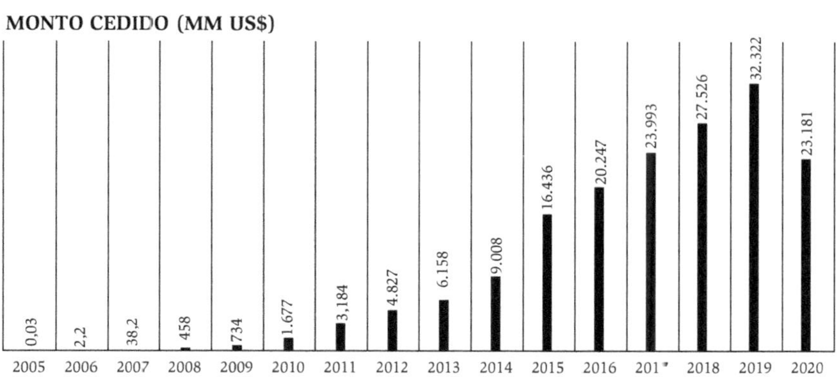

Source: SII, 2020. (Data as of September 2020)

A similar approach of annotation processes is being used in other countries by the respective tax administrations.

14. Barraza, F. (2018). Influencia de la Facturación Electrónica en el desarrollo del Factoring en Chile. In Barreix, A. & Zambrano, R. (eds), *La Factura Electrónica en América Latina*. Washington – Panamá: BID – CIAT.

3.4 Tax Refunds

Tax refunds of VAT, for instance to exporters, is a process that could clearly benefit from electronic invoices. Usually, this type of refund goes through a revision or even an audit by the tax administration. This whole process could be expedited with the electronic invoicing system, thus improving the competitiveness of the country.

One very interesting scenario concerns Ecuador. In Ecuador, the elderly and disabled people have the right, under certain limitations, to claim back the VAT they pay on regular purchases. The existing refund process is slow and requires verification, but it has been significantly improved by electronic invoicing. The new approach that will begin as of March 2021 is automatic, and the refund will be processed at the same time the invoice is issued. The process requires the incorporation of 160,000 individuals into the new automated process, and these taxpayers have requested refunds in the past. The inclusion would follow a risk analysis process. After that, participating issuers use a web service provided by the tax administration that immediately authorizes or refuses the refund.

Beyond providing a service for these individuals, this practice shows the potential of an online decision-making process associated with individual invoices. It also brings new possibilities to tax administrations and even to tax policy in the coming years.

4 BENEFITS OF ELECTRONIC INVOICES IN A BROADER SENSE

The implementation of a national electronic invoicing system is an effort that requires resources from all parties involved, including a large number of taxpayers. But this effort should result in benefits that go beyond an increase in voluntary tax compliance.

Removing paper from the invoicing process helps to reduce costs for companies, not only because it reduces the physical costs associated with paper invoices being delivered to customers through traditional mail services, but also because there is no need to file the physical invoice copies and retain them for a number of years, as is required in many jurisdictions.

A study conducted in Mexico, however, shows that the benefits for taxpayers may even go beyond this due to two other factors:[15] the first is the reduction in compliance costs; the second is linked to improved operational processes, which include better communication with customers and suppliers; accounts receivable; accounts payable; accounting; inventory management; and vertical integration in some industries. The study also suggests that the relationship between taxpayers and tax administrations has improved due to electronic invoicing systems. In Chile, for example, through its purchases and sales registry, continuous transaction controls by the tax administration allow for reporting obligations to be reduced.

The improvements that electronic invoicing systems bring for businesses come in part from the ability to automate, and this ability – in turn – relies on the use of a mandatory standard that must be used for all operations by all taxpayers in a country: the exchange of documents that anyone can prepare and read is thus easier, as is the

15. AMEXIPAC (2016). Impactos Sectoriales del uso de Factura Electrónica en México. Mexico City.

validation against a common schema, regardless of whether a company issues the document or receives it. Although this is beneficial for the majority of taxpayers in a country, companies that operate in multiple markets might be forced to work with different standards in different countries, and that would require dealing with an increasing set of regulations. In this vein, there is an initiative by the International Chamber of Commerce to improve the situation for international operations with a set of principles for the implementation of continuous transaction controls.[16]

The question of whether the introduction of a national electronic invoicing system will increase government revenue should be addressed with some care. If VAT compliance in a country is very high, there is not much financial gain, yet if there is room for improvement in terms of compliance then there is most certainly an opportunity to reduce the VAT gap through the introduction of such a system in combination with developing control measures and efficient services built around that system. Revenue from VAT as a percentage of GDP in general rose in the Latin American region after the introduction of electronic invoices. The Inter-American Development Bank has sponsored some studies conducted by independent researchers to verify whether there have been gains in revenue due to electronic invoicing systems being implemented.[17] The studies conducted in Argentina, Ecuador, Mexico, and Uruguay used techniques of regression discontinuity, difference in differences, and propensity score matching. The studies confirm that the introduction of electronic invoicing systems has had a positive effect on tax revenue in these countries.

16. International Chamber of Commerce (2020). Practice Principles for Implementation of Continuous Transaction Controls. Paris (2020).
17. Hernandez, C. & Robalino, J. (2018). *Evidence of the Impact of Electronic Invoicing of Taxes in Latin America*. In Barreix, A. & Zambrano, R. (eds), Electronic Invoice in Latin America. English Summary. Washington: IADB.

CHAPTER 6

The Potential for Emerging Technologies and Blockchain to Better Secure VAT in the Context of Missing Trader Intra-community and Carousel Frauds

Jérôme Duperrut & Philippe Thevoz

1 INTRODUCTION

Most tax authorities already have experience with digital technologies for the administration of taxes:[1] they generate a secure taxpayer identification number recorded in a database, they digitalize various tax declarations and accept electronic files, they allow for the payment of taxes through digital channels, they make use of software for recording international trade and taxation, they rely on digital technologies to track and trace their excisable goods,[2] they adopt electronic fiscal devices at the point of sale,[3] and many more things. These technologies sometimes represent an incremental improvement, while others are part of a fundamental modernization in tax administration. In any case, they all aim at enhancing trust in the tax authority.[4] Strong buy-in both at the highest political level and inside the tax authority is needed to drive the adoption of new technologies. This first stage of digital administration measures is well

1. International Monetary Fund, *Fiscal Monitor: Capitalizing on Good Times* (2018) and Emmanouil Kitsios et al., *Tax Evasion from Cross-Border Fraud: Does Digitalization Make a Difference?*, 245 IMF Working Paper (2020).
2. Jerome Duperrut & Pablo Chico de la Camara, *Methods to Assess the Fiscal Impact of Adopting Secure Track and Trace Solutions*, 6 Revista de Fiscalidad Internacional y Negocios Transnacionales (2017) and International Monetary Fund, *supra* n. 1.
3. Peter Casey & Patricio Castro, *Electronic Fiscal Devices: An Empirical Study of Their Impact on Taxpayer Compliance and Administrative Efficiency*, 73 IMF Working Paper (2015).
4. Philippe Amon, *Toward a New Economy of Trust*, in: *Revitalizing the Spirit of Bretton Woods*, Bretton Woods Committee (2019).

documented as a key contributor to strengthening domestic revenue mobilization, increasing tax compliance, and facilitating tax administration for both the tax authorities and the taxpayers.

A next stage in the digitalization of tax authorities is currently starting with the adoption of emerging technologies.[5] These new technologies include digital identity, the cloud, artificial intelligence, and blockchain. It is still early days to state whether these emerging technologies have the potential to transform tax administration, or if they will make more modest incremental improvements. That is not to say that incremental improvements cannot have a large impact on the reduction of the tax gap or on the increase in revenue collection. A number of international surveys report that the use of blockchain by governments is still relatively limited and small scale,[6] with Estonia emphasized as an early and reliable adopter.[7] It is not always clear what type of blockchain is most suitable for governments, and for tax authorities in particular. There is sometimes a disconnect between tax practitioners and technology specialists, which might go as far as mixing tax administration issues with blockchain-based currencies. All this might explain why case studies of blockchain for tax administration are even rarer;[8] it is learning by doing that will provide concrete examples for generating new processes and adapting standards. Tax authorities are likely to have an appetite for emerging technologies that mobilize a small portion of their budget resources and that can be mastered by their staff relatively easily.

These technologies are necessary not only because of their intrinsic characteristics, but also because they will increase the level of trust in the tax authority and in the manner it conducts its tax administration functions. In this context, they are likely to first be used on existing policies and legacy systems. These technologies could impact various aspects of tax administration, including the registration of taxpayers, the filing of tax declarations, the way information is submitted, stored, and analysed, and the types of audits conducted. As ripple effects, they may also alter practices such as withholding taxes, minimum taxation, and tax refunds. This paper focusses on their usefulness in the area of value added tax (VAT), in particular to address the question of missing trader intra-Community (MTIC) fraud. These emerging technologies should be able to largely operate within the current tax policy system of most countries, with relatively minor legal adjustments.

The rest of the chapter is organized as follows: section 2 presents a stylized description of the VAT MTIC fraud and sets the stage for the problem. Section 3

5. Organisation for Economic Co-operation and Development, *Tax Administration 3.0: The Digital Transformation of Tax Administration* (2020).
6. Jamie Berryhill et al., *Blockchains Unchained: Blockchain Technology and Its Use in the Public Sector*, 28 OECD Working Papers on Public Governance (2018) and Juho Lindman et al., *The Uncertain Promise of Blockchain for Government*, 43 OECD Working Papers on Public Governance (2020).
7. Sanjeev Gupta et al., *Digital Revolutions in Public Finance*, International Monetary Fund (2017) and International Monetary Fund, *supra* n. 1.
8. David Allessie et al., *Blockchain for Digital Government*, Publications Office of the European Union (2019); Inter-American Center of Tax Administrations (CIAT), *ICT as a Strategic Tool to Leapfrog the Efficiency of Tax Administrations* (2020) and Jeffrey Owens & Julia de Jong, *Taxation on the Blockchain: Opportunities and Challenges*, 87 Tax Notes International (2017).

introduces the proposed solution to address the identified problem, which is based on the secured certification of the taxpayers. Section 4 elaborates on the applications of the secured certification for VAT. Section 5 describes the emerging technologies enabling the secured certification, including blockchain. Section 6 discusses possible next steps. Section 7 concludes.

2 STYLIZED FACTS OF MTIC FRAUD AND ASSOCIATED TYPES

There are many kinds of frauds linked to VAT.[9] Some of the most prominent ones are the well-documented cases of MTIC fraud and carousel fraud. These types of frauds are generally large scale, contribute significantly to the VAT gap, and represent an important fiscal loss in many countries.[10] They occur typically across national and sub-national borders within a single market or a fiscal union – the European Union (EU) is a prime example. The main enablers of these frauds are: (i) the registration of VAT taxpayers; (ii) the place of taxable transaction; (iii) the zero-rating for VAT of exports and corresponding imports; (iv) the opportunity for deferred payments for VAT on imports, and eventually but not necessarily (v) the possibility to claim input VAT refunds when goods are re-exported.

In more detail, the registered taxpayer who imports a good or a service in this configuration does not have to pay the VAT on these imports, because of the zero-rating for VAT of the related exports. Typically, VAT on imports is levied at the border, but within some fiscal unions, it is levied when the importer files its next regular VAT return. In many countries, domestic VAT rules require this filing to take place on a periodic basis, which can extend to several months, especially for small taxpayers. The payment of the VAT is often due on the same date as the filing, but can sometimes take place at a later date. There can thus be a long time-lag between the onward sale of the imported good, the filing of the tax return, and the payment of the VAT to the tax authority.

In the meantime, the taxpayer will have generated income through his business activity by selling the goods and charging a price including VAT at the applicable rate, as VAT becomes chargeable on any subsequent domestic sale. This taxpayer's income is made of the net value of his sales plus VAT. He could then disappear before having had to submit a VAT return or, at the latest, before effecting a VAT payment to the tax authority. As he does not return the VAT to the tax authority, he makes an undue gain on his activity. Since the VAT rate is typically in the range of 15%-25%, this taxpayer makes a significant additional return on his sales. The tax authority makes an equivalent loss in tax collection. This is a key stage of the MTIC fraud, which is sometimes referred to as 'acquisition fraud'.

9. Michael Keen & Stephen Smith, *VAT Fraud and Evasion: What Do We Know, and What Can be Done?*, 31 IMF Working Paper (2007) and Michael Walpole, *Tackling VAT Fraud*, International VAT Monitor (2014).

10. European Commission, *The Concept of Tax Gaps: Report III: MTIC Fraud Gap Estimation Methodologies* (2018), International Monetary Fund, *supra* n. 1 and Loukia Sergiou, *Value Added Tax (VAT) Carousel Fraud in the European Union*, 2 Journal of Accounting and Management (2012).

Further down the line, these goods can be exchanged between other taxpayers and be re-exported and even reimported, to create the loop of carousel fraud. In aggregate, there will be an accumulation of VAT liabilities on imported goods and services that are not paid. This is because the importer liable for this VAT disappears. If the entire carousel fraud takes place, this can be accompanied by claims for VAT refunds on exported goods that are paid for by the tax authority. Beyond this basic description, various more complicated schemes have been developed to further complicate tax administration.

Let us assume the simple case as depicted in Figure 6.1. A small taxpayer T1 registers with the tax authority in the country of Utopia, which happens to be inside a fiscal union. Taxpayer T1 trades with exporter E1 in the country of Extopia. This trade – on one side, an export from exporter E1 and on the other side, an import from taxpayer T1 – does not include VAT, because of the zero-rating for VAT exports inside this fiscal union. Then, taxpayer T1 sells this good (or service) in a domestic transaction onward to taxpayer T2, at a price inclusive of VAT. Taxpayer T1 should declare the corresponding VAT liability and pay it. However, as a small taxpayer, it could be that his VAT filing is due on a quarterly basis or even annually. He could yet disappear before filing and keep the VAT, as an additional profit. The national tax authority does not collect the VAT due. Furthermore, taxpayer T2 is entitled to be refunded the VAT on this transaction (provided he is not an end-user). This VAT is equivalent to the VAT declared by taxpayer T1. The national tax authority thus loses on two fronts: it does not collect the VAT due by taxpayer T1, while it refunds the VAT to taxpayer T2.

Figure 6.1 Simple Case of MTIC Fraud with No VAT Remitted to the Tax Authority

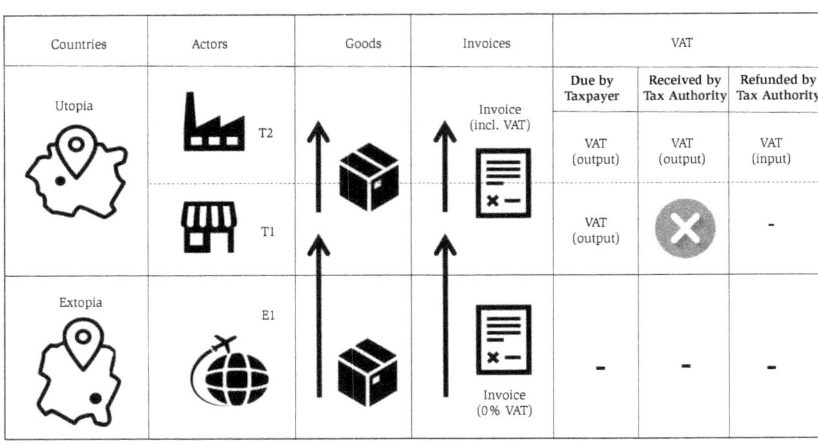

Faced with this problematic, compliance schemes have been implemented by tax authorities to address this fraud. A common one is tax audit. The first issue is to identify and select which taxpayers to audit. In many countries, less than 5% of taxpayers are audited on a yearly basis. Typically, large taxpayers are targeted and audited more often than smaller ones. The targeting can also focus on a specific sector of activity or on a region. The audits can be of different types, from basic audits to comprehensive ones. However, there are major drawbacks with tax audits: (i) they take place several months/years after the submission of the tax declaration; (ii) they take time to complete; (iii) they involve significant resources for the tax authority; and (iv) their success rate is uncertain. In the case of MTIC fraud as depicted in Figure 6.1, an audit of taxpayer T1 is unlikely to even take place, since he will have already disappeared. The timing of implementation of the tax administration measure is of the essence.

3 THE SECURED CERTIFICATION OF TAXPAYERS

While audits are an ex-post tax administration measure, the problem of MTIC fraud requires a strengthening of the control measures at the stage of the first enabler, i.e., the registration of taxpayer T1. This registration - which can largely remain based on current practices - has to be strengthened along three dimensions. First, the tax authority should issue a Smart Tax/VAT Registration Certificate to all taxpayers, in the form of a quick response (QR) code (*see* Figure 6.2). Second, the taxpayers must be required to add this secure QR code to most, if not all, of his invoices. Third, the buyer - taxpayer T2 - must be given the means to check that the supplier - taxpayer T1 - is indeed a correctly registered taxpayer and that the invoice is legitimate. This due diligence can be done via checking the QR code before agreeing to the invoice and effecting the buy. Sections 3.1-3.3 describe these three dimensions.

3.1 Smart Tax/VAT Registration Certificates:[11] The First Dimension

In most countries, the registration process of a taxpayer and/or the registration for VAT have been simplified and accelerated. It is typically a self-reporting registration. A new business, such as taxpayer T1 in Figure 6.1, classically needs to register as a taxpayer by filling out forms and providing information on: (i) the legal name of the company; (ii) the date of establishment; (iii) the address; (iv) the contact details; (v) the type of entity; (vi) the type of taxes; and (vii) the type of activity. A new VAT registration might ask for additional information such as the (expected) turnover and the intention to import goods and services. The tax authority will then process this registration with routine checks. The registration process for VAT is seldom coupled with a visit to or an inspection of the premises of the taxpayer, as this would be too costly for the tax authority. Some taxpayers could, however, be required to leave a deposit when they register for VAT, but this could introduce a degree of inequality of treatment. Assuming that the application is in order, the taxpayer T1 will be issued with a tax identification number (TIN) and/or a VAT number by the tax authority. These numbers are typically

11. In the rest of this chapter, the term 'Smart VAT Registration Certificate' is used. In countries where taxpayers have a unique tax registration for all taxes, a 'Smart Tax Registration Certificate' has the same function.

mandatory for all transactions and must appear on all invoices, including on the sales made by taxpayer T1.

In the new system to create a secure certification for taxpayers, all of these registration steps can remain as they are, in particular the information required from the taxpayer. The added task for the tax authority would be to issue not only a TIN number but also a secure QR code[12] to the designated taxpayer. This QR code would include relevant information as mentioned above and as currently collected by the tax authority, such as: (i) the TIN; (ii) the (expected) turnover of the company; and (iii) the type of activity. The QR code is flexible enough to encompass any relevant information as defined by the tax authority.

In addition, the tax authority could decide to grant a certain limit for the taxpayer's transactions at the time of the registration, based on the information he submits. In some countries, taxpayers are segmented according to their size, between small taxpayers, medium taxpayers, and large taxpayers. The invoice limit could be linked to these taxpayer segments. Other criteria to set the invoice limit could be the type of activity or the declared intention to import goods and services. In countries that have reported the creation of a number of small 'ghost' taxpayers issuing a large number of small invoices, the invoicing limit could be set at a low level.

This QR code could be issued by the tax authority and delivered to the taxpayer within a few seconds. It could be sent by email, as it is secured by emerging technologies including blockchain (*see* section 5).

Figure 6.2 Smart VAT Registration Certificate in the Form of a QR Code for a Taxpayer

3.2 Issuance of Secure Invoices: The Second Dimension

The QR code is typically taxpayer-specific and not transaction-specific. The same QR code is applied by taxpayer T1 on all his invoices (*see* Figure 6.3). This QR code should be such that it could easily be included in the company's fields that fit into the invoice template. This QR code will enable taxpayer T2 to verify the legitimacy of taxpayer T1, and of the invoice.

Such a QR code can easily be applied to a digital invoice (e.g., a PDF document) as well as to a paper-based invoice; many countries require invoices in a paper-based format, and the same level of security is achieved in both cases.

12. The QR code is the secured representation of the 'Smart VAT Registration Certificate'. Thus, in the rest of this chapter, the two should be considered as equivalent.

In order to reduce the administrative burden, invoices of small amounts could be excluded from the requirement to display the QR code on the corresponding invoices. In case the taxpayer sees his activity grow in a legitimate manner and he thus needs to issue invoices of higher amounts, he could request that the invoicing limit be increased. This request would have to be made to the tax authority, which would be informed about the increased activity of this taxpayer, investigate the request, and eventually grant it. The tax authority is the sole authority issuing the certification. Thereafter, the taxpayer will apply the new QR code with the higher invoicing limit.

A taxpayer might be awarded an exceptional contract (the 'contract of the century') and need to invoice a very large amount, above the invoicing limit set by the tax authority. In this context, the tax authority might want to issue a transaction-specific QR code, valid for a given customer for a given period of time, or for a single invoice; the flexibility exists to cater for exceptional cases.

On the contrary, if the supplier is found guilty of a tax offence the tax authority could expire or revoke altogether the Smart VAT Registration Certificate. After this revocation, the QR code loses its validity, and the affected taxpayer is unable to generate a valid invoice and make a legitimate transaction. This is likely to be less cumbersome for the tax authority than requiring that taxpayers renew their licence on a regular basis – in some countries, this is requested on a quarterly basis. Such a revocation or expiration can similarly take place if the company closes down, is bankrupt, changes its name, or merges.

Figure 6.3 Secure Invoice

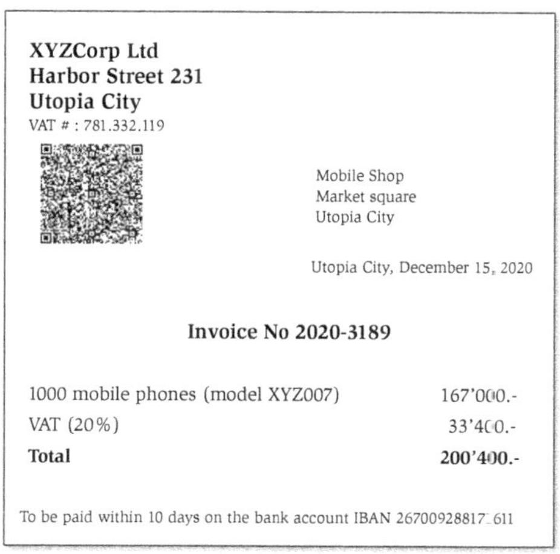

XYZCorp Ltd
Harbor Street 231
Utopia City
VAT # : 781.332.119

Mobile Shop
Market square
Utopia City

Utopia City, December 15, 2020

Invoice No 2020-3189

1000 mobile phones (model XYZ007)	167'000.-
VAT (20%)	33'400.-
Total	**200'400.-**

To be paid within 10 days on the bank account IBAN 26700928817[illegible]611

3.3 Strengthened Due Diligence: The Third Dimension

It is currently not easy for a buyer to sufficiently identify who is behind the invoice, in particular, if it is a potential fraudster. Typically, the TIN does not give useful information to the buyers, such as the size of the company or the area of trade. In the

EU, cross-border actors can check the validity of a VAT number issued in any of the Member States, through the VAT Information Exchange System (VIES) number validation. However, the VIES suffers from shortcomings, including those related to the availability, quality, and timeliness of data.[13]

Emerging technologies give a simple and efficient way to detect that the supplier is a legitimate taxpayer. This check can be done with a smartphone or a computer, by any taxpayer (*see* Figure 6.4). This represents an action that taxpayers can reasonably be expected to take.

This way of ensuring that the taxpayer enters into a lawful transaction is much easier than other due diligence actions, such as obtaining certificates of incorporation, VAT registration certificates, signed letters from the supplier, or credit checks.[14]

With these emerging technologies, an option would be to extend the requirement for due diligence and the liability rules of taxpayers. It could become an expectation – or even an obligation – that taxpayers check the secure certification of their suppliers; the onus would be on the buyer of the good.

At the time of returning the VAT declaration, the taxpayer typically has to join the invoices. The tax authority could easily spot if the taxpayer has checked the validity status of the invoices. In case the taxpayer entered into an unlawful transaction, he could be exposed to sanctions and penalties, such a losing his right to VAT refunds.

The added interest of this solution is that the data privacy of taxpayer T1 is safeguarded. The Smart VAT Registration Certificate does not require any transfer of data on the part of taxpayer T1. A check of its validity accesses neither the supplier's database nor that of the tax authority.

Figure 6.4 Due Diligence with a Smartphone Application

13. Richard Ainsworth & Andrew Shact, *Blockchain Technology Might Solve VAT Fraud*, 83 Tax Notes International (2016).
14. Revenue, *How to Protect Your Business from Becoming Involved in VAT Fraud*, Tax and Duty Manual (2018).

3.4 Possible Implications for Domestic Legislation

The adoption of the secured certification of taxpayers – with its three dimensions as explained in sections 3.1-3.3 – is unlikely to require fundamental and/or large-scale changes to domestic tax legislation or to rules governing VAT. This will probably be an important driver for a tax authority in its decision to adopt this measure. However, and depending upon countries and legislations, legislative changes could be needed to account for the following points:

(1) role of the tax authority:
- specification, introduction, and delivery of the Smart VAT Registration Certificate, which should replace the functions of the current VAT certificates;
- setting of invoicing limits for taxpayers;
- possibility to modify, expire, or revoke a Smart VAT Registration Certificate;
- extension of the due diligence rules to include the checking of the Smart VAT Registration Certificate as a required action; and
- possibility to sanction taxpayers who do not check the Smart VAT Registration Certificate of their suppliers; and

(2) role of the taxpayers:
- obligation for sellers to add the Smart VAT Registration Certificate to invoices accordingly;
- obligation for sellers to issue invoices that are compliant with the Smart VAT Registration Certificate; and
- obligation for buyers to check the compliance of invoices.

4 APPLICATIONS OF SECURED CERTIFICATION FOR VAT

4.1 Ensuring a Legitimate Transaction

A transaction potentially exposed to acquisition fraud has its origins in invoices. For a buyer, it is impossible based upon invoices alone to detect that one invoice comes from a legitimate supplier and another does not. Figure 6.5 illustrates two invoices from two different suppliers, but for the same transaction.

Figure 6.5 Example of Two Invoices

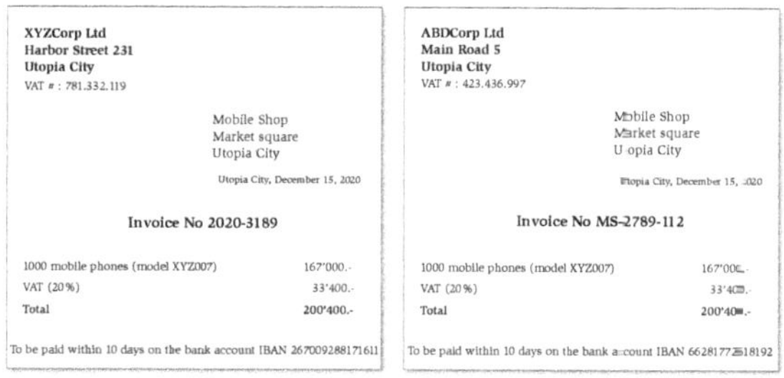

XYZCorp Ltd
Harbor Street 231
Utopia City
VAT # : 781.332.119

Mobile Shop
Market square
Utopia City

Utopia City, December 15, 2020

Invoice No 2020-3189

1000 mobile phones (model XYZ007)	167'000.-
VAT (20 %)	33'400.-
Total	200'400.-

To be paid within 10 days on the bank account IBAN 26700928817161l

ABDCorp Ltd
Main Road 5
Utopia City
VAT # : 423.436.997

Mobile Shop
Market square
Utopia City

Utopia City, December 15, 2020

Invoice No MS-2789-112

1000 mobile phones (model XYZ007)	167'000.-
VAT (20 %)	33'400.-
Total	200'400.-

To be paid within 10 days on the bank account IBAN 6628177[illegible]18192

In the case illustrated in Figure 6.5, the buyer cannot know easily and with certainty the key characteristics of the suppliers. It is unknown to him that company XYZCorp (left invoice in Figure 6.5) is a large company with 1,200 employees active in the field of electronics, whereas company ABDCorp (right invoice in Figure 6.5) is a 'shell' company of just a few employees, officially active as a restaurant. If the buyer had access to such information from the tax authority (as shown in Figure 6.6), he would detect right away that ABDCorp is not a legitimate company for the sale of large quantities of mobile phones, whereas XYZCorp is. However, as such information is not easily available, or could be counterfeited (such as through fake websites), the buyer is uninformed and could easily be abused.

Figure 6.6 The Same Two Invoices with the Corresponding Registered Description of the Companies

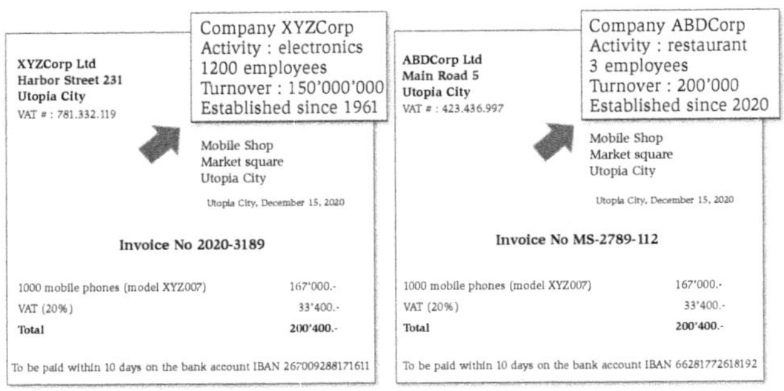

To solve this problem, the buyer should have a simple – yet trusted – means of accessing the corresponding registered description of the company. As explained in section 3, this can be done with the introduction of the Smart VAT Registration Certificate in the form of a secure QR code. This QR code, based upon the CERTUS™ solution,[15] cannot be forged. It is universally verifiable by anyone with a simple smartphone (or a computer), and it contains proof that it has been issued by the tax authority. For more detailed information about CERTUS, *see* section 5.

15. www.certusdoc.com.

Figure 6.7 Invoice with a QR Code, Acting as a Smart VAT Registration Certificate

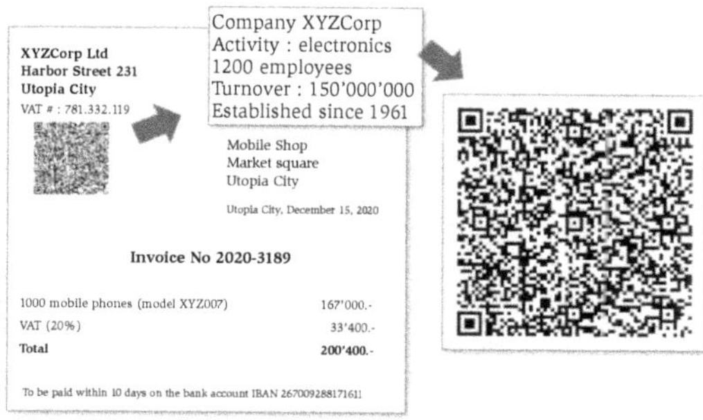

The smart VAT Registration Certificate should provide enough information to the buyer so that he can trust that the supplier is a legitimate taxpayer authorized to enter into such a transaction. In the examples shown in Figure 6.7, it is clear that a very small company of a few employees, such as ABDCorp, officially active as a restaurant, is not legitimate in its sale of thousands of mobile phones, whereas XYZCorp is.

The verification of the QR code can be done by the buyer by using a simple smartphone – via a mobile App (available on both iOS and Android) – or any computer – via a WebApp.[16] The result of this verification is shown in Figure 6.8. On the smartphone (or a computer), the following information is displayed:

- the validity of the CERTUS QR code (*see also* section 5 for more details): a green flag will be displayed if the CERTUS QR code is genuine; in all other cases, a red flag will be shown;
- the name of the issuer (here, the Utopia Tax Authority):[17] making sure that this document is indeed a valid Smart VAT Registration Certificate, and is officially issued;
- the name, address, and VAT number of the company;
- the domain of activity; and
- the invoicing limit.

16. All the QR codes shown in this chapter can be verified by the reader, using the WebApp, https://www.certusdoc.com/verify, as these are real CERTUS documents. They are issued by 'CERTUS-Demo' instead of the 'Utopia Tax Authority', for the sake of this chapter.
17. As Figure 6.8 portrays a demonstration document for the sake of this chapter, the name of the issuer is 'CERTUS-Demo'. In a real case, the name of the issuer would be the 'Utopia Tax Authority'.

Figure 6.8 Verification with a Smartphone of the QR Code

There is a secure link between the Smart VAT Registration Certificate, its verification, and the content of the invoice (*see* Figure 6.9). The buyer, after checking the validity of the CERTUS QR code, is assured that the content of the Smart VAT Registration Certificate corresponds to the information on the invoice, namely that the company name, address and VAT number match, that the field of activity (here, electronics) is relevant for the type of good sold (in this example, mobile phones), and that the size of the company (in this case, 1,200 employees) is realistic for this kind of supply. Finally, the buyer has the confirmation that the amount of the invoice (i.e., 200,400) is below the invoicing limit (of 250,000) for this company. Since these checks are all positive, the buyer can trust that the supplier is a registered taxpayer and that the transaction is legitimate.

Figure 6.9 Verification of the Conformity of the Invoice

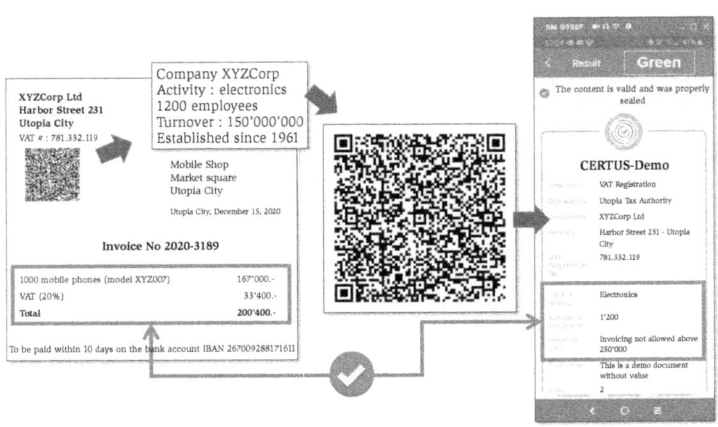

4.2 Transaction above the Invoicing Limit

The same transaction with ABDCorp would generate adverse findings by the buyer (*see* Figure 6.10). On the one hand, the CERTUS certificate is genuine (a green flag has been issued when checked). On the other hand, the activity of the company (in this case, a restaurant) and its size (3 employees) are not at all in line with the sale of large quantities of mobile phones. Moreover, the invoicing limit defined by the tax authority (in this case 5,000) is far below the amount of the specific invoice (200,400). In this context, the buyer cannot trust that he is entering into a lawful transaction. Because the Smart VAT Registration Certificate can be checked by everybody, the company ABDCorp will, in all likelihood, not be able to perform this type of transaction with any buyer, and will thus not be able to commit fraud.

Figure 6.10 Example of Fraud Concerning the Invoicing Limit

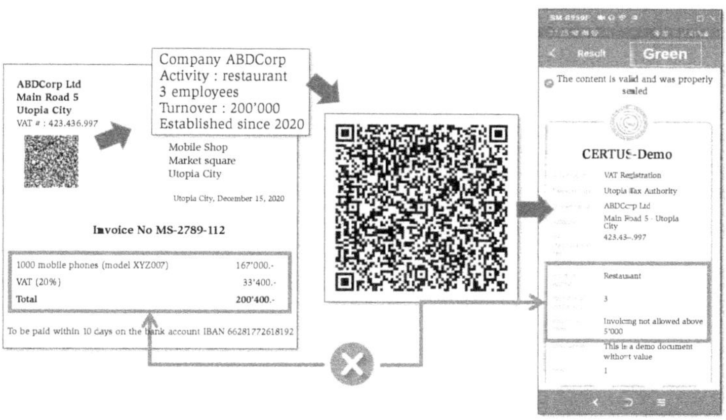

4.3 Attempt to Forge a Smart VAT Registration Certificate

To attempt to dupe buyers, the company ABDCorp might try to create a forged Smart VAT Registration Certificate. The QR code can be edited, as shown in Figure 6.11. The original QR code of the Smart VAT Registration Certificate of ABDCorp is reproduced on the left side. A scan of this QR code with a standard QR code scanner will produce the information displayed at the bottom left. Most information is in clear text, except a cryptographic link with the KSI® Blockchain (*see* section 5 for the technical details). In particular, the company's activity, size, and invoicing limit are in clear text. A fraudster could be tempted to change this information (bottom right) and to generate a new QR code, and thus a new Smart VAT Registration Certificate (top right).

Figure 6.11 Creation of a Forged QR Code

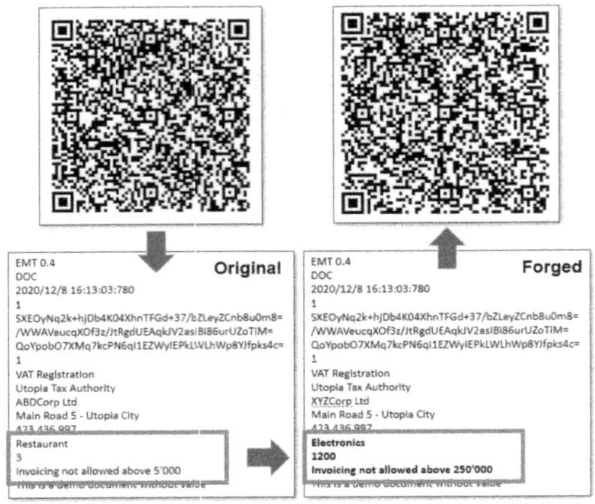

The buyer will immediately detect a forged QR code (*see* Figure 6.12). The tax authority would similarly be able to detect this anomaly. The CERTUS is flagged red, indicating a forged Smart VAT Registration Certificate. As a consequence, the buyer should not enter into this transaction, and he might even be disposed to inform the tax authority about this forgery.

Figure 6.12 Detection of a Forged QR Code

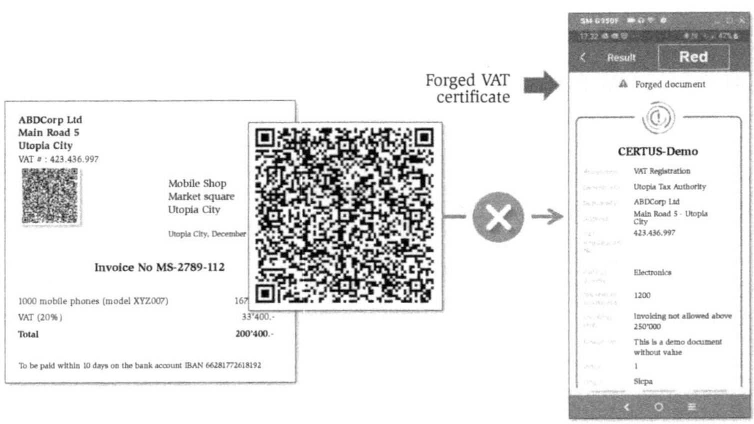

5 EMERGING TECHNOLOGIES ENABLING SECURED CERTIFICATION, INCLUDING BLOCKCHAIN

5.1 Combination of Emerging Technologies with CERTUS™

Smart VAT Registration Certificates are based on CERTUS technology, the characteristics of which are presented in Figure 6.13. This technology is a cost-effective, next-generation security solution that sets a new standard in securing sensitive paper-based and digital documents. It combines breakthrough digital seal technology protected by the blockchain with a secure QR code applied to documents. The result is a QR code marking that is impossible to tamper with or forge.

Figure 6.13 Characteristics of CERTUS

- One-click universal and independent verification
- Works for paper and digital certificates
- Privacy-preserving, does not store sensitive data
- Authenticates the issuer and the protected data
- Lifelong validity of issued certificates
- Immediate access to a simple and cost-effective online service, no infrastructure required
- Enables offline verification
- Versatility, protects any type of data structure

CERTUS enables independent and universal verification, safeguarding the value of holders' documents and the reputation of issuing authorities. The CERTUS tamper-proof QR code protects the claim – the sensitive data – directly, instead of the document itself.

The QR code contains the data to be protected in plaintext and a cryptographic signature, which acts as an undisputable mathematical proof of the link between the data to be protected and its digital security seal. Anonymized or encrypted data can also be included within the QR code in order to preserve confidentiality.

Personal and sensitive data are never stored, neither directly nor in an encrypted format, in any database or on the blockchain; only the indecipherable digital seals needed to verify a secure mark are secured by the blockchain to ensure their lifelong immutability.

Based on mathematical proofs, the issuer, the holder, and the verifier can be 100% confident of the origin and the legitimacy of the credentials. A CERTUS document certifies key information, as shown in Figure 6.14.

Figure 6.14 Certified Information Obtained upon Verification of a CERTUS Document

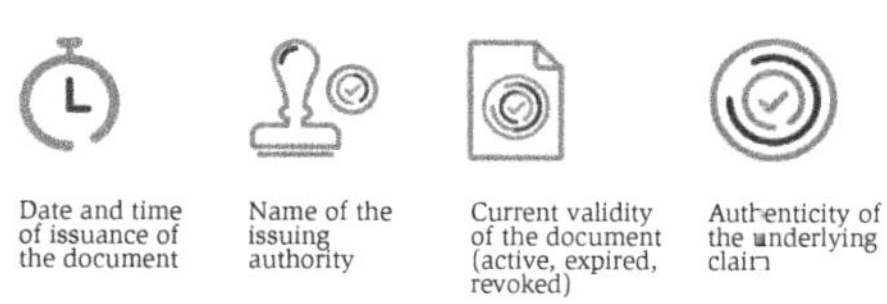

5.2 Technical Description

The CERTUS Platform generates CERTUS documents in batches.[18] The content of each document is secured by a QR code. Each QR code contains the data to be secured in the document which appear in clear text, as well as a cryptographic signature (or cryptographic link) – *see* Figure 6.15.

Figure 6.15 Structure of the QR Code Securing a CERTUS Document

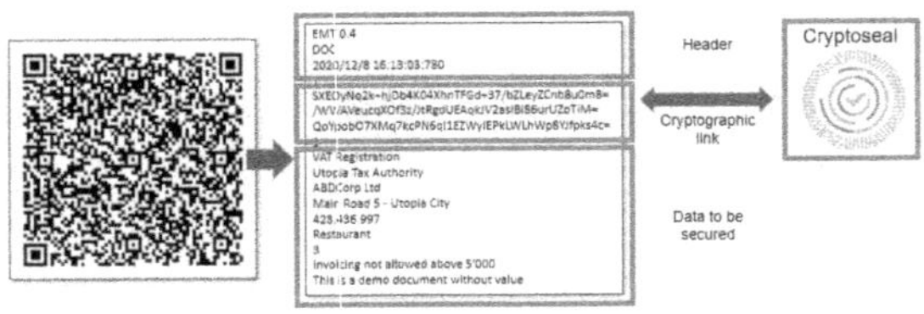

The cryptographic signature (or cryptographic link) is a unique and unforgeable link between the data in the document and the corresponding cryptographic seal (or 'cryptoseal') of the batch. The cryptoseal secures all documents in the batch. It also contains the name of the issuer, some metadata about the batch (e.g., issuance date, the gateway used for the document generation, and so on) and the hash root (or 'Merkel root').

The cryptoseal is signed on the KSI Blockchain once the batch is activated, as shown in Figure 6.16. In addition, the integrity of the CERTUS issuance process is guaranteed and can be independently proven, as it is also secured on the KSI Blockchain.

Figure 6.16 Path Showing How a CERTUS Document Is Secured by the KSI Blockchain, via the Cryptoseal

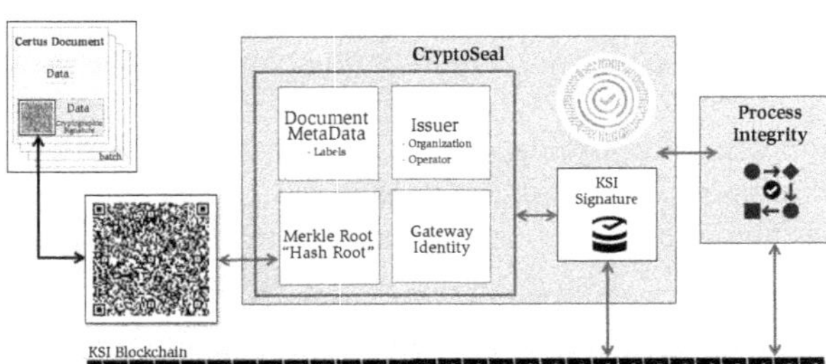

The cryptoseal, shown in Figure 6.16, is a JSON file that contains the four components highlighted inside the square, as well as the KSI signature, which seals the

18. A batch typically contains 1-500 documents. This upper limit can be increased, as needed.

whole cryptoseal. The integrity of each CERTUS document can be checked independently with the cryptoseal. The validity of the cryptoseal can itself be checked through its KSI signature on the KSI Blockchain (independently of the CERTUS platform). As neither the cryptoseal nor the blockchain are hosting any data from the CERTUS document, it fully preserves the privacy of the beneficiaries. In the context of the EU, this is compliant with its General Data Protection Regulation (GDPR).[19]

5.3 Universal Verification

A CERTUS document can be universally verified with a smartphone or a computer. The verification algorithms are fully open and transparent, allowing anyone to build his own verification tool.

5.4 Expiration and Revocation

An important feature of the CERTUS Solution is the possibility, for the issuing authority, to revoke or expire any document in real time and without any contact with the taxpayer. This revocation/expiration will be simultaneously valid for any digital and paper copy.

To expire or revoke a given CERTUS document (or a whole batch), the issuing authority has to connect to the CERTUS platform, select the document(s) to revoke or expire, and specify the expiry date. One second later, all corresponding CERTUS documents will exhibit a 'revoked' or 'expired' message upon verification. It is also possible to set a predefined expiration date at the issuance of a batch of CERTUS documents. This does not prevent expiring or revoking individual documents at a later stage.

5.5 A High-Security Solution to Fight Against Counterfeits

The QR code on a CERTUS document can be read by any standard QR-code reader, as its content is not encrypted. As shown in Figure 6.11, the content of a QR code can be changed. However, when it is verified, the counterfeit is immediately detected (*see* Figure 6.12), as the cryptographic link between the data and the cryptoseal is broken.

5.6 KSI Blockchain

The KSI Blockchain was invented by Guardtime in 2008, based upon patents filed in 2002. It first went live in April 2008, prior to the publication of the Bitcoin white paper by Satoshi Nakamoto in October 2008. The KSI Blockchain overcomes two major

19. EU General Data Protection Regulation (GDPR), *Regulation (EU) 2016/679 of the European Parliament and of the Council of 27 April 2016 on the protection of natural persons with regard to the processing of personal data and on the free movement of such data, and repealing Directive 95/46/EC (General Data Protection Regulation)*, Official Journal of the European Union L 119/1 (2016).

weaknesses of traditional blockchains - scalability and commitment time - making it usable at an industrial scale.

KSI makes use of cryptographic, one-way hash functions (such as SHA-256), which transform data of any type and size into non-reversible, fixed-size hash values: i.e., into a 'digital fingerprint' of the data. A user interacts with the system by submitting a hash value of the data to be signed by the aggregation service in a KSI gateway, and is then returned a signature, which provides cryptographic proof of the time of signature, integrity of the signed data, as well as attribution of origin, i.e., which entity generated the signature, as shown in Figure 6.17. KSI signatures have a small footprint (their size is just a few KB), so it is feasible to store them next to the data as an attribute, or separately in different types of data container.

Figure 6.17 Securing a Document on the KSI Blockchain

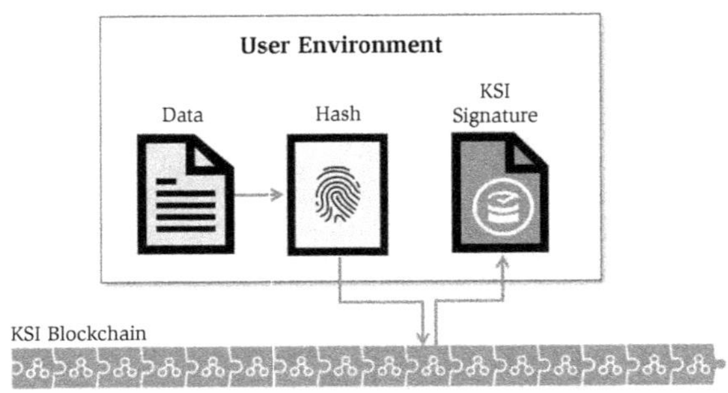

A KSI signature allows to prove three key things. First, it provides a timestamp (i.e., the time at which the document was signed on the blockchain). Second, the signing entity is given, which corresponds to the gateway used for the signing process. The signing entity can include not only the name of the signing organization but also (if desired) the name of the department of this organization, as well as the ID of the operator (or server) that triggered the signing. Third, the integrity of the signed document can be proven, as the hash of the document should match the corresponding hash embedded in the KSI signature. A KSI signature is only made out of hash functions (SHA-256) and does not need to rely on a public key infrastructure (PKI) to prove who signed the document.

As a consequence, the blockchain can be applied to any application or use case, as it is fully agnostic and generic - no data is stored in the blockchain (*see* Figure 6.18). Due to its pulse of 1 second, any data that is secured with this blockchain receives its corresponding timestamp the next second. Moreover, due to the fully decentralized architecture of the gateways that handle the signing process, the KSI Blockchain can secure up to a trillion (10^{12}) transactions/data per second.

Figure 6.18 The KSI Blockchain as the Trust Anchor to Secure Any Type of Data Anywhere

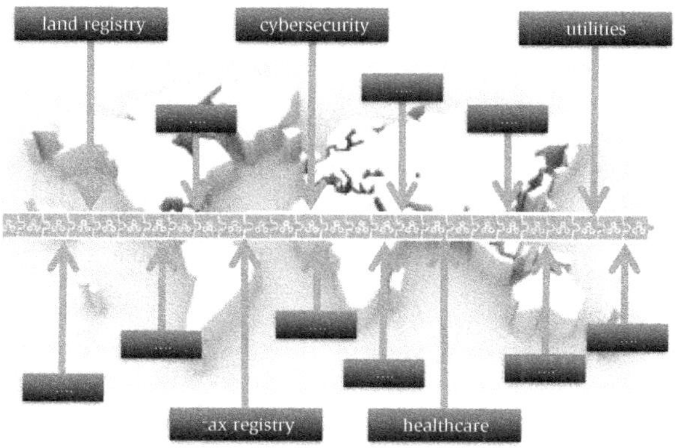

- o application agnostic
- o no data sharing/exposure
- o full scalability (10^{12}/s)
- o settlement time : 1 second
- o public trust anchor
- o no electricity consumption
- o no cryptocurrency
- o quantum proof
- o fully interoperable
- o running 24/7 since 2008
- o available to anyone

The KSI Blockchain is a private and permissioned blockchain, but it is publicly exposed through the public access to the blockchain on the one side, and its monthly publication in the Financial Times (and other public media) on the other side.

As of April 2020, the KSI Blockchain timestamping is accredited as a qualified trust service under the EU's eIDAS regulation,[20] giving it full legal recognition across the EU. This makes it the only blockchain-based service accredited for public sector and governmental use in the EU.

This blockchain has a number of advantages over traditional PKI-based integrity solutions, including scalability (to billions of transactions), easy and universal verifiability, and resistance to compromise or technological risks (such as quantum computing).

Guardtime's KSI Blockchain is widely used by the Estonian Government.[21] Since 2012, it secures all the data transactions of the Estonian administration,[22] something that represents millions of operations per second.

6 POSSIBLE NEXT STEPS

On the one hand, beyond the VAT-specific use of Smart VAT Registration Certificates, generic smart registration certificates based on the same emerging technologies and blockchain could be used for other types of taxes. The usefulness of digital integrity solutions and blockchain to strengthen the security of the automatic exchange of

20. https://guardtime.com/blog/guardtime-offers-first-eu-e-eidas-accredited-blockchain-based-trust-service. Guardtime's KSI Blockchain Timestamping Service is compliant with the eIDAS regulation and included in the European Trusted List, https://webgate.ec.europa.eu/tl-browser/#/tl/EE/1. The accreditation was conducted by TÜV Nord, Germany.
21. https://e-estonia.com/wp-content/uploads/2020mar-faq-ksi-blockchain-1-1.pdf.
22. Lindman, *supra* n. 6 and International Monetary Fund, *supra* n. 1.

financial account information for tax purposes has already been assessed.[23] In the context of property taxation, the secure certification of land registry and of the property registry would similarly be helpful. Smart registration certificates could also prove instrumental in strengthening trust in the certificates of origin used in international trade.

On the other hand, more complex suggestions propose to make use of emerging technologies, including blockchain, to secure the enforcement of VAT, for example by facilitating transaction-by-transaction monitoring.[24] These proposals would require systemic policy changes to VAT and are likely to require more time to gain traction.

Beyond the tax area, the same concept of Smart VAT Registration Certificates and their underlying technologies can be applied to many different domains. For instance, CERTUS could also be applied to:

- official documents (licences to operate, vehicle registrations, company registrations, conformity documents, attestations, permits);
- business records (trade licences, tax certificates, origin certificates);
- legal records (notarial acts, property title deeds, wills, apostilles);
- academic records (degree and diploma certificates, course completion certificates, credentials);
- civic records (certificates of birth, death, marriage; breeder's documents);
- financial records (grants, loans, proofs of insurance, attestations);
- health records (prescriptions, personal medical records, licences to practice, health passes, vaccination certificates); and
- identity documents (IDs, photo IDs, access controls).

7 CONCLUSION

Most tax authorities already have experience with digital technologies for the administration of taxes. A next stage in the digitalization is currently starting with the adoption of emerging technologies, including blockchain. Emerging technologies can help address VAT fraud, in particular, the case of the MTIC fraud. They can enable the secured certification of taxpayers and of transactions: a legitimate transaction is issued by a taxpayer which possesses a Smart VAT Registration Certificate, is based on an invoice which includes a secure QR code, and is easily verifiable by a simple digital application. Transactions above an invoicing limit set by the tax authority and embedded in the Smart VAT Registration Certificate, and transactions based on altered information about the taxpayer will be easily spotted and should facilitate due diligence. The buyer will have an increased role as an enabler of tax compliance. All this is allowed by a combination of technologies based on the CERTUS tamper-proof QR code and the KSI Blockchain, as a trust anchor. The resulting improvement in tax administration could have a large impact on the reduction of the VAT gap. It could also

23. Jerome Duperrut et al., *Why: And How – African Countries Should Use Technology for Automatic Information Exchange*, 96 Tax Notes International (2019).
24. Ainsworth & Shact, *supra* n. 13 and Gijsbert Bulk, *How Blockchain Could Transform the World of Indirect Tax*, Ernst & Young (2018).

reduce the cost of compliance, increase the level of trust in the tax authority, support the ease of doing business, improve the efficiency of tax administration, and raise transparency, while preserving data privacy.

CHAPTER 7

Introduction to Invoice Hashing for Governments: Securing Real-Time Reporting with Cryptography

Sascha Jafari

1 INTRODUCTION

This chapter discusses how invoice hashing can help to create a secure real-time reporting system, which can assist tax authorities to increase their value added tax (VAT) revenue in a confidential way. Section 2 discusses how and why real-time reporting systems are currently implemented. Section 3 will elaborate on security issues related to existing real-time reporting solutions. Furthermore, the section zooms in on the consequences of a data breach. Afterwards, in section 4, it is explained how this security issue can be tackled, namely through invoice hashing. After having created a firm understanding of what invoice hashing is, section 5 will explain how it can help to implement a real-time reporting system in a secure manner. Furthermore, the section will elaborate on the additional benefits that such a secure real-time reporting system brings to businesses. In section 6, the findings of this chapter are summarized.

2 REAL-TIME REPORTING

Globally, an estimated EUR 500 billion in VAT is lost on an annual basis.[1] In order to close this so-called VAT gap, an increasing number of governments are implementing real-time reporting systems. Such a system requires all companies within a certain

1. Christiaan van der Valk, *INSIGHT: How Are Governments Tackling the Great VAT Gap?* (12 May 2021), https://news.bloombergtax.com/daily-tax-report-international/insight-how-are-governm ents-tackling-the-great-vat-gap.

jurisdiction to report their invoices (in real-time or near-time) to the tax authority. This allows the tax authority to perform (automated) checks that will make it harder for the ill-intended to commit fraud and easier for the willing to comply. The first countries to implement such a system can be found in Latin America. Countries such as Brazil, Chile, and Mexico have successfully been using this technology for many years. For example, Brazil managed an increase of USD 58 billion in tax revenues, while Chile and Mexico reduced their overall VAT gap by 50%.[2] This success has led to the implementation of real-time reporting systems by tax authorities all over the world. Now, this trend has also reached the European Union (EU).

Over the last couple of years, more and more EU Member States have introduced a real-time reporting system to combat VAT fraud (EUR 50 billion in the EU per year) and close the VAT gap (EUR 140 billion in the EU per year). Examples are Greece, Hungary, Italy, and Spain. It is important to note that all countries are implementing real-time reporting in a different way. For instance, Italy combines real-time reporting with a mandatory e-invoicing regime and asks for actual real-time invoice information, while in Spain e-invoicing is not mandatory and data is required to be reported in near-time (within four working days). Plenty more variants of real-time reporting exist, and discussing all of these variants is outside the scope of this chapter. But what is important to emphasize is that all of these systems are storing invoice data in a centralized and clear text way. Furthermore, many of the systems allow public officials to have access to the data in plain text, for the purpose of analyses. Although the data should indeed be analysed in order to increase VAT compliance, this way of working comes with enormous security risks. As will be explained in section 3, these security risks can result in significant damage both to the tax authority and to the taxpayers.

3 SECURITY RISKS OF EXISTING REAL-TIME REPORTING SYSTEMS

As discussed in section 2, existing real-time reporting systems have proved to increase VAT revenue and close the VAT gap. However, real-time reporting systems in their existing forms do have a serious security issue: they store data on a central database. This can be extremely problematic and expensive for three reasons.

First, protecting databases is a difficult endeavour. Conceptually, this is easy to see once you realize that defenders and attackers have very different targets. While a defending government has to ensure that no serious flaw exists in its entire design and operation, attackers only need to find the single right flaw in order to gain unprivileged access to data. Empirical data show that companies and governments spend billions of dollars each year just to secure their data.[3]

Second, if the protection fails to deliver, the data might be lost because of a security breach. Such security breaches are becoming more frequent every year. A very

2. Bruno Koch Billentis, *Thee-Invoicing Journey 2019-2025* (12 May 2021), https://www.billentis.com/The_einvoicing_journey_2019-2025.pdf.
3. Summitto, *The Cost of Cyber Attacks* (12 May 2021), https://blog.summitto.com/posts/cost_of_cyber_attacks/.

recent example was the data breach in Brazil that exposed data from potentially 220 million people.[4] Especially relevant for tax authority officials: the information exposed included the CPF number[5] of almost all Brazilians.

The third reason why it is risky that real-time reporting systems collect data is that, often, data is made available in plain text to government officials. This can be problematic because 'humans are the weakest link in cybersecurity'.[6] Humans make mistakes. These mistakes can result in massive data breaches. An often-quoted example is the exposure of information of 191 million US voters. The reason for the data breach was a misconfigured database.[7] In other words, it was a simple human error. Allowing government officials to see taxpayers' data in plain text also leaves room for corruption. For instance, research institution Bellingcat recently showed how easy it is to buy detailed personal information of Russian Federal Security Service agents.[8]

All of these security breaches are extremely relevant for real-time reporting systems, as these systems deal with invoices, and invoices contain valuable pricing information. Companies do not want this data to be exposed, because this would allow their competitors to outbid them on the market. Furthermore, if this data were to be exposed, it can become public that a supplier is charging different prices for the same goods to different business partners. Lastly, the exposure of invoice data can even have consequences for the entire economy. Think of a situation in which a foreign company acquires the pricing information of a local company. This would allow the foreign company to outcompete the local company, potentially resulting in significant damage to the entire economy.

4 CONFIDENTIALLY FINGERPRINTING DATA

Before diving deeper into how invoice data can be protected, it is important to have a clear understanding of a technique called 'hashing'. In English, 'to hash' means 'to chop', 'to confuse' or 'to muddle',[9] or, according to the Oxford English Dictionary:

> hash something out (...) from French *hacher*, from *hache* 'axe'.[10]

---

4. Leonard Manson, *Giant Leak Exposes Data from Almost All Brazilians* (12 May 2021), https://www.somagnews.com/giant-leak-exposes-data-from-almost-all-brazilians/.
5. The CPF number is the identification number of Brazilian individual taxpayers.
6. Mus Huseyin, *Why Humans Are the Weakest Link in Cybersecurity* (12 May 2021), https://www.treasurers.org/hub/treasurer-magazine/why-humans-are-the%E2%80%93weakest-link-in-cybersecurity.
7. Jim Finkle, Dustin Volz, *Database of 191 Million U.S. Voters Exposed on Internet: Researcher* (12 May 2021), https://www.reuters.com/article/us-usa-voters-breach-idUKKBN0UB1E020151229?edition-redirect=uk.
8. Aric Toler, *Hunting the Hunters: How We Identified Navalny's FSB Stalkers* (12 May 2021), https://www.bellingcat.com/resources/2020/12/14/navalny-fsb-methodology/.
9. Merriam-Webster, *Search 'Hash'* (12 May 2021), https://www.merriam-webster.com/dictionary/hash.
10. Oxford Learner's Dictionaries, *Search 'Hash'* (12 May 2021), https://www.oxfordlearnersdictionaries.com/definition/english/hash_2?q=hashing.

To give an analogy: just like stones can be cut up into unrecognizable pieces (*see* Figure 7.1), data can be *hashed* by means of a 'hashing algorithm' or 'hash function'.

Figure 7.1 Stones Cut up into Unrecognizable Pieces

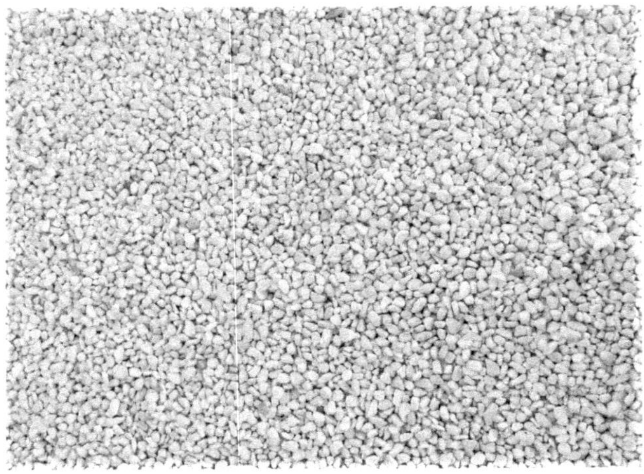

Source: Khadeeja Yasser – Unsplash.

What a hash function actually does is that it transforms input data (e.g., invoice data) into a fixed-size output. The output is also called the 'hash', 'message digest', or just 'digest'. In Figure 7.2, five simple hashing examples are shown. It shows that if a different input is hashed, it results in a different output of the same size. Even when changing just one letter (as is the case in the bottom four examples), the output is unrecognizably different. As a result, the hash function creates a kind of *fingerprint* of the input data. The hash function *hashes* (scrambles) the input data in such a way that the same input data will always hash to the same random-looking fingerprint.[11]

11. For a full technical deep dive of a famous hash function SHA-2, *see*, https://github.com/in3rsha/sha256-animation.

Figure 7.2 Hashing Examples

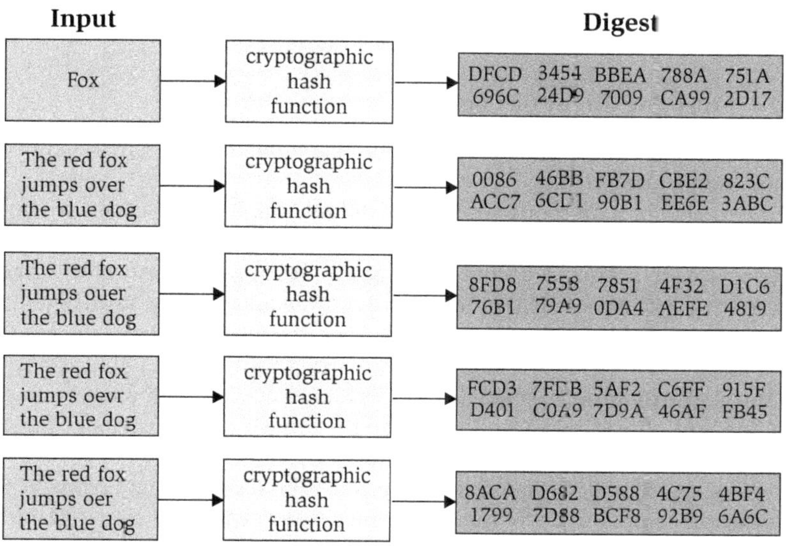

Source: Wikipedia. (2020). Retrieved from: https://en.wikipedia.org/wiki/Cryptographic_hash_function#/media/File:Cryptographic_Hash_Function.svg.

These hash algorithms can be used for many things. Hashes are essential building blocks for digital signatures, for example, which are used widely in the realm of e-invoicing and e-archiving. If two fingerprints are the same, the input data used must be the same as well. This can be a very powerful tool when used correctly (some best practices are discussed in section 4.1 including, for example, that it is not advised to use hash functions that are too old). Note that not all hash functions are equally strong or effective. For example, for a hash function to be strong it should be practically impossible for two inputs to hash to the same output. Furthermore, if someone knows a hash output but nothing else, it should be practically impossible to find the corresponding input.[12]

Over the years, cryptographers have built better and better hash functions, but people also have become better at 'breaking' these algorithms. The MD5 hash function was designed in 1992 by cryptographer Ronald Rivest and can nowadays be broken by generic laptops in seconds.[13] The Secure Hash Algorithm (SHA) 1, standardized in 1995, has been used around the world, but in 2017 it was broken in practice for the first

12. A full mathematical explanation of how these properties can be achieved is not within the scope of this chapter. *See* further, https://toc.cryptobook.us/.
13. Tao Xie, Fanbao Liu, Dengguo Feng, *Fast Collision Attack on MD5* (12 May 2021), https://eprint.iacr.org/2013/170.pdf.

time after years of attempts.[14] At the moment of writing, the renowned US National Institute of Standard and Technology advises the use of newer algorithms such as SHA-2 or even SHA-3. Note that many alternatives exist, each offering different technical trade-offs in order to be optimal for certain applications.[15]

4.1 Hashing: Best Practices

There are a number of things to keep in mind when building a system that uses hash functions to fingerprint data.

First, it is important to use a secure hash function. It is advisable that during the initial set-up, the latest and most secure hash functions available are used, and that the latest developments around secure hashing are being monitored. New attacks are discovered every year, but SHA-1 took over twenty years to break; in all likelihood the extensively and publicly tested SHA-3 will be usable for many years to come. Unfortunately, a number of tax authorities are using SHA-1 even today and with new systems. The use of these insecure algorithms allows anyone with a good computer to deliver different information resulting in the same hashes, which render fingerprints unusable for, for example, any auditing purposes.

Second, in order for the invoice fingerprints to be secure, it should not be possible for a random person to uncover the actual information when viewing a hash through brute-force methods.[16] In order to achieve this, fingerprints should be created or encrypted in such a way that only the sender, receiver, and anyone they specifically authorize can reconstruct the hash in order to verify from which information it was generated.

5 HOW CAN HASHING HELP SECURE REAL-TIME REPORTING SYSTEMS?

Section 4 explained how hashing works and elaborated on its best practices. This section will dive deeper into how hashing can help to implement a real-time reporting system in a secure way. By implementing a real-time reporting system, tax authorities can perform (automated) checks on the invoices of a company that are used for preparing the VAT return. Therefore, real-time reporting makes it no longer possible to report an amount of VAT that does not correspond with the VAT stated on the invoice without being detected. This even allows for pre-filled VAT returns, which some countries have already implemented or are planning to implement.[17] However, the tax authority does not have to see the actual invoice data to achieve the above-mentioned

14. Marc Stevens et al., *The First Collision for Full SHA-1* (12 May 2021), https://eprint.iacr.org/2017/190.pdf.
15. For more information, *see* NIST (12 May 2021), https://csrc.nist.gov/Projects/Hash-Functions/NIST-Policy-on-Hash-Functions.
16. Some attackers may try to simply guess how the invoice hash was made, by trying to hash many different combinations of invoice details, hoping to end up at a certain target invoice hash. For more information, *see*, https://en.wikipedia.org/wiki/Brute-force_attack.
17. David Borja et al., *ICT as a Strategic Tool to Leapfrog the Efficiency of Tax Administrations* (12 May 2021), https://www.ciat.org/Biblioteca/Estudios/2020-ICT_STL_CIAT_FMGB.pdf.

results; the tax authority just wants to know if the data on the VAT return correspond to the data on the invoices.

By applying invoice hashing to real-time reporting, tax authorities can close the VAT gap without storing any actual invoice information. In a world where the number of data breaches is becoming an increasing matter of concern, this is an excellent solution to make real-time reporting more secure. To illustrate how hashing can improve the way invoice information is verified, let us have a look at an example. In the example contained in Figure 7.3, Alice the auto mechanic sends an invoice to Bob the builder.

Figure 7.3 Alice Sends an Invoice to Bob

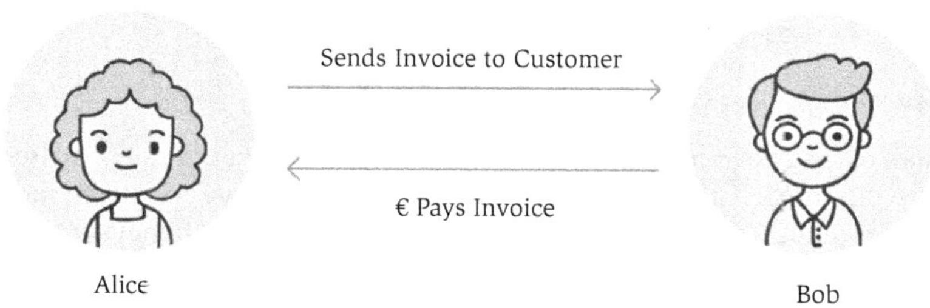

Source: Freepik.

A wide variety of auditors perform cross checks on the invoices in order to verify the correctness of the information (*see* Figure 7.4). Think of the following situations:

- tax authorities may want to know whether the counterparty registers the same amount of VAT;
- auditors may want to know whether all purchase and sales invoices in the bookkeeping are included; and
- financial institutions, such as lending providers and credit rating agencies, may want to know whether the same information is submitted to auditors and tax authorities as to the bank.

Figure 7.4 Many Parties Are Interested in Their Financial Information

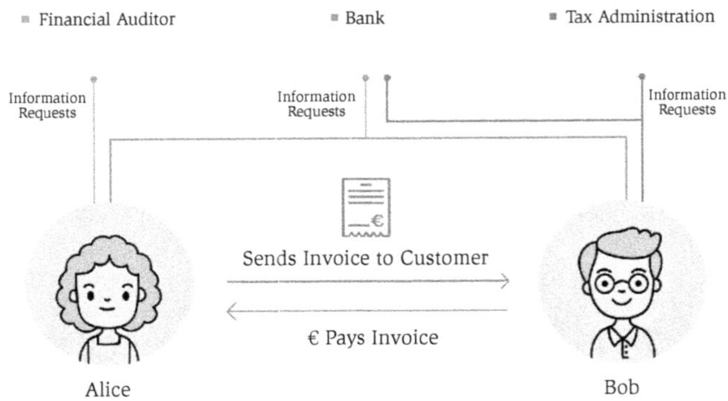

Source: Freepik.

In all of the above-mentioned cases, the auditing party does not actually need to see the invoice data. All they need to know is whether the data registered in different places is the same. This can be made possible by requiring companies to hash their invoices and to publicize the resulting invoice fingerprints:

- auditors can be sure that the invoices of the counterparty are in both registrations;
- tax authorities can be sure that the counterparty reports the same invoice for tax purposes; and
- financial institutions can be sure that the same information is submitted everywhere.

This is only possible if all parties can verify that the other parties are using the same source of information (*see* Figure 7.5).

Figure 7.5 Everyone Should Be Able to Access a Single Source of Truth

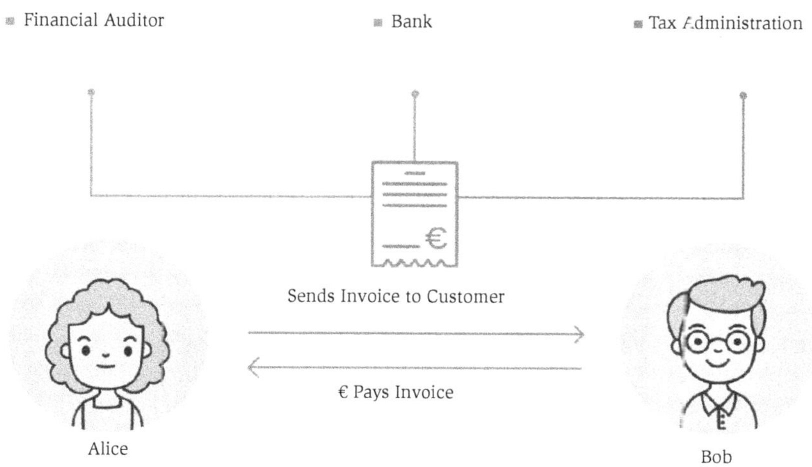

Source: Freepik.

Figure 7.6 gives an idea of how invoice hashing looks. On the top of the invoice, information can be found with several data fields. The resulting SHA-3 hash output is shown in Figure 7.6. If just one single character or number in the invoice is changed, the fingerprint will change completely.

Figure 7.6 Example of a Hashed Fingerprint

5.1 Additional Benefits for Businesses: Verified Financial Information

As previously explained, when applying hashing to real-time reporting the invoice fingerprints can be published for auditing purposes. This would create additional value for businesses because businesses can then provide mathematical proof that they used their invoices for tax purposes. In this way, publicly verifiable financial information is created. This would be in contrast with how the information is handled in most existing real-time reporting systems. Often, the data that is sent to the tax authority is solely used for tax purposes. By combining hashing with real-time reporting, this data can be taken out of the tax authority's silo in a 100% secure way. There is a wide variety of applications for verified financial information. For example, the information can be used to automate audits, or to allow a company to give their investors real-time access to its revenue.

There are many more use cases for verified financial information, but the key take away is that invoice hashing cannot only help to secure a real-time reporting system, but it can even provide additional benefits for businesses and the entire economy.

6 CONCLUSION

This chapter provided a high-level introduction to hash functions and their application to real-time reporting. This chapter started by explaining how more and more countries are making use of real-time reporting systems as they have proved to be an excellent tool to close the VAT gap. However, because existing solutions centrally store invoice data and often give public officials access to the data in plain text, these solutions come with serious security issues. It was shown that invoice hashing, which allows auditors to verify certain invoice data without revealing all of it by default, can help to make real-time reporting more secure. Furthermore, when implemented correctly, it can even provide multiple benefits to businesses through the creation of verified financial information. To conclude, this chapter by no means provides a complete deep dive; there is a lot more to discover and understand. However, the author hopes that it does provide a good toolkit for tax authorities to make real-time reporting not only more secure but also get more utility for tax payers.

CHAPTER 8

The Change of Paradigm of Tax Transparency and Its Challenges to Taxpayers' Rights to Privacy and Personal Data Protection

Shimeng Lan

1 INTRODUCTION

The notion of tax transparency has evolved over time. Traditionally, there was an information asymmetry between taxpayers and tax authorities favouring the former.[1] Yet, over the past years, we have witnessed an unprecedented move towards tax transparency.[2] Furthermore, the emergence of state-of-the-art technologies such as big data, artificial intelligence (AI), and the internet of things has significantly changed the way information is collected, analysed, stored, and exchanged.[3] These technological developments not only bring powerful engines for tax authorities but also result in a host of new questions regarding the privacy and data protection of taxpayers.

This chapter summarizes the trends and characteristics of data collection and analytics in the transparency era and identifies the challenges from a privacy and personal data protection perspective. It starts with a review of tax authorities' practices in the past (*see* section 2), which highlights the information asymmetry that favoured taxpayers. Then, it examines the major events and policy changes that have pushed forward tax transparency using different countries' practices as examples. The trends

1. Stan Stevens, *Cutting-edge Techniques to Collect Information from Taxpayers*, Chapter 5 of the *Tax Transparency, EATLP Annual Congress Zurich* (2018).
2. Johanna Hey, *The Notion and Concept of Tax Transparency*, Chapter 1, general report of the *Tax Transparency, EATLP Annual Congress Zurich* (2018).
3. Stan Stevens, *Cutting-edge Techniques to Collect Information from Taxpayers*, Chapter 5 of the *Tax Transparency, EATLP Annual Congress Zurich* (2018).

and characteristics of data collection and analytics from this stage form a clear comparison with the past (*see* section 3). Furthermore, it analyses the advanced data analytics deployed by tax authorities to enhance their power of processing tax data. Lastly, but most important of all, it identifies the challenges to taxpayers' right to privacy and personal data protection according to four different stages of the data processing: data collection, data analytics, data exchange, and data storage, and subsequently calls for more research and debates in a broader social context (*see* section 4).

Tax transparency has several meanings.[4] The Organization for Economic Co-operation and Development (OECD) and many authors use tax transparency to refer to the development in the international exchange of information.[5] However, in the context of this work, tax transparency is depicted generally as a two-way process: that of taxpayers' transparency towards tax authorities and, in turn, tax authorities' transparency towards taxpayers. Tax authorities access taxpayers' tax-related information through various means, including through taxpayers' self-reporting, third-party reporting, and exchange of information. Tax authorities should therefore also be transparent to taxpayers and openly disclose their 'tax rules, agency interpretations, decision-making processes, and enforcement practices'.[6]

2 THE INFORMATION ASYMMETRY IN THE PAST

Traditionally, tax collection has been based on taxpayers' declarations in the form of tax returns and supporting evidence, which is then subject to verification checks by tax authorities. In the course of verification, tax authorities may conduct tax audits on certain taxpayers based on risk assessment, or in some cases through random selection.[7] However, due to the volume of tax returns and the limited time and resources of tax authorities, it is impossible to verify and control all returns.[8] Most countries' audits are conducted on a 'more or less random basis', and the total audit rate remains relatively low; in some cases less than 1% of tax returns are audited.[9]

This suggests that, in the past, taxpayers had a more advantageous position vis-à-vis tax authorities since they had more complete information about themselves compared to the information known by the tax authorities. In such a situation, information about taxable events was not usually transmitted to the tax authorities in real time. As a result, an information asymmetry inherently existed which meant that

4. *See* Stefano Castagna, *The Benefits of Differentiated Transparency. Proposal for Graduated Confidentiality Regimes within International Tax Disputes*, 48(12) Intertax 1125-1144, 1130 (2020).
5. https://www.oecd.org/tax/beps/tax-transparency/, accessed 13 January 2021.
6. Joshua Blank, *The Timing of Tax Transparency*, 90(3) S. Cal. L. Rev. 459 (2017).
7. OECD (2020), *Tax Administration 3.0: The Digital Transformation of Tax Administration*, OECD, Paris, p. 11.
8. Tina Ehrke-Rabel, *Third Parties as Supplementary Sources of Tax Transparency*, in the book Tax Transparency – EATLP Annual Congress Zurich, Funda Basaran Yavaşlar and Johanna Hey (eds), IBFD (2019), p. 72.
9. *Ibid.*, p. 72. *See also* https://www.irs.gov/about-irs/irs-audit-rates-significantly-increase-as-income-rises, accessed on 30 March 2021.

tax authorities relied heavily on the voluntary compliance of taxpayers.[10] The current context of cross-border situations has also increased the difficulty for the tax authorities of a resident state to obtain information about taxable transactions.

In this regard, tax authorities have adopted different measures to alleviate the disadvantages of information asymmetry and to encourage voluntary compliance. Studies show that taxpayers are more compliant when the risk of detection of non-compliance is high.[11] Consequently, tax authorities often seek information from third parties to verify the information submitted by taxpayers.

There are different types of third parties.[12] There are those that are bound by law or professional ethics to disclose information to tax authorities, for example, financial institutions, tax advisers, and notaries. Others may have enhanced relationships with taxpayers, such as employers or contracting parties. Public authorities may also be third parties, for example other government institutions/departments, or tax authorities from other states. Other third parties may include private companies that collect user data – such as Uber and Airbnb – which can be passed to the tax authorities and other open sources, such as open databases.

Employers have to provide information on the income and wages of their employees to the tax authorities.[13] Some countries require notaries, telephone service companies, postal operators, or publishers to submit information on taxable events.[14] Other countries require third parties to report the tax-deductible payments of their debtors, such as donations, life insurance premiums, and loans for real estate.[15] Some tax authorities also require third parties to spontaneously report certain information on

---

10. OECD (2020), *Tax Administration 3.0: The Digital Transformation of Tax Administration*, OECD, Paris, p. 11; OECD (2019), *Tax Administration 2019: Comparative Information on OECD and other Advanced and Emerging Economies*, OECD Publishing, Paris, p. 34. *See also* Tina Ehrke-Rabel, *Third Parties as Supplementary Sources of Tax Transparency*, in the book Tax Transparency – EATLP Annual Congress Zurich, Funda Basaran Yavaşlar and Johanna Hey (eds), IBFD (2019), pp. 70-71.
11. Susan Cleary Morse et al., *Cash Businesses and Tax Evasion*, 20 Stan. L. & Pol'y Rev. 37, 50 (2009). Richard T. Ainsworth & Goran Todorov, *Stopping VAT Fraud with DICE –Digital Invoice Customs Exchange*, 72 Tax Notes Int'l 637, 637 n. 3 (2013) (*citing* Steven D. Levitt & Stephen J. Dubner, *Freakonomics: A Rogue Economist Explores the Hidden Side of Everything*, William Morrow Paperbacks, 25 August 2009, p. 238. See https://www.amazon.com/Freakonomics-Economist-Explores-Hidden-Everything/dp/0060731338. Citing, Leandra Lederman & Joseph Dugan, *Information Matters in Tax Enforcement*, Research Paper Number 396 2020 Byu L. Rev (forthcoming). Available on SSRN: http://ssrn.com/abstract=3325598.
12. This list is summarized from the article of Tina Ehrke-Rabel, *Third Parties as Supplementary Sources of Tax Transparency*, in the book Tax Transparency – EATLP Annual Congress Zurich, Funda Basaran Yavaşlar and Johanna Hey (eds), IBFD (2019), p. 80.
13. OECD (2019), *Tax Administration 2019: Comparative Information on OECD and other Advanced and Emerging Economies*, OECD Publishing, Paris, p. 34.
14. For example, Czech Republic, Greece, France. *See* Tina Ehrke-Rabel, *Third Parties as Supplementary Sources of Tax Transparency*, in the book Tax Transparency – EATLP Annual Congress Zurich, Funda Basaran Yavaşlar and Johanna Hey (eds), IBFD (2019), p. 87.
15. For example, in Denmark, a third party is required to report deductible charitable donations. *See* Christian Gillitzera & Peer Ebbesen Skovb, *The Use of Third-Party Information Reporting for Tax Deductions: Evidence and Implications from Charitable Deductions in Denmark*, 70(3) Oxford Economic Papers 892-916 (2018), https://doi.org/10.1093/oep/gpx055.

taxpayers' arrangements.[16] Furthermore, tax authorities generally have access to registers held by other government authorities, such as social security agencies. They also exchange information with different states and/or perform research into a taxpayer based on publicly available information to overcome the territorial limitations of the information. Last but not least, there are also so-called whistle-blowers who voluntarily provide certain leads to the tax authorities.

Despite the fact that these measures have always existed, the scale of tax information collection and exchange was limited because of technical constraints and low levels of digitalization: the IT systems of tax authorities were not sufficient to support large quantities of data processing; tax returns were mostly in paper format – non-digitalized, paper-based documents were not as convenient to transmit compared to digitalized data, and it was difficult for the tax authorities to keep up-to-date information; and international cooperation was not as active as it is today – mechanisms such as automatic exchange of information (AEOI) were not established. Therefore, information collection in the past was limited, and tax authorities conducted only limited checks on the information reported by taxpayers and on that obtained through tax audits.

3 THE TRANSPARENT ERA

In the last two decades, there has been increasing political momentum in the international community to act together to increase tax transparency. Tax authorities are expanding their sources of collecting tax-relevant data, and big data is becoming a reality thanks to technical advances. Consequently, tax authorities have more and more access to taxpayers' information.

3.1 International Political Momentum on Enhancing Transparency and Multilateral Cooperation

There is strong international political momentum to improve tax transparency and counter tax evasion and fraud, and close collaboration among many jurisdictions has greatly pushed forward the level of tax transparency. The OECD has been at the forefront of the international cooperation endorsed by the G20 establishing measures such as: the Common Reporting Standard (CRS) and the AEOI, its Action Plan on Base Erosion and Profit Shifting (BEPS) including country-by-country reporting (CbCR), and multilateral cooperative compliance programmes, such as the International Compliance Assurance Programme (ICAP).

16. For example, in Denmark, intermediaries who assisted taxpayers with the purchase of assets or financial instruments have to disclose the substance of such arrangements to tax authorities if the arrangements are for the purposes of reducing or deferring taxes. *See* Tina Ehrke-Rabel, *Third Parties as Supplementary Sources of Tax Transparency*, in the book Tax Transparency – EATLP Annual Congress Zurich, Funda Basaran Yavaşlar and Johanna Hey (eds), IBFD (2019), p. 88.

3.1.1 From FATCA to CRS

The focus of exchange of information has traditionally been on the exchange of information on request.[17] The introduction of the Foreign Account Tax Compliance Act (FATCA) by the United States (US) in 2010 was a milestone for AEOI[18] and inspired the G20 to move towards AEOI.[19] In 2013, the G20 leaders mandated the OECD to develop a CRS for tax authorities to obtain information from their financial institutions and automatically exchange that information with other jurisdictions on an annual basis.[20] Consequently, the OECD developed a Model Competent Authority Agreement (Model CAA) and the CRS.[21] In July 2014, the OECD released the full version of the Standard for Automatic Exchange of Financial Account Information (the AEOI Standard), which was subsequently endorsed by the G20 in September 2014.[22] It included commentaries on the Model CAA and the CRS, and it also included the XML Schema. In 2015, the OECD published the first edition of the Implementation Handbook to assist government officials and financial institutions with the implementation of the AEOI Standard and updated it in 2018. By November 2019, a total of ninety-four jurisdictions had completed around 6,100 bilateral exchanges.

3.1.2 BEPS Actions and Inclusive Framework

Multinational enterprises (MNEs) frequently exploit the gaps and mismatches in different countries' tax rules to erode the tax bases of the source state and artificially shift profits to low or no-tax locations without economic substance. This BEPS has become an increasing global concern, especially for developing countries that rely heavily on corporate income tax as their main source of tax revenue.[23] Against this backdrop, the OECD and G20 countries worked closely with developing countries to develop a package of actions to counter BEPS issues. As a result, the OECD published its BEPS Action Plan in 2013 and released its Final Reports on the fifteen BEPS actions in October 2015.

Increasing transparency is one of the three fundamental pillars of the OECD/G20 BEPS Project.[24] Among the fifteen BEPS actions, Action 5 (Harmful Tax Practices),

17. Xavier Oberson, *International Exchange of Information in Tax Matters – Towards Global Transparency*, 2nd ed., Elgar Tax Law and Practice, 2018.
18. Diane Ring, *Article 26: Exchange of Information – Global Tax Treaty Commentaries*, IBFD, 2014.
19. It 'urged all jurisdictions to move towards exchanging information automatically with their treaty partners, as appropriate'. *G20 Meeting of Finance Ministers and Central Bank Governors Communiqué* (Washington, 18-19 April 2013), available at http://www.g20.utoronto.ca/2013/2013-0419-finance.html.
20. *G20 Meeting of Finance Ministers and Central Bank Governors Communiqué* (Washington, 18-19 April 2013), available at http://www.g20.utoronto.ca/2013/2013-0419-finance.html, accessed on 30 March 2021.
21. Xavier Oberson, *International Exchange of Information in Tax Matters – Towards Global Transparency*, 2d ed., Elgar Tax Law and Practice, 2018.
22. https://www.oecd.org/tax/automatic-exchange/about-automatic-exchange/, accessed on 16 July 2020.
23. https://www.oecd.org/tax/beps/about/#mission-impact, accessed on 7 February 2021.
24. https://www.oecd.org/ctp/oecd-presents-outputs-of-oecd-g20-beps-project-for-discussion-at-g20-finance-ministers-meeting.htm, accessed on 2 February 2021.

Action 12 (Mandatory Disclosure Rules), and Action 13 (CbCR) contain measures requiring the disclosure of certain additional information to tax authorities and/or the exchange of the information between tax authorities.

Shortly after the release of the fifteen BEPS actions, the G20 Leaders pushed for a timely implementation and a more inclusive framework with the involvement of more countries and jurisdictions, including developing economies. Following the mandate of the G20, the OECD established the Inclusive Framework on BEPS in January 2016. Since then, over 125 countries and jurisdictions have been brought together to collaborate on standard setting for BEPS-related issues, and for the review and monitoring of the implementation of the BEPS Package to ensure a level playing field.[25]

3.1.3 *Multilateral Cooperation*

We can also observe a strong trend to enhance multilateral cooperation in the field of tax compliance, for instance with the OECD's multilateral cooperative compliance programmes such as the ICAP and joint audits. The first ICAP pilot took place in 2018 and brought together eight tax authorities. The second ICAP pilot was announced in March 2019 and nineteen jurisdictions participated in the programme.[26] In February 2021, the OECD released the Handbook for ICAP and expects a broader participation from more jurisdictions as a result.[27] During these cooperative compliance programmes, the information provided by taxpayers is fully transparent for all participating tax authorities, something that is beneficial for taxpayers in order to obtain multilateral tax certainty.

3.1.4 *EU Administrative Cooperation*

Alongside the work of the OECD, the European Union (EU) has also undertaken similar actions against tax evasion and to increase transparency. This can be found in the implementation of Directive 2011/16/EU on administrative cooperation in the field of taxation (DAC 1) which laid the foundation for the exchange of information (including spontaneous, on-request, and AEOI) as well as other forms of administrative cooperation.[28] DAC 1 has been intensively amended over the last ten years (*see* sections 3.2.1.2-3.2.2.3 for details of some of the amendments).

25. https://www.oecd.org/tax/beps/beps-about.htm/, accessed on 2 February 2021.
26. https://www.oecd.org/tax/forum-on-tax-administration/international-compliance-assurance-programme.htm, accessed on 2 February 2021.
27. OECD (2021), *International Compliance Assurance Programme – Handbook for Tax Administrations and MNE Groups*, OECD, Paris.
28. Council Directive 2011/16/EU of 15 February 2011 on administrative cooperation in the field of taxation and repealing Directive 77/799/EEC, OJ L 64, pp. 1-12.

3.2 Expanded Sources of Tax Data

Another significant characteristic of the transparent era is that tax authorities have expanded their sources of data. While taxpayers have always been required to submit tax information, today they face stricter time, format, and accuracy requirements. Meanwhile, countries impose more reporting obligations on certain client-facing third parties. Moreover, with the help of advanced technologies, tax authorities are able to harness big data, even though they are in unstructured forms. The expanded sources of data enable tax authorities to have better insights into taxpayers' tax situations, and from multiple perspectives.

3.2.1 More Stringent Self-Reporting Obligations for Taxpayers

Taxpayers remain the most important source of information for tax authorities. Nowadays most countries have stringent self-reporting requirements. Taxpayers may be required to report their information in real time or near real time, and in a standard format, for example in XML Schema.

3.2.1.1 Transfer Pricing Documentation

An example of transfer pricing documentation would be the three-tier transfer pricing (TP) documentation introduced by BEPS Action 13, which deals with transfer pricing documentation and CbCR. It proposed a three-tiered approach for transfer pricing documentation, namely the Master File, Local File, and CbCR. The CbCR is a minimum standard under Action 13. It requires large MNEs to report the aggregate data on the global allocation of income, profit, taxes paid, and economic activity among tax jurisdictions in which they operate. This information is shared with the tax authorities in the jurisdictions where the MNE operates to be used in high-level transfer pricing and BEPS risk analysis.[29] By the end of 2020, most of the OECD/G20 Inclusive Framework members had introduced, or were in the process of introducing, a CbCR obligation, and, significantly, every MNE above the consolidated group revenue threshold is already within the scope of CbCR.[30]

3.2.1.2 Mandatory Disclosure Rules

BEPS Action 12 provides states with recommendations to design mandatory disclosure rules for aggressive or abusive transactions, arrangements, or structures. It does not amount to a minimum standard, so states have the freedom to choose to design such rules based on their needs. Should states decide to do so, the BEPS Action 12 Final

29. OECD (2015), *Transfer Pricing Documentation and Country-by-Country Reporting, Action 13 – 2015 Final Report*, OECD/G20 Base Erosion and Profit Shifting Project, OECD publishing, Paris, p. 16.
30. OECD/G20 Inclusive Framework on BEPS, Progress report July 2018-May 2019.

Report provides a modular framework for the regime as well as recommendations on more effective information exchange and cooperation between tax authorities.[31]

BEPS Action 12 has had a profound influence on policy setting in the EU which enacted the Council Directive (EU) 2018/822 amending Directive 2011/16/EU (DAC 6).[32] Under DAC 6, intermediaries or taxpayers are required to disclose cross-border arrangements to the tax authorities if one of the hallmarks detailed in the Directive is fulfilled. Subsequently, the information will automatically be exchanged among EU Member States. The reporting obligation lies mainly with the intermediaries. However, in the absence of an intermediary, when the intermediary is exempt from reporting, or when the intermediary does not provide proof of reporting to taxpayers, the obligation to report falls to the 'relevant taxpayer'.[33] 'Relevant taxpayer' refers to any person to whom a reportable cross-border arrangement is made available for implementation, or who is ready to implement a reportable cross-border arrangement, or has implemented the first step of such an arrangement.[34]

3.2.1.3 SAF-T and E-Invoicing

Standard Audit File for Tax purposes (SAF-T) was initiated by the OECD in 2005.[35] It requires a set of accounting data to be directly extracted from the accounting systems of businesses in a standard XML format so that tax authorities can easily and effectively inspect the data for compliance purposes. Many countries have implemented regulations related to the provision of SAF-T filing. The submission of the SAF-T file can be on demand, on a regular basis, or in real time or near real time.[36]

Real-time SAF-T filing applies mainly to the field of value added tax (VAT). For example, Spain rolled out the *Suministro Inmediato de Información* (SII) system in VAT in July 2017.[37] It requires all VAT taxpayers to send their invoice details electronically to the tax authorities via an online platform where taxpayers can maintain all of their digital records in the VAT Record Books. The Record Books consist of books of issued invoices, received invoices, investment goods, and specific intra-Community operations. Taxpayers must provide much more comprehensive information – compared with the information required for the conventional Record Books – within four days of

31. OECD (2015), *Mandatory Disclosure Rules, Action 12 – 2015 Final Report*, OECD/G20 Base Erosion and Profit Shifting Project, OECD Publishing, Paris.
32. Recitals 2, 4 and 6 of the Council Directive (EU) 2018/822 of 25 May 2018 amending Directive 2011/16/EU as regards mandatory automatic exchange of information in the field of taxation in relation to reportable cross-border arrangements ('DAC 6').
33. Article 8ab(6) of the DAC 6.
34. Article 3(22) of the DAC 6.
35. For the history of the SAF-T, *see* Alicja Majdanska & Karol Dziwinski, *The Potential of a Standard Audit File – Tax in the European Union: A Chance for Coordinated VAT Administration?*, 72(10) Bull. Int'l Tax'n 582-594, 584 (2018).
36. Bianca Kuijper, Todd Cameron & Zsolt Szatmari, *Technology-Enabled Tax Compliance*, 74(10) Bull. Int'l Tax'n 583-597, 593 (2020).
37. OECD (2019), *Tax Administration 2019: Comparative Information on OECD and other Advanced and Emerging Economies*, OECD Publishing, Paris, https://doi.org/10.1787/74d162b6-en, p. 174. *See also* Rosa Prieto & Mercedes Jordán, *Impact of Digitalization on the Transformation of Tax Administrations*, IOTA, Budapest, 2018, p. 46. The information of the whole paragraph is summarized from these two reports.

the transaction. The SII system revolutionized the VAT administration in Spain, and it plays a significant role in risk management and fraud detection in the area of VAT.

Some countries go a step further and require instant filing and electronic invoicing (e-invoicing), for example, in Italy and Brazil. Under the Brazilian e-invoicing framework (*Nota Fiscal Eletrônica*, NF-e), all invoices and tax-related documents are transmitted to the tax authorities digitally.[38] They must be digitally signed online on the Public System of Digital Bookkeeping and obtain pre-validations from the tax authorities online before the payment at the point of sale.[39] E-invoicing enables tax authorities to inspect all parts of the transaction instantaneously, right up to the completion of sales.[40]

Italy is the first EU Member State to apply mandatory e-invoicing for B2B (business-to-business), B2C (business-to-consumer), and B2G (business-to-government) transactions from 1 January 2019. It applies to all taxable persons established in the territory of Italy except for small businesses. The e-invoices should be issued in XML format and be compliant with the technical specifications set out by the tax authorities. The e-invoices are transmitted to the Interchange System (*Sistema di Interscambio*, SDI) set up by the tax authorities where they are subsequently verified. The Italian tax authorities provide a host of free services in relation to e-invoicing and envisage developing prefilled VAT returns using real-time data, which will help with fraud detection and also provide better taxpayer services.

Last but not least, in 2018, China started pilot programmes on blockchain e-invoicing via a private-public partnership collaboration model between Shenzhen Tax Bureau and Tencent.[41] This new technology combines electronic payment, via WeChat Pay or Alipay for example, with electronic invoicing. From the perspective of business consumers, if an invoice is required to prove certain consumptions of employees are for business purposes, the employees can simply scan the payment QR code to pay, download the invoice from the WeChat Pay system, and apply for online reimbursement from their employer through the corporate WeChat Pay reimbursement system. The reimbursement information is synchronized and written onto the blockchain cloud computing node of the Shenzhen Taxation Bureau in real time, thus completing a closed loop.[42] The tax authorities can monitor the invoice issuance, circulation, and reimbursement process also in real time via the blockchain management platform. Furthermore, instead of traditional eighty-four-digit tax control passwords, blockchain electronic invoicing employs a hash number which is secure,

---

38. Raul Zambrano, Isaác G & Arias E, *Technology and Tax Administration Control in Latin America*, 74(10) Bull. Int'l Tax'n 608-618, 610 (2020).
39. Steef Huibregtse, Paola Ottoni & Sonia Catalina Muñoz Rodríguez, *How Technology Is Changing Taxation in Latin America*, 73(3) Bull. Int'l Tax'n (2019), section 4.2.4. *See also* Bruno Koch, *The E-Invoicing Journey 2019-2025*, 4th ed., Billentis, 2019.
40. *Ibid.*
41. Marta Olowska, Prerna Peshori & Shimeng Lan, *The Digitalization of Tax Administration in China (People's Rep.), India and Korea (Rep.) in the Fourth Industrial Revolution*, 74(8) Bull. Int'l Tax'n (2020), section 3.2.3.1.
42. *See* STA official website http://www.chinatax.gov.cn/n810219/n810739/c3482784/content.html, accessed on 2 February 2021.

unique, open to authentication, traceable, and non-changeable.[43] Therefore, it is an effective way to curb VAT fraud. Although currently the use of blockchain invoicing systems is limited to one type of invoice (Plain VAT Invoices), it is reasonable to expect that this system will become widespread in the near future.[44]

3.2.2 *Increased Reporting Obligations for Third Parties*

3.2.2.1 FATCA and CRS

Under the FATCA, Foreign Financial Institutions (FFIs) are required to register with the US Inland Revenue Service (IRS) and report on the foreign assets held by their US account holders.[45] FFIs that do not both register and agree to report may face a 30% withholding tax on certain US-source payments made to them.[46]

The CRS mandates Reporting Financial Institutions (RFIs) to collect and report information with respect to each Reportable Account. RFIs include depository institutions, custodial institutions, investment entities, and specified insurance companies.[47] The reportable information includes, among other things, the name, address, jurisdiction(s) of residence, tax identification number (TIN), date and place of birth, the account number, the name and identifying number (if any) of the RFI, and the account balance or value of the account.

3.2.2.2 DAC 6

Under DAC 6, intermediaries have the primary obligation to disclose any cross-border arrangement to the tax authorities if it contains at least one of the hallmarks set out in the Directive. The hallmarks aim to reflect the characteristics of aggressive tax planning, and some of them are linked to the 'main benefit test'.[48] One of the hallmarks has also incorporated the model rules targeting CRS Avoidance Arrangements and Offshore Opaque Structures set out in the OECD 2018 report on Model Mandatory Disclosure Rules for CRS Avoidance Arrangements and Opaque Offshore Structures.[49]

The term 'intermediaries' covers any person who designs, markets, organizes, makes available for implementation or manages the implementation of a reportable cross-border arrangement, and any person who knows or could be reasonably expected to know that they have undertaken to have directly or indirectly provided aid,

43. *Ibid.*
44. Marta Olowska, Prerna Peshori & Shimeng Lan, *The Digitalization of Tax Administration in China (People's Rep.), India and Korea (Rep.) in the Fourth Industrial Revolution*, 74(8) Bull. Int'l Tax'n (2020), section 3.2.3.1.
45. https://www.irs.gov/businesses/corporations/information-for-foreign-financial-institutions.
46. *Ibid.*
47. OECD (2018), *Standard for Automatic Exchange of Financial Information in Tax Matters – Implementation Handbook – Second Edition*, OECD, Paris, p. 61.
48. Kristin Resenig, *The Current State of DAC-6 Implementation in the European Union*, 60(12) Eur. Tax'n 527-535, 527 (2020).
49. OECD (2018), *Model Mandatory Disclosure Rules for CRS Avoidance Arrangements and Opaque Offshore Structures*, OECD, Paris, *www.oecd.org/tax/exchange-of-information/model-mandatory-disclosure-rules-for-crs-avoidance-arrangements-and-opaque-offshorestructures.Pdf.*

assistance, or advice with respect to designing, marketing, organizing, making available for implementation or managing the implementation of a reportable cross-border arrangement.[50]

3.2.2.3 *Sharing Economy Platforms*

The sharing economy is also often referred to as the 'gig economy',[51] the 'peer-to-peer economy',[52] or the 'platform economy'.[53] While the sharing economy challenges many aspects of the traditional tax system,[54] it provides an opportunity to make the informal cash economy more compliant. The OECD published its Model Rules for Reporting by Platform Operators with Respect to Sellers in the Sharing and Gig Economy (MRDP) in July 2020.[55] It requires digital platforms to collect and report information on the income realized by platform sellers that offer accommodation, transport, and personal services.

In parallel to the work of the OECD, the EU Commission has also proposed the so-called DAC 7.[56] According to the proposal, the reporting platform operators are first required to collect and verify the information on the income earned in line with due diligence procedures. Then, they are required to report the income information about the reportable sellers. The scope of the reportable activities is broader than the OECD MRDP. In addition to accommodation, transport, and personal services, it also includes the sale of goods, and investment and lending in the context of crowdfunding. The reported information will then be automatically exchanged to the competent authorities of the EU Member State where the reportable seller is a resident or to the competent authorities of the EU Member State where the immovable property is located within two months following the end of the reportable period.

50. Article 3(21) of the DAC 6.
51. G. Friedman, *Workers Without Employers: Shadow Corporations and the Rise of the Gig Economy*, 2 Rev. Keynesian Econ. 171-188 (2014), also referred to in, Giorgio Beretta, *VAT and the Sharing Economy*, 10(3) World Tax Journal 381-425 at 385 (August 2018).
52. S. Scanlon, *Peer-to-Peer Rental: The Rise of the Sharing Economy*, The Economist (9 March 2013), https://www.economist.com/leaders/2013/03/09/the-rise-of-the-sharing-economy, also referred to in *see* Giorgio Beretta, *VAT and the Sharing Economy*, 10(3) World Tax Journal 381-425 at 385 (August 2018).
53. C. Busch et al., *The Rise of the Platform Economy: A New Challenge for EU Consumer Law?*, 5(1) J. Eur. Consumer & Mkt. L. 3-10 (2016). *See* Giorgio Beretta, *VAT and the Sharing Economy*, 10(3) World Tax Journal 381-425 at 385 (August 2018).
54. *See* Shimeng Lan, *Sharing Economy: Challenges and Opportunities for Chinese Individual Income Taxation*, 26(2) Asia-Pacific Tax Bull. 2020.
55. https://www.oecd.org/tax/exchange-of-tax-information/model-rules-for-reporting-by-platform-operators-with-respect-to-sellers-in-the-sharing-and-gig-economy.htm, accessed on 14 January 2020.
56. European Commission, Proposal for a Council Directive Amending Directive 2011/16/EU on Administrative Cooperation in the Field of Taxation, COM (2020) 314 final (15 July 2020), https://ec.europa.eu/taxation_customs/sites/taxation/files/2020_tax_package_dac7_en.pdf, accessed on 14 January 2020.

3.2.2.4 *Payment Platform*

In the US, starting from 2011, processors of credit and debit cards, such as Visa and MasterCard, and electronic payment systems, such as PayPal, are required to report the gross annual receipts for each merchant to the IRS, as well as to the merchants who received them, unless a merchant's total payment transactions for the year do not exceed USD 20,000, or the total number of transactions does not exceed 200.[57]

Similar measures have also been adopted in the EU. In February 2020, the EU Council adopted Directive 2020/284/EU amending the current VAT Directive by imposing requirements for payment service providers (PSPs) to keep records on cross-border payments related to e-commerce that will be automatically exchanged.[58] The Directive will be effective from 1 January 2024. The information collected will subsequently be exchanged with the tax authorities of other EU Member States. Furthermore, a Central Electronic System of Payment information (CESOP) accessible only to Eurofisc liaison officers has been established pursuant to Regulation 2020/283/EU.[59]

3.2.3 *Big Data Being Harnessed More Than Ever*

Apart from data collected from taxpayers and third parties, in recent years, many tax authorities have started to explore the use of big data to enhance their knowledge of taxpayer behaviour and taxable transactions. Sources of big data may include data from the 'Internet, social media, sensors, text messages, video, images and audio files as well as other unstructured sources'.[60] Furthermore, the internet of things enables physical objects to transmit real-time data, which also provides tax authorities with opportunities to monitor taxpayer activities in real time.[61] Sections 3.2.3.1-3.2.3.2 provide some examples of big data being harnessed by tax authorities.

3.2.3.1 *Data from Cash Register and GPS Trackers*

Since the popularization of online cash registers, many countries have been able to collect transactional data in real time. For instance, Russia has introduced the

57. Department of the Treasury. Internal Revenue Service, 26 CFR Parts 1, 31, and 301 [TD 9496], RIN 1545-BI51 Information Reporting for Payments Made in Settlement of Payment Card and Third Party Network Transactions. Access via: https://www.irs.gov/tax-professionals/third-party-reporting-information-center-information-documents, accessed on 30 March 2021.
58. Council Directive (EU) 2020/284 of 18 February 2020 amending Directive 2006/112/EC as regards introducing certain requirements for payment service providers, OJ L62 (2020).
59. *See* Council Regulation (EU) 2020/283 of 18 February 2020 amending Regulation (EU) 904/2010 as regards measures to strengthen administrative cooperation in order to combat VAT fraud, OJ L62 (2020). *See also* European Commission, Central Electronic System of Payment Information (CESOP), available at https://ec.europa.eu/taxation_customs/taxation/central-electronic-system-payment-information-cesop_en, accessed on 15 January 2021.
60. OECD (2016), *Technologies for Better Tax Administration: A Practical Guide for Revenue Bodies*, OECD Publishing, Paris, p. 48.
61. OECD (2016), *Technologies for Better Tax Administration: A Practical Guide for Revenue Bodies*, OECD Publishing, Paris, p. 51.

mandatory use of online cash registers in all retail businesses starting from 1 July 2019. Similar measures have also been implemented in Hungary.

GPS data could also help tax authorities to keep track of the transportation process of goods, beneficial for VAT or customs purposes. For example, since April 2017, Poland has established the Poland has establisehed a system to monitor and control the road system to monitor and control the road and rail transportation of certain 'sensitive' goods for state budget revenues, including motor and heating fuels, liquefied petroleum gas, lubricants, and oils.[62] In Switzerland, the tax authorities use data from tachographs installed in cars to detect under-declaration in the tax returns of taxi drivers or others who drive for commercial purposes (e.g., Uber drivers).[63]

3.2.3.2 Internet Open-Source Data, Including Social Media

Open-source data has always been a source of information for tax authorities. The difference when using open-source data compared to more traditional practices of gathering information is that tax authorities have stronger capacity to automatically retrieve data in bulk instead of searching for specific data on a small scale. Take the two following examples of how tax authorities have used open-source data:

(1) The Spanish tax authorities collect rental information in bulk from the internet in an effort to increase voluntary compliance in income tax returns. They use this data to double-check if taxpayers have declared immovable property income, or to remind taxpayers of their obligation to declare this income in their tax return.[64]

(2) The Swedish tax authorities gather information on poker players via online tournaments in order to find individuals who have not declared their gains.[65]

Tax authorities may also resort to social media to find tax-related information. At the end of 2019, France enacted a new legislation authorizing a three-year experimental *ciblage de la fraude et valorisation des requêtes* (fraud targeting and valuation of requests, CFVR) programme.[66] It allows the tax and customs authorities to automatically collect and analyse the information published by all taxpayers on social media as well as information from e-commerce platforms regarding the sale or exchange of goods, or the provision of services. Upon the collection of data, the tax and customs

62. Anetta Janda-Brzezińska, *The SENT System – An Effective Tool in Combating Crime*, in IOTA book 2020, Applying New Technologies and Digital Solutions in Tax Compliance, p. 31. The bases of the articles were presentations given at the IOTA Annual International Conference, 16-17 October 2019, Tbilisi, Georgia.
63. OECD (2019), *Tax Administration 2019: Comparative Information on OECD and other Advanced and Emerging Economies*, OECD Publishing, Paris, p. 47.
64. José Borja Tomé, *Data Analytics in the Spanish Tax Agency*, in Data-driven Tax Administration, Published by IOTA, Budapest, 2016, p. 22.
65. OECD (2019), *Tax Administration 2019: Comparative Information on OECD and other Advanced and Emerging Economies*, OECD Publishing, Paris, p. 48.
66. Article 57, Projet de loi de finances pour, which is the draft 2020 Financial Bill. Later on, it was incorporated in Article 154 of the Final Financial Bill, LAW n ° 2019-1479 of 28 December 2019 on finance for 2020 1).

authorities will carry out undifferentiated data mining to detect any non-compliance or fraudulent behaviour and conduct further investigations.

The IRS in the US also allegedly mines data from social media as well as private emails as part of its data mining and analytics to detect tax evasion,[67] and the HM Revenue and Customs (HMRC) in the United Kingdom (UK) also monitors open-source data including social media to foster compliance and detect tax fraud or evasion.[68]

3.3 Characteristics of Current Data Collection

The following characteristics pertain to data collection in this transparency era:

- Advanced technologies enable tax authorities to process much larger quantities of data than before, regardless of the data being in structured or unstructured format. Structured data is transmitted through a fixed format and is generally easier to process. Unstructured data has been more difficult to analyse in the past due to technical restrictions. However, tax authorities now have more power to analyse this type of data even though it requires pre-processing to transform the raw data into a useable format.
- With the aid of advanced data analytics techniques, tax authorities are able to collect and analyse more and more (near) real-time data rather than mere historical data. Examples of this can be seen in the near real-time SAF-T filing in Spain and the e-invoicing system adopted in Italy (*see* section 3.2.1.3) where the VAT-related data are collected shortly after the taxable transactions take place.
- Data tend to be collected automatically in bulk instead of merely targeting specific (types of) taxpayers that the tax authorities suspect are non-compliant or fraudulent. The French CFVR programme reflects this approach and collects social-media data on all taxpayers without distinction. The automatic collection of tax information by e-commerce platforms (detailed in section 3.2.2.3) is also a good example of this approach.
- Tax authorities tend to collect all tax-related data, even if some data are redundant.[69] The collected data are usually stored in a centralized tax authority database for an extended period.[70]

---

67. *See* K.A. Houser & D. Sanders, *The Use of Big Data Analytics by the IRS: Efficient Solutions or the End of Privacy as We Know It?*, 19 Vanderbilt J. Ent. & Tech. L. 4 (2017). *See also* Justin Rohrlich, *The Taxman Browseth: The IRS Wants to Use Social Media to Catch Tax Cheats, Quartz*, https://qz.com/1507962/the-irs-wants-to-use-facebook-and-instagram-to-catch-tax-evaders/, accessed on 20 January 2021; Monique Claiborne, *2 Ways the IRS May Be Stalking You on Social Media and How to Avoid Being Singled Out*, https://www.inc.com/monique-claiborne/2-ways-the-irs-may-be-stalking-you-on-social-media.html, accessed on 20 January 2021; Dara Kerr, *Tax Dodgers Beware: IRS Could Be Watching Your Social Media, Cnet*, https://www.cnet.com/news/tax-dodgers-beware-irs-could-be-watching-your-social-media/, accessed on 20 January 2021.
68. https://www.pinsentmasons.com/out-law/news/hmrc-social-media-tax-evaders, accessed on 20 January 2021.
69. For an evaluation of the digital response of tax authorities to optimize tax administration within the digitalized economy, *see* Helena Strauss, *Tyson Fawcett and Danie Schuttee*, 18(2) J. Tax Res.

4 TECHNOLOGICAL OPPORTUNITIES AND LEGAL CHALLENGES

4.1 Advanced Data Analytics Making It Possible to Harness the Ocean of Data

Recently, sources of tax-related information have been significantly broadened, but merely owning the data without an effective means to process it will not translate 'Big Data' into 'Big Improvements'.[71] Thanks to the Fourth Industrial Revolution that stimulated the marriage of big data and advanced data analytics, tax authorities are able to turn this ocean of previously unused data into actionable information to enhance compliance.[72]

To make use of this data, tax authorities first need to deploy data science techniques to convert raw data into useable information. After this step is carried out, tax authorities can employ advanced data analytics techniques to use this information in multiple ways.

First, data can be used to carry out 'automated machine actions' using rule-based approaches to perform defined functions.[73] For example, in Austria, the tax authorities can issue automated notifications to taxpayers under defined conditions without human approval.[74] In the UK, HMRC uses an automated system to serve notices to file returns and to issue penalties for late filers.[75] Similarly, the Irish tax authorities deploy an automated robotics system to validate taxpayer records and relationships based on the data reported in their tax returns.[76]

Second, data can be used for predictive modelling.[77] Tax authorities can use the large amount of data to profile taxpayers for the purpose of debt management, risk assessment, and fraud detection. Audit case selection is a typical example of predictive analytics: tax authorities apply a supervised and an unsupervised model to identify and/or predict non-compliance or fraud, and prioritize the case for further investigation or audit.

383-401 (2020). In this study, thirty different tax administrations from developing and developed countries were interviewed: 'The majority of tax authorities interviewed still collect and store all tax-related data collected from either taxpayers and/or third parties such as financial institutions, international authorities and government institutions. It was, furthermore, observed that the majority of participating tax authorities maintain redundant data that are not utilized to add value to the tax administration process.' The study suggested: 'an optimised data management strategy that identifies critical tax administration data that must be collected and other relevant data which can be accessed through secure data connections, is thus critical'.

70. *Ibid.*
71. OECD (2016), *Advanced Analytics for Better Tax Administration: Putting Data to Work*, OECD Publishing, Paris, p. 3.
72. OECD (2016), *Technologies for Better Tax Administration: A Practical Guide for Revenue Bodies*, OECD Publishing, Paris, p. 52.
73. OECD (2019), *Tax Administration 2019: Comparative Information on OECD and other Advanced and Emerging Economies*, OECD Publishing, Paris, p. 57.
74. *Tax transparency – EATLP Annual Congress Zurich*, p. 373.
75. https://www.pinsentmasons.com/out-law/news/law-change-will-confirm-that-hmrc-decisions-can-be-made-by-a-computer, accessed on 3 February 2021.
76. OECD (2019), *Tax Administration 2019: Comparative Information on OECD and other Advanced and Emerging Economies*, OECD Publishing, Paris, p. 57.
77. OECD (2019), *Tax Administration 2019: Comparative Information on OECD and other Advanced and Emerging Economies*, OECD Publishing, Paris, p. 87.

Supervised models by definition require labelled data, for example historical data, from tax audits where the outcome of the audit is known. Subsequently, during training, they learn to extract the most efficient pattern from the data to predict the outcome.[78] For example, many tax authorities build statistical models using data arising from the high volume of VAT payment and repayment claims to predict VAT fraud or error,[79] and some tax authorities carry out social network analysis to identify the relationship between individuals to detect VAT carousel fraud and other group-level risks.[80] Where feasible, tax authorities may deploy multiple models to identify distinct risks. For example, in Norway, the tax authorities use distinct models for VAT fraud or error detection and carousel fraud detection.[81]

Unsupervised models learn to cluster the data based on interesting or anomalous patterns they identify themselves in the data, instead of learning from the outcomes of specific cases.[82] This helps tax authorities identify previously undetected types of risks.[83] Examples of the application of unsupervised models can be found in Australia where the 'nearest neighbour model' is used to identify incorrect income tax deductions, and also in Ireland's 'income-consumption model' which is used to identify under-declaration of income.[84]

Moreover, data can be used to carry out taxpayer services and simplify tax compliance procedures. Many countries have implemented prepopulated tax returns for personal income tax or VAT purposes using the data received from third parties.[85] For example, Italy conducted a three-year experiment from 2015 to 2017 to apply a prefilled tax return for employment and pension income. In such a scenario, the tax authorities collect taxpayer information related to their employment and pension income, and automatically process the information to generate tax returns. Taxpayers can then review the prefilled tax report online and choose to accept it if all the information is correct, or modify it in case of error. Upon the acceptance of the prefilled tax return, the return will become final and not be subject to tax audit afterwards.[86]

78. OECD (2016), *Advanced Analytics for Better Tax Administration: Putting Data to Work*, OECD Publishing, Paris, p. 23.
79. OECD (2016), *Advanced Analytics for Better Tax Administration: Putting Data to Work*, OECD Publishing, Paris, p. 21. Examples are France, Ireland, Mexico, the Netherlands, Norway, Sweden, Switzerland, and the United Kingdom.
80. *Ibid.* Examples are Ireland, Malaysia, the Netherlands, New Zealand and Singapore.
81. *Ibid.*
82. OECD (2016), *Advanced Analytics for Better Tax Administration: Putting Data to Work*, OECD Publishing, Paris, p. 23.
83. OECD (2016), *Advanced Analytics for Better Tax Administration: Putting Data to Work*, OECD Publishing, Paris, p. 23.
84. *Ibid.*
85. OECD (2019), *Tax Administration 2019: Comparative Information on OECD and other Advanced and Emerging Economies*, OECD Publishing, Paris, pp. 81-83.
86. All the information about this programme comes from Gianluca Mazzoni, *(Re)defining the Balance between Tax Transparency and Tax Privacy in Big Data Analytics*, 72(11) Bull. Int'l Tax'n (November 2018).

Countries may also use AI in the form of chat bots or virtual assistants to enhance communication between the tax authorities and taxpayers. For example, Spain introduced a VAT virtual assistant subsequent to the launch of SII (*see* section 3.2.1.3),[87] and Singapore has used text mining in taxpayers' email enquiries to obtain better insights.[88] Tax authorities may also provide tailored services using AI, such as sending notifications, alerts, and warnings for the payment of taxes or debts as a way to nudge taxpayers into compliance. For example, in Italy, automatic compliance letters will be sent out to taxpayers when the automated system identifies discrepancies between the information submitted by taxpayers and that obtained from third parties.[89]

Of course, one piece of data may not only be used for one single purpose; it is reasonable to assume that some data could be used multiple times to perform multiple functions. For example, income data could be used not only for auditing case selection and for generating prefilled tax returns, but also for training AI assistants to better communicate with taxpayers. While data can be used to provide taxpayer services and to simplify the tax compliance process, such use can also be double-edged; as discussed in section 4.2, data use may interfere with the fundamental rights of taxpayers.

4.2 Challenges to Privacy, Personal Data Protection and Beyond

More data collection and efficient data analytics mean greater transparency of taxpayers' information for tax authorities. Through using data for compliance by design, tax evasion and fraud are becoming easier to detect, meaning that the compliance gap is also effectively being alleviated. Taxpayers also benefit from simplified compliance procedures and smoother communication with tax authorities as a result. However, this increased transparency also leads to new issues in respect of privacy and personal data protection, as well as other fundamental rights of taxpayers.

In terms of data collection, the first question arises from the potential over-collection of data. Machine learning usually requires a large amount of data to produce strong results.[90] The more data the tax authorities have, the higher the quality of their analytical results.[91] Consequently, there is an incentive for tax authorities to increase the amount of data they collect.[92] Furthermore, there may well be a fundamental clash between the characteristics of big data (volume, variety and velocity, and veracity and validity) and the basic principles of data protection, i.e., purpose limitation and data

87. OECD (2019), *Tax Administration 2019: Comparative Information on OECD and other Advanced and Emerging Economies*, OECD Publishing, Paris, p. 174.
88. OECD (2019), *Tax Administration 2019: Comparative Information on OECD and other Advanced and Emerging Economies*, OECD Publishing, Paris, p. 167.
89. Rosa Prieto & Mercedes Jordán, *Impact of Digitalization on the Transformation of Tax Administrations*, IOTA, Budapest, 2018, p. 20. *See also* p. 34 for example in Portugal.
90. Karl Manheim & Lyric Kaplan, *Artificial Intelligence: Risks to Privacy and Democracy*, 21 Yale J.L. & Tech. 106 (2019).
91. *Ibid.*
92. *Ibid.*

minimization.[93] In this regard, the limitations of the information tax authorities can collect from third parties and other open resources should be questioned.

Second, as stated in section 3.2.3.2, some tax authorities already routinely collect data from digital sources, such as from taxpayers' digital identities in the form of social media, in order to identify non-compliance behaviours and select targets for tax audits. In this regard, questions arise as to whether tax authorities have fulfilled their fair information duty – for example, Articles 12-15 of the GDPR – in collecting this type of information. For example, when tax authorities collect information from third parties, they are required to provide taxpayers with certain information, including information on the purposes of the processing as well as the categories of personal data concerned. It would be interesting to research whether, in practice, this information is duly notified to taxpayers. Moreover, an automated system could result in an automatic assessment of the taxpayer's tax position, yet the legitimacy of such an assessment is also worth discussing from a data-protection perspective.

Data analytics gives rise to many intriguing issues. First, the potential misuse of certain sensitive information could raise questions about fundamental human rights and freedoms.[94] One example of this is the freedom of expression: if taxpayers know that their posts on social media might be used against them, they may be reluctant to post. Another example would be sensitive information such as medical records: if taxpayers know that such information is routinely monitored, they may feel restricted in how open they can be.[95]

Second, there is also the question of data mining: Is it appropriate and/or proportionate to perform routine data mining into the digital presence of all taxpayers in order to identify non-compliance behaviour and be selected for audit?[96] As argued by Yavaşlar, by doing so, all taxpayers are presumed to be potential tax evaders.[97]

A further issue about data analytics is its transparency. As stated in section 1, tax transparency refers to a two-way process: it does not only require taxpayers to disclose their information to tax authorities but also requires tax authorities to make public the way they process tax information. The issue of transparency here revolves around the second aspect, i.e., the way that tax authorities process taxpayer data and whether it is transparent to taxpayers.

As discussed in section 4.1, tax data may be used for automated machine actions such as automated notifications and tax assessments executed by machines without human interventions. Ideally, the legislation and use of such automated actions should be fully transparent. Taxpayers should be informed when tax-related decisions are

93. Gianluca Mazzoni, *(Re)defining the Balance between Tax Transparency and Tax Privacy in Big Data Analytics*, 72(11) Bull. Int'l Tax'n (2018).
94. Michael Hatfield, *Taxation and Surveillance: An Agenda*, 17 Yale J.L. & Tech. 319 (2015); Michael Hatfield, *Privacy in Taxation*, 44 Fla. St. U. L. Rev., 359 (2008).
95. *Ibid.*
96. Houser & D. Sanders, *Houser and Sanders* (2017) believe that it would, the consent requirement of Fair Information Practices. K.A. Houser & D. Sanders, *The Use of Big Data Analytics by the IRS: Efficient Solutions or the End of Privacy as We Know It?*, 19 Vanderbilt J. Ent. & Tech. L. 4 (2017).
97. Chapter three of the *Tax Transparency, EATLP Annual Congress Zurich* (2018).

being made about them automatically without human intervention.[98] Furthermore, they should be in a position to query the decision-making process and to correct any mistakes made by the automated decision-making system.[99] In practice, however, taxpayers may not be aware of the existence of automated systems, and therefore may not be aware of their legitimate rights in relation to such an automated decision-making process.

For example, in Finland, more than 80% of all tax decisions are handled automatically without human involvement, not only related to the sending of reminders but also to decisions on additional taxes, tax collection, and the monitoring of payments.[100] However, in the past, there were complaints about mistakes made by the tax authorities using such automated systems. In light of such complaints, the Deputy Parliamentary Ombudsperson of Finland conducted investigations and concluded that such systems are unlawful in November 2019. According to the Deputy Ombudsperson, one aspect of the consideration was the transparency requirement. The principle of good governance requires that taxpayers be informed when they are subject to automated procedures. Taxpayers also have the right to know the basis of the automated processes, as well as when an issue has been resolved automatically.[101] The application of the Finnish automated systems is not fully in compliance with such requirements. Therefore, the Deputy Ombudsperson challenged the lawfulness of this practice.

Furthermore, the nature of advanced machine learning algorithms may prove challenging to integrate with taxation systems. Ideally, a tax system should be transparent in relation to the disclosure of the process of assessment and decision-making by the tax authorities concerning tax affairs.[102] However, deep learning – the engine of the current advances in machine learning – is a black box model. This means that taxpayers may not be able to understand how a model has reached a certain decision, even if the decision is relatively good. In other words, we are not able to understand what patterns are actually discovered, which may have bias in the underlying data.[103]

---

98. Michael Hatfield, *Taxation and Surveillance: An agenda*, 17 Yale J.L. & Tech. 319 (2015); Michael Hatfield, *Privacy in Taxation*, 44 Fla. St. U. L. Rev., 365 (2018). Karl Manheim & Lyric Kaplan, *Artificial Intelligence: Risks to Privacy and Democracy*, 21 Yale J.L. & Tech. 106, 153 (2019).
99. *Ibid.*
100. Helsingin Sanomat (2019d): Verottajan robotti on karhunnut ihmisiltä liikaa rahaa, ja apulaisoikeusasiamiehen mukaan automaattinen päätöksenteko rikkoo myös perustuslakia (The Tax Robot Has Rotted too Much Money from People, and the Deputy Ombudsman Says Automatic Decision-Making also Violates the Constitution), https://www.hs.fi/kotimaa/art 2000006321 422.html, reproduced in Automating Society Report 2020 October 2020, AlgorithmWatch gGmbH, Bertelsmann Stiftung, available online at: https://automatingsociety.algorithmwatch .org, accessed on 15 February 2021, p. 90.
101. *Ibid.*
102. Michael Hatfield, *Taxation and Surveillance: An Agenda*, 17 Yale J.L. & Tech. 319 (2015); Michael Hatfield, *Privacy in Taxation*, 44 Fla. St. U. L. Rev., 366 (2018). Karl Manheim & Lyric Kaplan, *Artificial Intelligence: Risks to Privacy and Democracy*, 21 Yale J.L. & Tech. 106, 153 (2019).
103. Will Knight, *The Dark Secret at the Heart of AI*, Mit Tech. Rev. (11 April 2017), https://www .technologyreview.com/s/604087/the-dark-secret-at-the-heart-of-ai (describing the 'black box' effect of unexplainable algorithmic functions).

A typical example of the use of the black box models is the 'System Risk Indication' (*Systeem Risico Indicatie*, SyRI) in the Netherlands.[104] It aims to detect fraud concerning social benefits, allowances, or taxes by cross-referencing a wide scope of personal data including data about work, fines, penalties, taxes, properties, housing, education, retirement, debts, benefits, allowances, subsidies, permits, and exemptions, amongst other things. The system is algorithm-based and identifies 'risk indicators', flagging citizens in certain neighbourhoods as high risk. Many government agencies have access to the system, the employment agency and the tax authorities included. Since the system uses 'black box' methods, the lack of transparency was a pressing matter. Citizens of particular neighbourhoods were not informed that they were being analysed, neither were they warned when they were flagged as high risk, nor were they informed of the reasons for such judgements made by the algorithms. Furthermore, the 'risk indicators' identified by the algorithm may not reflect the reality. For example, one of the indicators used in the algorithm was a low usage of running water. The reasoning behind this indicator was that the beneficiary of an allowance for single persons might be living with someone else at another address, thus disqualifying them from receiving the said benefit. However, this method could be highly arbitrary, since it may also just be the case that the person was absent from their home for an extended period. The SyRI was ruled as unlawful by the Court of the Hague as it violates Article 8 of the European Convention on Human Rights. The Court maintained that governments have the responsibility to safeguard human rights when implementing such automated decision-making systems, and ensuring transparency is a crucial element of this.

Furthermore, the black box model may induce data-dependent biases, such as discrimination against certain races, religions, or groups of taxpayers, and result in the unequal treatment of citizens in the area of public services.[105] For example, the Die Österreichische Öffentliche Arbeitsverwaltung – Austrian Public Employment Service (AMS), Austria's state-owned employment agency, applies an algorithm to automatically attribute scores to job seekers and divide them into three groups, to which different accesses to job-seeking support resources are allocated.[106] According to the method mentioned in the paper published by the AMS,[107] women, disabled people, and

104. The following facts ware summarized from the Automating Society Report 2020, October 2020, AlgorithmWatch gGmbH, Bertelsmann Stiftung, available online at: https://automatingsociety.algorithmwatch.org, accessed on 15 February 2021, p. 8 and pp. 161-163.
105. Manheim and Kaplan, *supra* n. 4, pp. 158-160. Melissa De Zwart, Sal Humphreys & Beatrix Van Dissel, *Surveillance, Big Data and Democracy: Lessons for Australia from the US and UK*, 37 U. New S. Wales L.J. 713, 718 (2014); Bart van der Sloot, Dennis Broeders & Erik Schrijvers (eds) *Exploring the Boundaries of Big Data;* cited in K.A. Houser & D. Sanders, *supra* n. 67
106. Paola Lopez, *Reinforcing Intersectional Inequality via the AMS Algorithm in Austria*, Conference Proceedings of the STS Conference Graz 2019, 6-7 May 2019, pp. 289-309, DOI: 10.3217/978-3-85125-668-0-16.
107. Holl, J., Kernbeiß, G. & Wagner-Pinter, M., 2018. *Das AMS-Arbeitsmarktchancen-Modell. Dokumentation zur Methode*, available at: https://www.google.com/url?sa=t&rct=j&q=&esrc=s&source=web&cd=&cad=rja&uact=8&ved=2ahUKEwj-sL6T3tjvAhUsy4UKHZqoCrcQFjABegQIBBAD&url=https%3A%2F%2Fwww.ams-forschungsnetzwerk.at%2Fdownloadpub%2Farbeitsmarktchancen_methode_%2520dokumentation.pdf&usg=AOvVaw1ESEVR9ofL_zZ9G39rFUjs, accessed on 30 March 2021.

people over 30 are given a negative weight, as are women with children.[108] Therefore, even under comparable circumstances, women are likely to be assigned lower scores than men. This algorithm has received much criticism in Austria, as it is manifestly discriminatory and results in unequal treatment. It is also likely to violate the non-discrimination law under the EU legal framework.

In terms of data exchange between tax authorities and other government departments, it is worth discussing whether exchanged information used at a later stage beyond the original purposes of the exchange is compatible with the purpose limitation principle. Moreover, it is important to examine whether taxpayers' procedural rights are guaranteed in the course of exchange of information. Such rights are:

- right to notification;
- right to participate in the procedure;
- right to access the file;
- right to rectification of data;
- right to erasure of data; and
- right to appeal.

For example, in many countries, taxpayers do not have the right to be notified when their information is exchanged further to a request by another jurisdiction.[109] The reasoning for not granting such rights to taxpayers is that the Exchange of Information (EOI) is an administrative cooperation procedure taking place between two states, and a taxpayer is not party to such a procedure. However, it is questionable whether this non-notification is in compliance with taxpayers' rights to privacy and data protection, since the information being exchanged constitutes the personal information of a taxpayer.

Last but not least, since tax authorities usually maintain large amounts of data for an extended period of time, they are prone to being targets for internet hacks and cyberattacks. Therefore, data security is imperative for safeguarding the confidentiality of taxpayer information. A number of such incidents have taken place in recent years. In June 2019, the database of the Bulgarian tax authorities was hacked, and the information of around five million individual taxpayers is understood to have been leaked.[110] This data hack was considered to be the most serious hack ever to have been

108. *Ibid.*

109. For example, Australia, Austria, Bahamas, Bahrain, Barbados, Bermuda, Botswana, Canada, Costa Rica, Croatia, Denmark, Dominica Republic, France, Guernsey, India, Indonesia, Italy, Kazakhstan, Malaysia, Marshall Islands, Micronesia, Nauru, the Netherlands, New Zealand, North Macedonia, Norway, Panama, Peru, Tunisia, Saudi Arabia, Spain, TCI, UAE, Vanuatu, China, Greece, Papua New Guinea. The information can be found in the Global Forum on Transparency and Exchange of Information for Tax Purposes peer review reports: https://www.oecd-ilibrary.org/taxation/global-forum-on-transparency-and-exchange-of-information-for-tax-purposes-peer-reviews_2219469x, accessed on 16 February 2021.

110. M. Santora, *5 Million Bulgarians Have Their Personal Data Stolen in Hack*, The New York Times (17 July 2019), https://www.nytimes.com/2019/07/17/world/europe/bulgaria-hack-cyberattack.html.

targeted at a country's tax authorities.[111] This incident reveals the security risks surrounding the large amount of data collected by tax authorities, especially in the wake of the AEOI and CRS being implemented by the OECD.[112] In the UK, between June and September 2020, HMRC was subject to an average of over 5,000 spam, phishing, and malware attacks per day.[113] This begs the question of what actions tax authorities can take to avoid such large-scale data hacks, and what they should do to mitigate the loss of personal data should such incidents occur in future. Such questions must be given due consideration in light of the tendency for storing more and more data and the increasing exchange of information.

5 CONCLUSION

The ways in which tax authorities collect and process tax data have been revolutionized with the advent of big data, AI, and other new technologies. As tax authorities are able to glean more and more insights into taxpayers' situations, the information asymmetry that favoured taxpayers in the past is gradually being alleviated. Yet, the methods used by tax authorities may not be fully transparent to taxpayers. Consequently, the balance has shifted and tax authorities may well have a more advantageous position in this respect over taxpayers. Although we appraise the convenience and efficiency that technology brings for tax authorities, the protection of the fundamental rights of taxpayers, including the right to privacy and the right to protect personal data, must not lag behind technological advances.

Some issues concerning fundamental rights related to the use of advanced data analytics by public authorities are also common in other fields. In addition to tax authorities, automated decision-making AI and machine learning are used by public health authorities, social welfare authorities, and law enforcement authorities, where concerns and even real-life examples of bias and discrimination generated by automated decision-making also exist. Therefore, in this author's opinion, it is imperative that this debate be conducted in light of the broader social context of deploying advanced technology while protecting fundamental rights. And it should start sooner rather than later, otherwise such technology may be broadly deployed without thoroughly considering the impacts on taxpayers' fundamental rights. Failing to do so may, in turn, give rise to more discriminatory practices. In the face of such urgent issues, we must prepare for the future of digital tax administration, and not only from a technological perspective but also from a human rights perspective.

111. Baker Phillip, *Bulgarian Data Hack Provides a Timely Warning of Data Breaches to Come*, 47(11) Intertax (2019).
112. *Ibid.*
113. https://www.internationalinvestment.net/news/4021134/uk-hmrc-bombarded-malicious-email-attacks-day, accessed on 16 February 2021.

CHAPTER 9

Using New Technologies to Improve Existing VAT Systems

*Marta Olowska**

1 INTRODUCTION

Around the world we may observe an increasing number of tax administrations and businesses altering their value added tax (VAT) compliance processes to take advantage of the available technological developments. The digitalization of society, moving at an increasingly rapid pace, now offers opportunities as well as challenges to all parts of society, including tax administration. These changes provide an opportunity to address some of the structural limitations of the current system of tax administration, moving away from sequential taxpayer-facing processes and beginning to integrate taxation processes into the systems used by taxpayers as part of their daily lives and businesses. Such integration will allow compliance-by-design outcomes to an increasing extent, as well as possible step-change reductions in compliance costs for taxpayers.[1] Over recent years, the opportunities offered by digital tools, new communication channels, and the large increase of internal and external data sources have allowed to improve services to taxpayers and to better target compliance activities.[2] As a result, digitalization is transforming how tax administrations operate, helping to improve process efficiency and service delivery.[3]

This chapter will analyse what the current problems of VAT systems are and what the potential to transform VAT systems using emerging technologies is. In particular, it will focus on aspects such as the European Commission's agenda on

* The author would like to thank Prof. Jeffrey Owens for his valuable comments.

1. OECD (2020), *Tax Administration 3.0: The Digital Transformation of Tax Administration*, OECD, Paris, http://www.oecd.org/tax/forum-on-tax-administration/publications-and-products/tax-administration-3-0-the-digital-transformation-of-tax-administration.htm.
2. *Ibid.*
3. IMF, *Corruption, Taxes and Compliance*, Working Paper No. 17/255, 17 November 2017.

counteracting VAT fraud utilizing new technologies, how real-time reporting – and in particular e-invoicing – is implemented in different countries, and finally how COVID-19 has influenced the planned digitalization of VAT compliance.

2 WHAT ARE THE CURRENT PROBLEMS OF VAT?

VAT has already been adopted in over 160 countries, and today is the single largest source of government's revenue, accounting for approximately 20% of the total government's revenue. In general, consumption-based taxes, which include VAT, goods and services taxes, sales taxes, excise taxes, and other forms of taxes on goods and services, account for 33% of total taxation across the Organisation for Economic Co-operation and Development (OECD) member countries.[4] They are now only marginally behind taxes on income, profits, and capital gains (essentially, personal income tax and corporate income tax combined, which is at 34%) in terms of total revenue collected. Taking into account the current difficult economic situation deriving from the COVID-19 pandemic, it is possible that the role of consumption taxes will grow over the coming years, and that more countries are already moving in that direction.

Yet many existing VAT systems are imperfect in their structure and administration, which leads to revenues from the tax being substantially less than if a uniform tax imposed at the standard were to be imposed. This is known as the 'VAT gap'. This gap has two major components, usually called the 'policy gap' and the 'compliance gap'. The policy gap measures the extent to which VAT revenues are reduced as a result of the design of the tax law, especially by zero-rated exemptions or reduced rates granted to particular activities. The remaining share of the VAT gap – that not explained by explicit policy decisions – is the compliance gap, measuring the extent to which the taxes legally due (under the existing law) are not collected.[5]

From an economical point of view, in order to collect more revenues from VAT, focus on reducing the policy gap, the compliance gap, or both, rather than increasing the VAT rate should be the priority. This is of particular importance nowadays, as the current COVID-19 crisis has shown enormous budgetary pressure on governments.

Furthermore, VAT currently exists in several different forms across the world, and has been implemented and reported on in different ways. Thus, the administrative compliance burden varies significantly between countries, even between those in which VAT systems are built on similar principles, such as in the European Union (EU). This makes compliance more time-consuming and costly, especially for the businesses operating in many countries.

Finally, most countries have decided to adopt a narrow tax base with a range of rates, which is often down to political reasons. This challenge will take time to overcome; but through simplifying the system, broadening the base and decreasing the number of tax rates, it would become easier to get the full benefit.

4. OECD unweighted average based on the OECD 2018 Consumption Tax Trends, p. 42.
5. R.M. Bird, *VAT in and after the Pandemic*, Tax Notes International, 28 September 2020, p. 1747 available at, https://s3.amazonaws.com/pdfs.taxnotes.com/2020/2020tni39-14.pdf.

3 HOW THE EUROPEAN COMMISSION'S AGENDA ON COUNTERACTING VAT FRAUD UTILIZES NEW TECHNOLOGIES

The two main problems plaguing the EU VAT system are the complexity of rules and their vulnerability to fraud. Although the VAT gap decreased from EUR 147 billion in 2015 to EUR 137 billion in 2017, the amounts at stake are still high, even exceeding the gross domestic product (GDP) of some smaller EU Member States. The EU VAT gap is 11% on average (the range in individual Member States is from 7% to 35.5%). The 'VAT gap' measures the difference between potential VAT revenue – the amount that would be yielded if the standard tax rate applied to all final consumption by households, governments, and non-profit organizations – and actual VAT revenue as a share of the potential revenue.[6] A significant difference in the VAT gaps of the various Member States exists, and this creates a lack of trust among the States.

While VAT is a major source of tax revenue and benefits from relatively low administrative costs,[7] it is susceptible to fraud, as it relies on self-reporting. It is also a disjointed system of rules, and enforcement varies among EU Member States. Moreover, it has been recognized that the current system no longer reflects the reality of the digitalized economy. With these considerations in mind, using new technologies for the purpose of simplifying compliance, fighting fraud in a more efficient manner, and adapting to new business models is of the utmost importance for the EU.

Since the adoption of the European Commission's recent VAT Action Plan,[8] the Commission has submitted to the Council several proposals in order to modernize, make fraud-proof and reboot the VAT system, trying to address the challenges posed by the digitalization and globalization of the economy.[9] The 2019 Action Plan assumes three types of action:

(1) moving to a single EU VAT registration;
(2) modernizing VAT reporting obligations and facilitating e-invoicing; and
(3) updating VAT rules for the sharing economy.

All the efforts should lead to the legislative proposal in 2022. For the purpose of this chapter, we will focus on the second point.

In the area of VAT obligations, Member States enjoy a wide margin of flexibility within the boundaries laid down by the EU VAT Directive.[10] Therefore, the situation among Member States differs significantly. Several EU Member States are already employing new technologies in order to fight VAT fraud, in particular, in areas such as

6. Grzegorz Poniatowski et al., *Study and Reports on the VAT Gap in the EU-28 Member States: 2019 Final Report*, CASE Reports No. 500 (2019).
7. *See also* R. de la Feria, *Tax Fraud and the Rule of Law*, University of Leeds Working Paper 18/02, 2018, p. 2.
8. European Commission, *An action plan for fair and simple taxation supporting the recovery strategy*, Brussels 15.07.2020, COM(2020) 312 final.
9. VAT Expert Group, *Upgrading the EU VAT System: A Reflection on Possible Ways Forward*, VEG N° 086, Brussels, 12 November 2019, p. 2.
10. Council Directive 2006/112/EC of 28 November 2006 on the Common System of Value Added Tax, OJ L 347, 11 December 2006, 1-118.

real-time reporting or e-invoicing. The rest are either still considering the introduction of transaction-based reporting or have no reporting requirements. This has led to excessive fragmentation and high administrative burdens for businesses operating across borders in the EU.

For real-time reporting in the EU, there are two types of transactions that require harmonization: (1) intra-Community transactions and (2) domestic transactions. Currently, there is no real-time reporting system for intra-Community transactions. For the registration of intra-Community transactions, the VAT Information Exchange System (VIES) is used. Based on monthly declarations of turnover to each client in another Member State, it is an old-fashioned system that was put in place at the time of the Single Market. It lacks flexibility for risk-analysis purposes and causes difficulties when crosschecking data and performing joint analysis. Finally, the availability, quality and timeliness of data is problematic along with the limited services provided to businesses. One of the outcomes of the discussion during the recent Fiscalis workshop was that 'there is a preference for a harmonized real-time reporting system regarding intra-Community transactions. The VIES system should be revised accordingly in order to coordinate and avoid duplicates in data sharing.'[11]

The costs of changing the current system could be high, especially for countries that have already implemented unilateral solutions. Nevertheless, the increasing compliance cost for businesses has to be altered in a way that balances the interests of all parties involved. Thus, an increased level of harmonization and the coordination of actions are needed. The preference would be for an EU-wide system that builds on a convergence of domestic systems with an intra-Community system.

The EU strategy assumes that 'new technologies should provide for a win-win situation: tax authorities should have improved instruments in the fight against VAT fraud and businesses should benefit from a reduction in the overall compliance costs by the suppression of burdensome reporting obligations'.[12] Moreover, the European Commission plans on using artificial intelligence (AI) to identify fraud profiles, a system which in Italy has had a success rate of 80%. Ideally, such an approach could lead to a situation in which auditing all taxpayers would not be necessary, as the high-risk taxpayers would be identified at the initial stage and dealt with accordingly.

4 HOW REAL-TIME REPORTING IS IMPLEMENTED ACROSS THE WORLD

Frequently, tax administrations require the same data to be included in different reports, such as in VAT returns, recapitulative statements, and standard audit file for tax (SAF-T) reports. Tax administrations also require the use of e-invoicing and the introduction of logical algorithm systems that capture additional data on VAT returns.[13] Examples of the reporting obligations are shown in Figure 9.1.

11. European Commission, *Questionnaire for the discussions on the background note*, 26 June 2020.
12. VAT Expert Group, *supra* n. 9, p. 4.
13. PwC, *VAT Compliance: The Impact on Business and How Technology Can Help*, 2017, p. 3.

Figure 9.1 Digital Tax Reporting in Europe

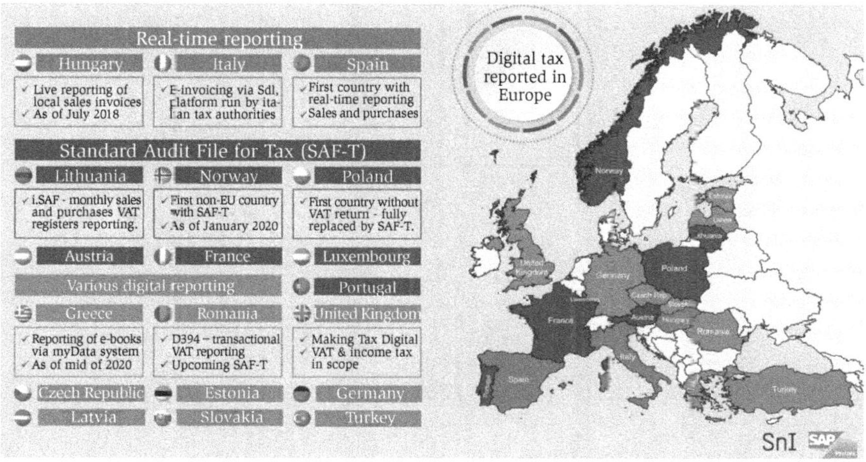

Source: C. Yurdakul, How would SAP S/4HANA impact on your tax reporting&compliance solutions?, November 9, 2017, available at: https://www.linkedin.com/pulse/sni-saf-tsii-add-ons-has-been-certified-s4-hana-hot-topic-yurdakul/?hcb = 1.

In recent years, EU Member States have implemented a wide variety of measures aimed at combating VAT fraud. At the national level, we are witnessing a proliferation of new reporting obligations including online cash registers, split payments, and real-time reporting.[14] There are significant variations in the reporting requirements across the EU, and the format and type of data to be communicated to the tax administration differ by country (*see* Figure 9.2). Among those requirements, we can see a significant increase in the implementation of electronic reporting systems, including real-time transaction reporting systems. Interestingly, many countries, and especially those in the EU, have chosen to adopt the less interventionist approach of real-time reporting. That is, to obtain the transaction-level data on a real-time basis. Eventually, VAT fraud thrives because of delays in reporting time, which is why real-time compliance (instead of monthly delays) is the key. This is a step short of government-regulated invoicing where the government effectively seeks to interpose itself into the transaction/invoicing chain.[15]

14. A. Bal, *Between Hype and Disillusionment: Will a VAT Blockchain Ever Be Possible in the EU?*, Tax Notes International, 24 February 2020, p. 893.
15. https://www.internationaltaxreview.com/article/b1j8ydd4qghx0w/vat-and-technology-the-first-fully-automated-tax.

Figure 9.2 European Compliance Landscape

- Increasing real time reporting requirements globally
- Non-uniform approach from member States within the EU

Adoption timeline in Europe

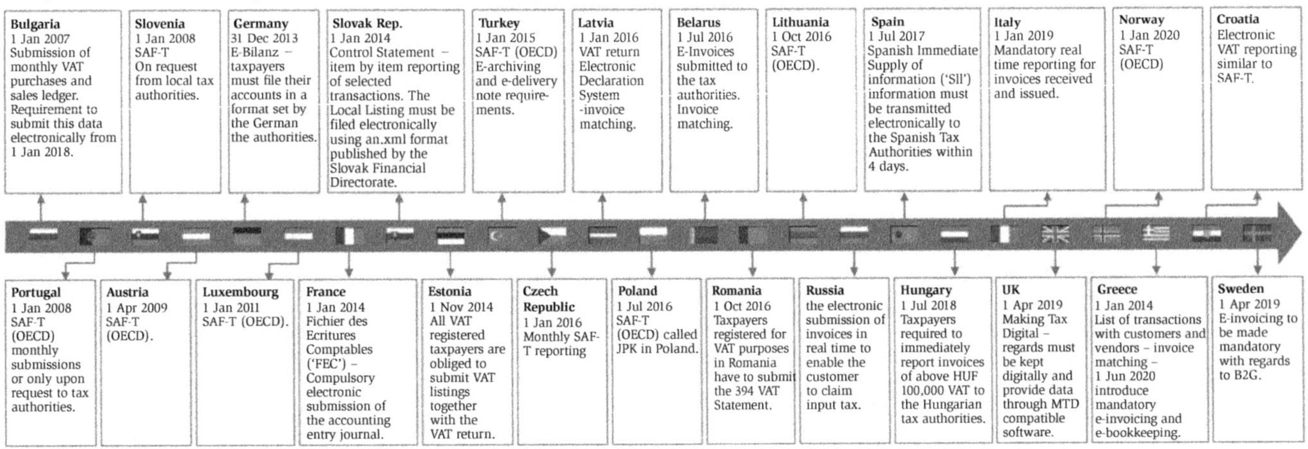

Source: PwC, Making Tax Digital for VAT, October 2020.

Figure 9.1 indicates a non-uniform approach even among the EU Member States. Even though real-time reporting is high on the agenda of the European Commission as reflected in July 2020s Tax Package,[16] the European Commission should develop a more comprehensive standard set of requirements that can be deployed across the EU. It is important to observe that this window of opportunity is brief – as outlined above, several EU Member States have begun adopting new e-compliance requirements unilaterally (*see* Figure 9.3). With more Member States adopting their own rules, the likelihood that a common EU standard can be developed decreases – and that means a substantially higher compliance burden for companies and tax departments.

Figure 9.3 National Strategies and Their Impacts

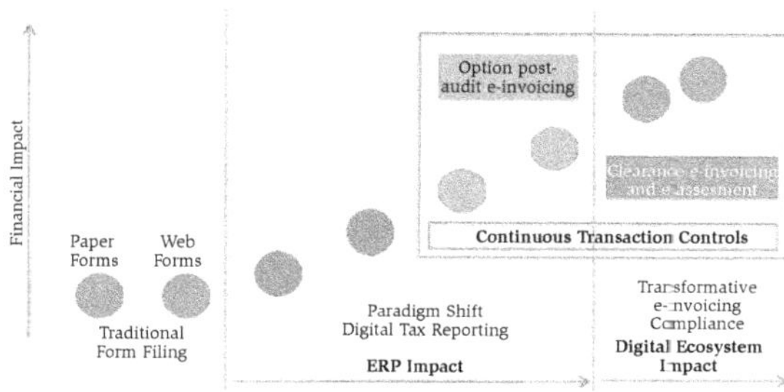

Source: Trends in Continuous Global VAT Compliance, 11th Edition, Sovos Compliance, LLC.

One economic factor driving e-compliance adoption is high budget deficit levels. Budget deficits help to explain why Spain introduced its *Suministro Inmediato de Información* (SII, Immediate Supply of Information System), why Bolivia and Uruguay introduced invoice clearance, and why France announced that it intends to implement an invoice clearance model. Budget deficit numbers may also explain why some countries – such as Bulgaria, Greece, and Lithuania – are all moving slowly, or not at all, towards e-compliance despite relatively high VAT gaps. Among those EU Member States that have introduced or announced an invoice clearance or near real-time reporting obligation, some – for example, Greece, Italy, and Poland – appear to be primarily driven by the desire to reduce their VAT gaps. The examples of Russia or Spain prove a significant reduction in the VAT gap (accounting for up to two-thirds) through the use of technology. Other countries – for example, France, Hungary, and Italy – appear to be more interested in leveraging new e-compliance requirements to address budget deficits.

As Figure 9.4 indicates, not only European countries have implemented real-time reporting solutions. Some of the most efficient and effective uses of technology among tax administrations around the world may be observed in Latin American countries,

16. https://ec.europa.eu/taxation_customs/general-information-taxation/eu-tax-policy-strategy/package-fair-and-simple-taxation_en.

where all documents are transmitted to the tax administration in a common format,[17] signed with public key infrastructure technology (a national primary key infrastructure for electronic signature). Thanks to the low-cost infrastructure, digital solutions are available also for small and medium-sized enterprises, as only an Internet connection is required. Moreover, Latin American countries use the e-invoicing system for electronic audit, which has led to a significant change in processes and culture. Through the use of advanced analytics and AI, tax administrations in Latin American countries are able to identify anomalies and detect fraudulent documents.

Figure 9.4 Real-Time Reporting Outside of Europe

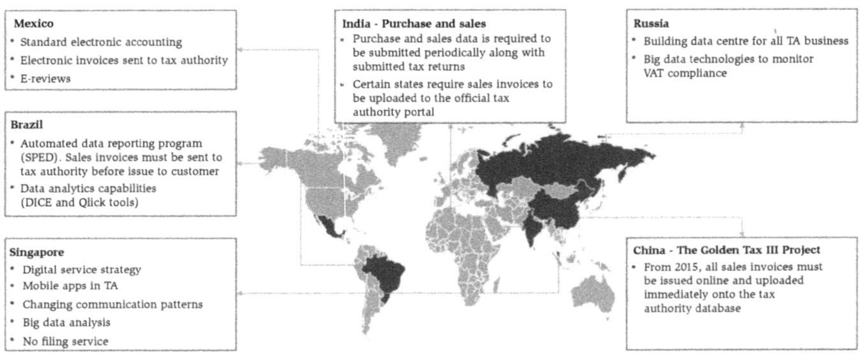

Source: Trends in Continuous Global VAT Compliance, 11th Edition, Sovos Compliance, LLC.

5 E-INVOICING IMPLEMENTATION IN DIFFERENT COUNTRIES

Even as recently as 2008, businesses in the EU were filing paper returns to satisfy VAT compliance requirements. At that time, only a few countries had begun to use e-invoicing. Brazil was one of those countries, and its electronic compliance approach was widely considered an anomaly in VAT reporting. Fast-forward to 2020, e-compliance requirements for VAT – including continuous transaction control – seem likely to become the new normal, both within and outside the EU.[18] The need to reduce the VAT gap is widely considered the main driver behind e-compliance requirements.

The positive effects of a mandatory e-invoicing regime, such as achieving simplification of the invoicing process, reducing costs for businesses, and creating effective anti-counterfeiting measures for VAT control, have become clear to governments across the world. Drawn by its potential to strengthen tax compliance and reduce costs, more than fifty countries around the world have already implemented

17. Over 160 billion documents in Latin American countries.
18. P. Boerhof, *Navigating the EU VAT's Road to E-compliance*, Tax Notes International, Volume 100, 2 November 2020, p. 66.

e-invoicing, including ten countries in Latin America and the Caribbean region.[19] Mandatory e-invoicing is implemented to collect transactional data for downstream compliance automation and data analytics. The main difference between the models used by countries is the moment at which the tax authorities receive information on the particular business transaction and thus are able to recognize potential frauds and react to them.

Generally, taxpayers are free to decide how to issue an e-invoice and how to transmit it; as long as the invoice contains all of the elements required by law, it is valid. Ensuring the authenticity of the invoice's origin and the integrity of the content are required. These can be guaranteed by different means, such as electronic signature or business controls. Businesses, by using new technologies, could significantly reduce compliance costs (even by up to 60%). Ultimately, the more we can reduce such costs the better for everybody.

In the EU, Spain was the first country to implement the near real-time reporting of transaction data. In July 2017, the SII system took effect, requiring taxpayers to report their sales and purchase invoices within four days of the issuance date or the posting date of incoming invoices – hence why the system adopted by Spain is referred to as 'near' real-time reporting. The information has to be provided in XML format and is used in audit and preparation of tax returns. The Spanish tax administration requires businesses that have a revenue of EUR 6 million or higher to report details of their billing records.

Another interesting system was introduced in Russia in 2016. The Russian Federation's updated VAT transaction system offers a more complete and transparent view of tax data. The system has created an environment of tax compliance, rather than of tax evasion, reducing the so-called VAT gap from 10%-11% to less than 1%. E-invoices between companies have been permitted since 2012. Invoices must be produced in XML as a UTD format set by the Federal Tax Service. Once information has been automatically sent, the tax administration can compare purchasers' and suppliers' electronic reports in just a few days. Should there be any incoherence, sales partners must transmit digitized invoices electronically to justify their transactions. At this point, an electronic signature is required for each invoice. Invoices are submitted for a local digital signature via encryption software. This is provided only by certified Russian software providers.

E-invoicing can bring several benefits to taxpayers, including cost savings (such as lower printing, storing and administrative costs), more secure and accessible information storage, and integration of invoice issuance with other internal (accounting, payment, billing) and external processes (such as accounting, payment, and procurement systems of suppliers, clients, and the public sector). At the same time, by improving control over the invoicing process and allowing for real-time monitoring of taxable transactions, tax administrations may also be able to reduce sales omission,

19. *See also* EY, *2018 Worldwide Electronic Invoicing Survey*, https://www.actuel-expert-comptable.fr/sites/default/files/ey-worldwide-electronic-invoicing-survey-2018.pdf. A.D. Barrei and R. Zambrano eds. *Electronic Invoicing in Latin America*, Inter-American Development Bank, 2018, available at, http://dx.doi.org/10.18235/0001038.

purchase over-invoicing (including the reporting of purchases that are not related to business operations), fraudulent transactions, and general tax submission errors, thus reducing tax non-compliance and informality at a lower cost.[20]

Previous studies for other countries have also found that e-invoicing leads to a gradual increase in reported sales and VAT collection.[21]

6 HOW COVID-19 INFLUENCED THE PLANNED DIGITALIZATION OF VAT COMPLIANCE: HAVE THE REFORMS BEEN POSTPONED OR ACCELERATED?

While this dramatic shift was underway before the onset of COVID-19 (*see* Figure 9.5), the economic distress caused by the global pandemic is likely to accelerate the implementation of e-compliance requirements in many countries around the world.

Figure 9.5 Adoption of Tax Technology 2018/2019

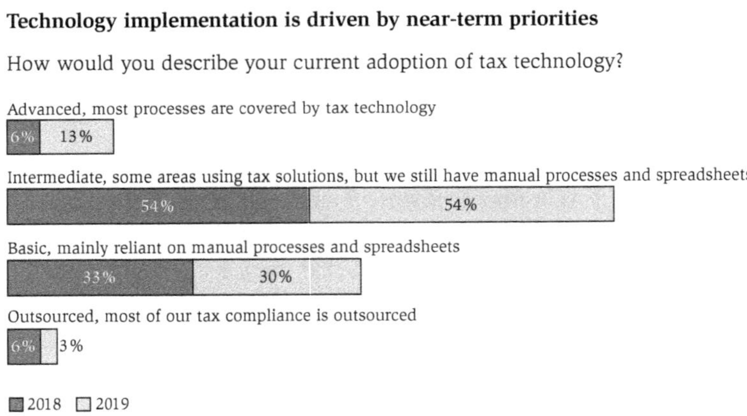

Source: 2019 Thomson Reuters European Tax Technology Survey, p. 8.

During a recent plenary meeting,[22] heads of the OECD Forum on Tax Administration agreed on an ambitious agenda for the next year, focussed on enhancing resilience and tax certainty. Because of the COVID-19 pandemic, the European

20. IMF, *Digitalization to Improve Tax Compliance: Evidence from VAT e-Invoicing in Peru*, WP/19/231, 2019, p. 6.
21. *See also* J. Ramírez, José, O. Nicolás and A. Mauro, *Facturación Electrónica en Ecuador: Evaluación de impacto en el cumplimiento tributario*, Inter-American Development Bank Discussion Paper No. 563, 2018; M. Bérgolo, C. Rodrigo and S. María, *Factura electrónica y cumplimiento tributario: Evidencia a partir de un enfoque cuasi-experimental*, Inter-American Development Bank Discussion Paper No. 561, 2018; Ch. Hyung, *Can Electronic Tax Invoicing Improve Tax Compliance? A Case Study of the Republic of Korea's Electronic Tax Invoicing for Value-Sdded Tax*, World Bank Policy Research Working Paper No. 7592, 2016.
22. The Thirteenth Plenary Meeting of the OECD Forum on Tax Administration (FTA) on 7-8 December 2020.

Economic Forecast predicts that budget deficits as a percentage of GDP will significantly increase in 2020 and 2021, thanks to increased expenditures and stalling revenue.

Countries are likely to turn to environmental taxes and VAT, with VAT being the larger source of revenue. However, increasing VAT rates is less appealing economically because doing so is likely to reduce overall consumption. Broadening the tax base for VAT by eliminating reduced rates and exemptions has also proven to be politically challenging. In contrast, focussing on fighting fraud, decreasing the VAT gap, and increasing compliance through the use of new technologies could generate few objections, especially in the political arena. This agenda could pave the way for a wider acceptance of e-compliance.

The impacts of COVID-19 could provide the spark that generates more technology and innovation in VAT functions worldwide, helping to secure essential resilience. The pandemic has accelerated thinking about the use of digital technology and tools, including how digitalization might lead to fundamental changes in the administration of tax. Learning lessons from the crisis, in which tax administrations have played a pivotal role, will be critical during the recovery period and in building future resilience.

As outlined in section 2, problem areas in VAT derive less from the allocation of taxing rights, but rather from poorly designed systems. Improvements are needed in collection mechanisms based on a simple and consistently applied international VAT framework, together with the efficient use of modern technology and expanded availability of cooperative compliance procedures. As the OECD concluded, our collective work on the steps to realize this vision may be an important legacy of this crisis. VAT compliance is the ideal area to start the implementation of digital solutions, which could later serve as the example for the remaining tax branches, and eventually other government departments.

The COVID-19 pandemic has challenged the capacity of governments to use digital technologies and data strategically in order to adapt to the change and respond to the crisis with agility. Governments that had invested in sound digital governance, policy levers and skills were better prepared to leverage digital technologies and data to provide rapid and effective responses to the COVID-19 outbreak.[23] While the public dealt with the uncertainty of the pandemic, many tax administrations played a key role in helping their governments deliver emergency measures to support those in need.[24] Technology alone will not ensure a fully functioning VAT system, but it is nevertheless important to evaluate what kind of impacts technological developments could have on the design and operation of future VAT systems.

7 CONCLUSION

VAT is an important source of revenue and its importance can only increase over the coming years. It is inevitable that VAT and the way it is collected will continue to

23. OECD (2020), *Digital Government Index: 2019 Results*, OECD Public Governance Policy Papers, No. 3, OECD Publishing, Paris, p. 6, available at, https://doi.org/10.1787/4de9f5bb-en.
24. 2020 FTA 'Amsterdam' Plenary Communique, p. 1.

evolve. VAT requirements may become more demanding, but hopefully less complex. Disruptive technologies are changing the way taxpayers and tax authorities interact and, more importantly, are altering the way taxes are being paid and information is stored and used. The digital age is also reshaping tax systems. Big data, cloud computing, social media, blockchain, the internet of things, 3D printing, and machine learning are all examples of disruptive technologies that are transforming businesses and governments.[25] Appropriate technology is the key to fulfilling the reporting requirements and reducing the manual effort in the VAT process.

When analysing how tax administrations can benefit from these disruptive technologies, it is very important to bear in mind that Information and Communication Technologies is not an end but a means for this journey. Technology alone can only provide tools; to achieve meaningful and impactful goals, a comprehensive strategy must be defined, covering aspects of the regulatory, institutional, and operational fields. The introduction of new technologies requires changes to tax legal frameworks and procedures, organizational structures, human resources, business processes, and, in general, tax administration business models.

Finally, the way that tax administrations have used new technologies to respond to COVID-19 and the accompanying economic crisis makes the broader adoption of e-compliance highly likely. Despite the challenges that these new requirements may pose, they could ultimately benefit companies by significantly reducing the overall VAT compliance burden. It also seems likely that blockchain and other advanced technologies will be deployed across the value chain in ways that facilitate the integration of financial, logistical, and VAT data. No European country has yet adopted blockchain as the basis for its VAT compliance system, but tax practitioners around the world agree that blockchain is a promising tool for combatting fraud, particularly in the EU's VAT system. Such a change would allow VAT payments to be automated and would also create a history of transactions that authorities across the EU could easily access if they suspect fraud or errors.

25. OECD, *Technologies for Better Tax Administration: A Practical Guide for Revenue Bodies*, OECD Publishing, Paris 2016, https://doi.org/10.1787/9789264256439-en.

CHAPTER 10

Tax Administration in a Post-digital Era: A Tax Authority Perspective

Helena Strauss

'The measure of intelligence is the ability to change'
- Albert Einstein

1 INTRODUCTION

The digital saturation of reality has granted organizations globally with exceptional capabilities. Organizations can now understand their customers with a new depth of granularity, and they have more channels than ever to reach their customers. With a significant number of organizations finally converging on the same digital footing, there are more digital ecosystems and more potential partners to assist in creating holistic experiences.

Businesses, clients, consumers, and taxpayers globally operate in a 'post-digital' era. 'Post-digital' describes a world where organizations are no longer exploring emerging technologies, but are implementing disruptive technologies, such as mobile, social, cloud, artificial intelligence (AI), distributed ledgers, and robotics as the standard.[1] This is the era where demand is communicated instantly, and gratification is expected immediately. Demand and expectations constantly change and create an infinite and never-ending stream of opportunities to be met through various business models. These include business-to-business (B2B), business-to-consumer (B2C), customer-to-customer (C2C), and customer-to-business (C2B). Many governments also changed their models to e-governments which include new ways of interaction

1. Cloudgeeni, 2019. *What does it mean to be post-digital?*. Available at: https://cloudgeeni.co.uk/what-does-it-mean-to-be-post-digital/.

and service delivery. These include government-to-government (G2G), business-to-government (B2G) and government-to-citizens (G2C).

The post-digital world is one where technology has become the fabric of reality, and organizations use this to meet clients and consumers wherever they are and at any moment in time – all under the assumption that these organizations and service providers have risen to the challenge by adopting and implementing technology-driven solutions and innovation.

Organizations have not been alone in their journey of digital transformation. Consumers, workers, threat actors, and markets have also accelerated their digital transformation, demands, and expectations expeditiously. Research reflects that this transformation, in many cases, has taken place at a higher rate than in the case for businesses and organizations.[2]

Post-digital consumers enjoy the results of technology saturation and display strong sentiments about technologies to be – or not to be – adopted. These sentiments and preferences should be critical for organizations who wish to be competitive in the post-digital era. Post-digital threat actors have an almost infinite amount of entry points to organizations; these do constitute cyber threats not only to the organization itself but also to every supplier, consumer, and client that forms part of the organization's ecosystem.

Post-digital markets consist of consumers, business partners, and governments that enjoy the benefits of digital transformation. Fully on-demand or fully customized products and service offerings have become standard, and it is inevitable that customers and consumers will expect every business and government organization to offer both on-demand and customized service offerings and products.[3]

Organizations face a world of new expectations, and core digital technologies have become a critical backbone for this digitally saturated reality. The time for pilots and experimentation is, however, over and leaders must strategically position themselves for the post-digital era. Elements associated with the post-digital era include, but are not limited to, distributed ledger technology, artificial intelligence, extended reality, and quantum computing (DARQ).[4]

As with all other business models, markets, and industries, this technology 'disruption' has had a material impact on international and domestic tax administration systems. The world is consentaneous with the fact that the traditional tax system needs to reform to remain relevant and effective in a post-digital era. However, research points out that the reform that is taking place is occurring at a slow-moving pace. This is especially true if compared to digital transformation of the global business

2. Accenture, *The post-digital era is upon us, are you ready for what's next?*, Accenture Technology vision 2019 (2019), https://www.accenture.com/_acnmedia/PDF-94/Accenture-TechVision-2019-Tech-Trends-Report.pdf.
3. Accenture, *The post-digital era is upon us, are you ready for what's next?*, Accenture Technology vision 2019 (2019), https://www.accenture.com/_acnmedia/PDF-94/Accenture-TechVision-2019-Tech-Trends-Report.pdf.
4. Accenture, *The post-digital era is upon us, are you ready for what's next?*, Accenture Technology vision 2019 (2019), https://www.accenture.com/_acnmedia/PDF-94/Accenture-TechVision-2019-Tech-Trends-Report.pdf.

sector, markets, and industries. The slow pace of reform of tax administration systems leaves tax authorities in a compromised position, as the successful fulfilment of their mandates to enforce tax legislation and collect tax revenue is heavily dependent on their ability to change along with this ever-changing digital reality.

This chapter considers the status quo of the reform of domestic and global tax administration as well as what a post-digital tax authority should look like to meet both government and taxpayer expectations. It is, however, imperative to first understand the tax administration system as an organization, as well as the tax ecosystem in which it operates.

2 THE TAX ADMINISTRATION SYSTEM

The traditional international and domestic tax administration 'ecosystem' consists of various elements which, in combination, assist tax administrations globally to achieve their respective mandates to enforce tax legislation and collect tax revenue. The organizational structure and components of a typical revenue authority[5] are illustrated in Figure 10.1.

Figure 10.1 A Typical Revenue Authority's Organizational Structure

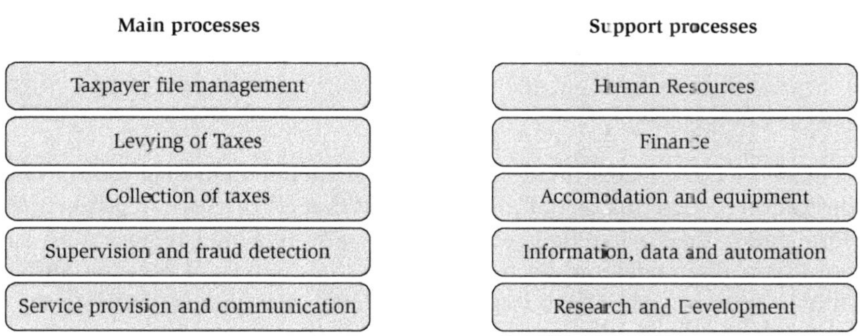

Source: Author's own (2021).

The revenue authority structure as illustrated in Figure 10.1 in turn fits into a larger tax administration 'ecosystem'. A typical but simplified tax administration ecosystem can be illustrated as in Figure 10.2:

5. Allink & Van Kommber, *Handbook on tax administration* (2nd ed., IBFD, 2016).

Figure 10.2 A Simplified Tax Administration Ecosystem

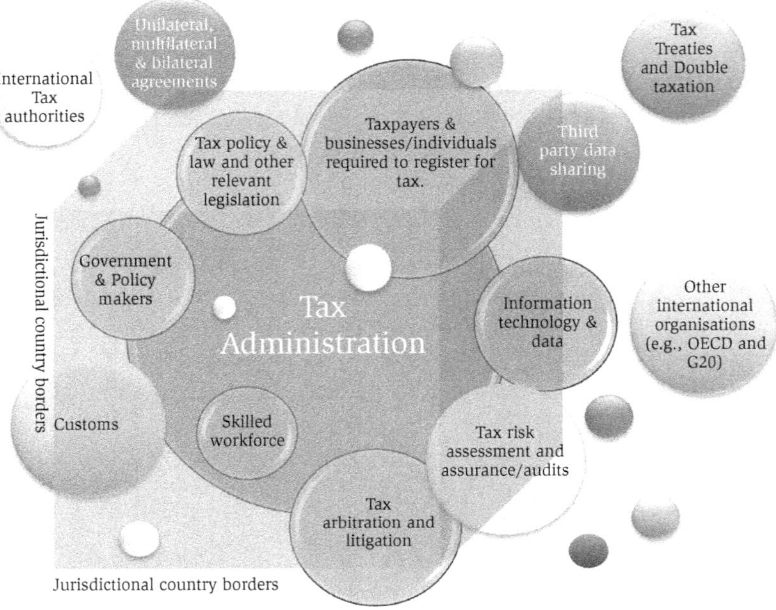

Source: Author's own (2021).

Figure 10.2 illustrates the multifaceted and multidimensional nature of a tax administration system. It should further be noted that all elements depicted in Figure 10.2 form part of their own unique ecosystems. Figure 10.2 only demonstrates one tax authority, yet this model can be multiplied by the number of revenue authorities currently in existence globally to visualize the global international tax system.

Although a significant amount of focus has been placed on tax policy and legislative reform in response to the digitalized economy, Figures 10.1 and 10.2 demonstrate that the reform required is much broader than tax policy and legislation. Tax authorities will have to reform their organizational structure as well as the overall global tax ecosystem to ensure relevance and optimized tax administration in a post-digital era.

Successful reform will, thus, require that tax authorities not only take into consideration all the aforementioned elements, but also the technology available to them to ensure optimized tax administration ecosystems that can interact, adapt, and coexist with any other ecosystems within both the traditional and the digitalized economy.

This brings us to the question of the current state of transformation of global tax authorities and the related ecosystems, as well as their current ability to administer taxes in a post-digital era. Section 3 will explore this reform.

3 THE STATUS QUO OF GLOBAL TAX REFORM IN A POST-DIGITAL ERA

3.1 Legislative and Policy Reform

Steinmo[6] and Peters[7] deliberate extensively on the topic of tax policy. 'Tax policy' can be described as 'a compilation of tax norms in a form of a legal document that determine rules on taxes, on who pays and how much'.[8] These are multifaceted instruments with significant impact on political and economic relations.

The economy became globalized with its digitalization, and country borders were virtually eliminated with the introduction of the Internet. The technological advancement and innovation associated with the Third and Fourth Industrial Revolutions resulted in exponential change in an array of areas, including the global economy: a significant amount of businesses now trade globally, new business models have been introduced, new employment models and platforms exist, products have been converted into services, and new investment, financing, and payment options such as crypto currencies and altcoins have also been introduced globally.

In addition to the above, significant reliance is now placed on intellectual property and intangible assets as important sources of income generation – and to a large extent, a lot of this is invisible to the naked eye. Traditional tax legislation and policy revolve around the nexus of a business or taxpayer. In terms of traditional tax law, taxes are, in general, levied at the source, i.e., at the place where the main business or asset that generates taxable income is situated.

The legislative and policy reform to date with regard to the main tax types impacted by the digitalization of the economy are discussed in sections 3.1.1-3.1.3.

3.1.1 Direct Taxes

Elements that have impacted direct taxes include, but are not limited to, the new business models associated with the digitalized economy and the introduction of cryptocurrencies, altcoins, digital currencies and related investment, speculation, payment, and financing methods.

New business models of highly digitalized multinational enterprises (MNEs) and the gig and sharing economy enable businesses and individuals to reduce their tax liability significantly, or even evade taxes. This is done with complex tax structures that usually include tax havens, or by simply not declaring – or under-declaring – taxes in the jurisdictions where it is due. A general overview of the direct tax legislation and policy reform that has taken place to date is detailed in sections 3.1.1.1-3.1.1.2.

6. Steinmo, *Taxation and democracy: Swedish, British and American approaches to financing the modern state* (New Haven: Yale University Press, 1993).
7. Peters, *The Politics of Taxation: A comparative perspective* (Basil Blackwell, Cambridge MA & Oxford UK, 1991).
8. Peters, *The Politics of Taxation: A comparative perspective* (Basil Blackwell, Cambridge MA & Oxford UK, 1991).

3.1.1.1 *Corporate Income Tax*

Recent studies reflect that only a limited number of countries have changed their corporate income tax legislation and policy to accommodate taxation in a post-digital era.[9] Australia, for example, has adjusted its legislation and policy to include a multinational anti-avoidance law (MAAL) and diverted profit tax (DPT). The MAAL and DPT were designed to address the tax arrangements of significant global entities (SGEs) of which the main objective was to shift taxable profits out of the country. Structuring arrangements addressed by the DPT include, but are not limited to, intellectual property transfers, royalty arrangements, offshoring services, and procurement hubs.[10]

The United Kingdom (UK) has also introduced DPT rules with the main focus being on contrived arrangements designed to erode the UK tax base. DPT aims to deter and counteract the diversion of profits from the UK by large MNEs that seek to avoid the creation of a permanent establishment that would result in UK corporate taxes being levied. DPT is set at a higher tax rate than the set corporate income tax rate that would apply in normal circumstances. The UK tax authorities, HM Revenue and Customs (HMRC), indicated that DPT was introduced to encourage MNEs to restructure their taxes to take advantage of the normal corporate income tax rate instead of the higher DPT rate.[11]

Countries such as India, Israel, and Nigeria have introduced new nexus rules referred to as 'significant economic presence' (SEP) or 'significant digital presence' (SDP) rules. These rules expand the scope of taxable income of non-residents to income that resulted from a 'business connection' within the respective country. Revenue that results from digital and digitalized services that is subject to tax in the respective country includes, but is not limited to, the provision or downloading of data or software, systematic or continuous soliciting of business activities, and engaging in interaction with users in the respective country through digital means. The SDP rules in Israel apply to revenue derived by non-resident entities that resulted from contracts for online services with Israeli customers and/or consumers, and where there is a high volume of web traffic between Israel and the foreign supplier.

The European Commission issued two directives in 2018, one of which proposed a 3% tax on turnover for companies regarded to have a 'digital permanent establishment' within the European Union (EU).[12,13] This was expected to complement the

9. Strauss, Schutte & Fawcett, 2020. *An evaluation of the legislative and policy response of tax authorities to the digitalisation of the economy.* (South African Journal of Accounting Research, *2020)*, https://doi.org/10.1080/10291954.2020.1810504.
10. Australian Tax Office, *Tax avoidance taskforce helps net $5,6 billion in first two years* (2018), https://www.ato.gov.au/Media-centre/Media-releases/Tax-Avoidance-Taskforce-helps-net-$5-6-billion-in-first-two-years/.
11. HM Revenue & Customs, *Diverted profits tax: Guidance* (2018), https://assets.publishing.service.gov.uk/government/uploads/system/uploads/attachment_data/file/768204/Diverted_Profits_Tax_-_Guidance__December_2018_.pdf.
12. European Commission, *Proposal for a Council directive on the common system of a digital service tax on revenues resulting from the provision of certain digital services* (2018), https://ec.europa.eu/taxation_customs/sites/taxation/files/proposal_common_system_digital_services_tax_21032018_en.pdf.

current 'permanent establishment' concept, but both directives were rejected by the EU finance ministers.[14]

The United States (US) introduced 'base erosion and anti-abuse tax' (BEAT), which aims to prevent large MNEs from reducing their US tax liability by making deductible payments to foreign related parties in low-tax countries. The BEAT is a minimum tax add-on and related entities are taxed at a rate of 21%. In cases where the regular tax is lower than the BEAT, the entity is liable for the regular tax plus the amount by which the BEAT exceeds the regular tax liability.[15]

In terms of corporate income tax, it is evident that only limited reform has taken place thus far if considered from a global perspective. The reforms that have taken place are inconsistent, complex, and the actual enforceability of these policy and legislative changes is questionable, especially if cross-border assistance is required, for example, during the tax assurance process.

3.1.1.2 *Personal Income Tax*

Personal income taxes have mainly been impacted by the disruption to traditional employment and service-rendering models. Individuals can now enter a global job market and economic ecosystem via digital platforms. This is known as the 'gig' or 'sharing' economy. Examples of such platforms include Airbnb, Soothe, Freelancer, and Uber.

These platforms enable employees and/or consultants to deliver services globally, and limit the amount of revenue declared (if any) for tax purposes due to the fact that the services are not 'visible' to tax authorities. The reform of tax legislation and tax administration systems to assist with tax risk management, tax enforcement and collection within the gig or shared economy is, however, limited if evaluated from a global perspective.

Traditional personal income tax laws and policies revolve around the fact that employees or individuals are located in a specific country, and that employers automatically deduct personal income taxes as per the applicable tax law. The gig and sharing economies, however, have changed this concept in its entirety, and pose various challenges to tax authorities. This is mainly because the digital services are 'invisible' to tax authorities and because of the global location of these platforms which seldom coincide with the location of actual service delivery. Both of these business model characteristics complicate the enforceability of country-specific tax laws.

The reforms that have taken place to date include the requirement (in some countries) of digital platforms to withhold taxes on behalf of the participants in the gig

13. European Commission, *Proposal for a council directive on the common system of a digital service tax on revenues resulting from the provision of certain digital services* (2018), https://ec.europa.eu/taxation_customs/sites/taxation/files/proposal_common_system_digital_services_tax_21032018_en.pdf.
14. Wessing, *Taxation of the digital economy – updated Progress at OECD/G20 level* (2020), https://www.lexology.com/library/detail.aspx?g=70eecc42-1a28-4e09-9015-2f5eab6ed29e.
15. Tax Policy Center, *Key elements of the U.S. tax system* (2020), https://www.taxpolicycenter.org/briefing-book/what-tcja-base-erosion-and-anti-abuse-tax-and-how-does-it-work.

and sharing economies. Other recommendations include the implementation of reporting requirements and information sharing for digital platforms to the relevant tax authorities. These proposed measures seem to be under consideration in Australia, the EU, and the US,[16] but it is debatable whether these requirements will be legally enforceable at this stage if a digital platform is established in a jurisdiction that differs from the tax authority's jurisdictional borders.

A matter that requires further clarity with regard to the gig and sharing economies relates to the debate as to whether gig and sharing economy workers are regarded as 'employees' or 'contract workers' as defined by the respective domestic tax laws. This classification impacts the nature of the expense deductions available in terms of the relevant domestic tax laws, as well as whether a digital platform will be regarded in some way as an 'employer', which, in most instances, will require the withholding of taxes in terms of current tax law.

Impactful tax reform related to the gig and sharing economies - and, importantly, tax reform that is suitable in a post-digital era - thus remains limited to date.

3.1.2 Indirect Taxes

Technological innovation reformed many products into services that can be delivered globally. Examples include the online sale of music and 3D printing capabilities that enable a 'blueprint' of a product to be purchased online then printed in the comfort of the customer's home. These disruptions have impacted the taxation of physical goods and services due to the 'intangible' nature of online services.

Reform that has taken place to address these tax challenges includes the broad adoption of taxation at the place of consumption. Foreign suppliers who supply digital services to consumers are thus liable to pay taxes in the jurisdiction where the service is consumed. It should be noted that there are still countries that have not made specific changes to their tax legislation and policies in this regard.

For the countries that have changed their tax laws and policies to accommodate digital services, the reform is complex, inconsistent, and the compliance costs for highly digitalized MNEs are high.[17] This is mainly due to material inconsistencies, if considered from a global perspective, regarding the definition of 'digital services', applicable indirect tax rates, and registration thresholds.

Another development regarding indirect taxes relates to the introduction of 'digital services tax' (DST). Countries such as Austria, Canada, the Czech Republic,

16. White, J, 2019. *The OECD's digital tax plans more costly than BEPS.* (International Tax Review, *2019*). Available at: https://www.internationaltaxreview.com/article/b1fydc23lrbzg4/the-oecdsdigitaltax-plans-more-costly-than-beps. Edwards, Ratcliffe, Granby, Murdoch & Kirsch, 2019. *The taxation of workers in the Gig Economy – A European perspective.* Available at: https://www.lexology.com/library/detail.aspx?g=64dc2851-1e5e-4695-aca7-4411af9c9c30. IRS, 2020. *Gig Economy Tax Center.* Available at: https://www.lexology.com/library/detail.aspx?g=64dc2851-1e5e-4695-aca7-4411af9c9c30.
17. Strauss, Schutte & Fawcett, 2020. *An evaluation of the legislative and policy response of tax authorities to the digitalisation of the economy.* (South African Journal of Accounting Research, *2020)*, https://doi.org/10.1080/10291954.2020.1810504.

France, Hungary, Italy, Latvia, Norway, Slovakia, Slovenia, Spain, Turkey and the UK have implemented or have shown an intention to levy, DST.

DST specifically targets highly digitalized MNEs that generate global income derived from digital services. A substantial amount of criticism with regard to DST has, however, been expressed. This includes, but is not limited to, the hybrid nature of the tax type, as it displays elements of both direct and indirect taxes. Other criticism includes the lack of coordination or consent of trading parties, including with Third-World countries and the US. DST creates complexity and legal uncertainty due to, amongst other things, the definition and scope of the tax as well as the size thresholds. It increases the tax burden of domestic companies and fails to 'equalize' the tax burden and liability for domestic and highly digitalized MNEs. There are also other difficulties related to this tax that have been discussed, including the fact that challenges will be faced if countries try to verify or audit the tax due to a lack of mutual agreement and assistance across jurisdictions. DST can also potentially lead to double taxation that could not be resolved by international treaties and might consequently lead to an increased number of international tax disputes and arbitrations.[18]

It is evident from the above that current global reform efforts with regard to indirect taxes in response to the digitalization of the economy do not provide for optimized tax administration in a post-digital world.

3.1.3 *Direct and Indirect Taxes on Crypto and Similar Currencies or Assets*

The post-digital era is associated with payment, investment, speculation, and financing options such as cryptocurrencies, altcoins, digital currencies, and other similar innovative instruments. In a world where the economy is uncertain, return on investments is low, corruption is rife, and (legal) tax revolts remain ongoing, cryptocurrencies provide a welcome financial alternative to many businesses and individuals globally. Together with the various benefits of cryptocurrencies and the like, this disruption to the financial industry has also created an opportunity for taxpayers to reduce their tax liabilities or evade taxes.

Most tax authorities that have considered the tax implications of cryptocurrencies have classified these currencies as 'assets' for tax purposes. They also apply, in most instances, the same direct tax rules to cryptocurrencies as would be the case with any other taxable business or individual. However, research highlights global inconsistencies with regard to matters such as the definitions and scope of cryptocurrencies, the classification of transactions as speculative or investment in nature, the tax registration thresholds, the nexus of mining activities as well as the applicable tax rates.[19]

18. Becker & Englisch, *EU Digital Services Tax: A populist and flawed proposal* (2018), http://kluwertaxblog.com/2018/03/16/eu-digital-services-tax-populist-flawed-proposal/; Lampreave, *Spain has approved the digital service tax: the controversy is served* (2020), http://kluwertaxblog.com/2020/02/24/spain-has-approved-the-digital-service-tax-the-controversy-is-served/#_ftn6.
19. Strauss, Schutte & Fawcett, 2020. *An evaluation of the legislative and policy response of tax authorities to the digitalisation of the economy.* (South African Journal of Accounting Research, *2020)*, https://doi.org/10.1080/10291954.2020.1810504.

Evaluated from a global perspective, the tax reform in response to the introduction of cryptocurrencies remains limited.

Overall, the tax policy and legislative reform that has occurred so far in order to address the challenges associated with the digitalized economy still seems to be country-border specific as per the traditional tax models; limited evidence has been identified to suggest that the global and digital nature of the digitalized economy, which is not defined by traditional jurisdictional borders, have been fully embraced in order to create international tax policies and legislation that are relevant, enforceable, and suitable for a post-digital era.

3.2 Tax Authorities' Digital Responses to the Digitalization of the Economy

As illustrated in Figure 10.2, the tax system or tax 'ecosystem' comprises an array of elements which, in combination, enable tax administration. These elements (individually and as an ecosystem) all require reform to optimize tax administration in a post-digital world.

While tax policy and legislative reforms provide the legal basis for tax administration, the tax authority must be able to practically enforce this legislation. Technology and data form a critical part of this process, and consequently require reform due to the digitalization of the economy. These elements form part of a broader transformation that is required, also known as 'digital transformation'. A synthesis of research results that reflects the current digital transformation of thirty global tax authorities (including developed and developing economies) [20] is set out in Figure 10.3.

20. Strauss, Schutte & Fawcett, 2020. *An evaluation of the digital response of tax authorities to optimize tax administration within the digitalised economy.* (eJournal of tax research, *2020*), https://www.business.unsw.edu.au/research-site/publications-site/ejournaloftaxresearch-site/Documents/An-evaluation-of-the-digital-response-of-tax-authorities-to-optimise-tax-administration-within-the-digitalised-economy.pdf.

Figure 10.3 Global Digital Response of Tax Authorities as at 31 December 2020

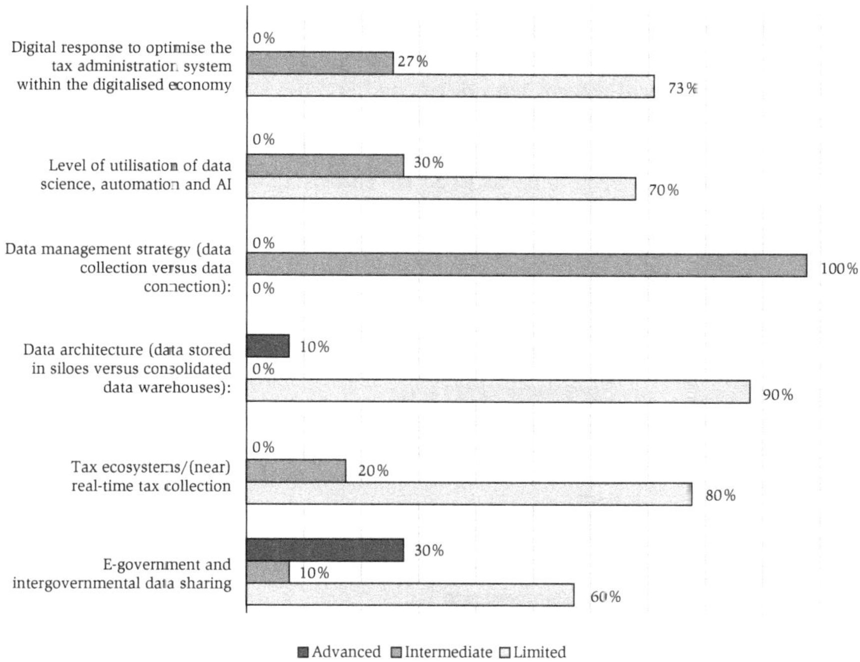

Source: Author's own (2021).

The research results depicted in Figure 10.3 indicate that the majority of tax authorities globally still reflect a 'limited' digital response when compared to the technology and capabilities currently available in a post-digital era. A limited digital response will negatively impact tax authorities' ability to administer taxes in a post-digital era.

3.3 Tax Risk Management Within the Digitalized Economy

A third critical element of the tax administration ecosystem that requires reform is the tax risk management and assurance process. This process includes the implementation of effective and efficient tax risk identification, prevention, detection, and correction measures. The tax assurance or audit process forms part of the tax risk 'correction' process.

The digitalization of the economy has had a material impact on the traditional tax risk prevention, detection, and assurance/audit process. This is mainly due to the intangible nature of highly digitalized MNEs, individuals participating in the gig and sharing economy, and cryptocurrency users and transactions. The multiple jurisdictions in which highly digitalized MNEs, gig and sharing economies as well as crypto platforms operate further impacts the enforceability of tax law and complicates the assurance process.

A risk management and assurance process suited to a post-digital era heavily relies on technology and data tools as well as international collaboration. Figure 10.4 synthesizes the research results of the tax risk management and assurance responses of thirty global tax authorities from both developed and developing economies.[21]

Figure 10.4 Global Risk Management and Assurance Response as at 31 December 2020

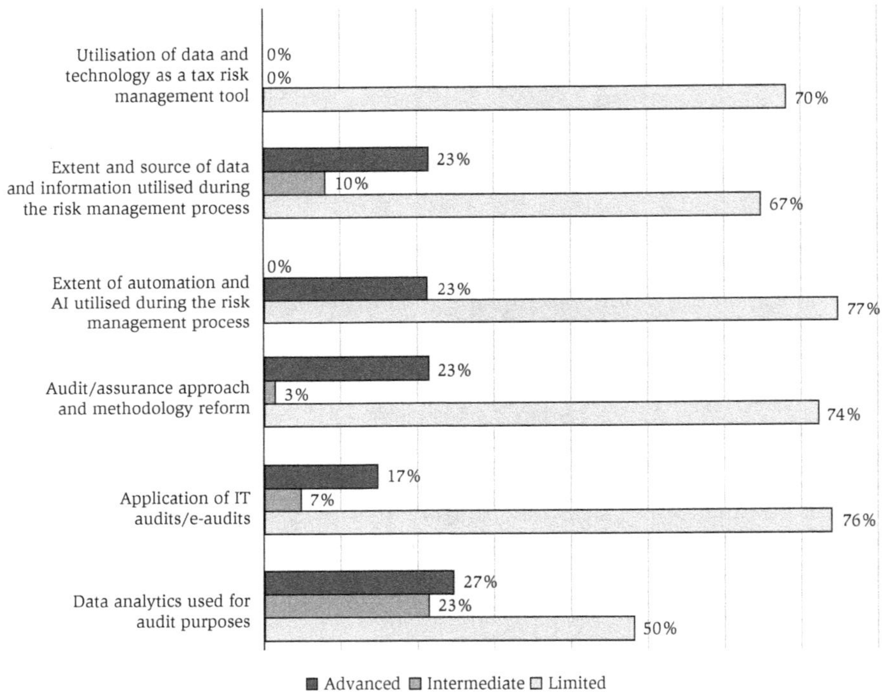

Source: Author's own (2021).

The research results depicted in Figure 10.4 reflect an overall 'limited' response to the digitalization of the economy. This raises general concerns about the optimization of tax administration systems and, more broadly, the international tax ecosystem within a post-digital era. An inefficient tax risk management and assurance system increases the risk of tax leaks, increased tax avoidance and evasion as well as unidentified tax fraud.

21. Strauss, Schutte & Fawcett, 2020. *Tax risk assessment and assurance reform in response to the digitalised economy.* (Journal of telecommunications and the digital economy, *2020*). Available at: https://jtde.telsoc.org/index.php/jtde/article/view/306.

Section 4 provides a short overview of the global transformation of tax authorities in terms of economic classification.

4 GLOBAL DIGITAL TRANSFORMATION BASED ON ECONOMIC CLASSIFICATION

The United Nations[22] has classified global economies into 'developed economies', 'developing economies', and 'economies in transition'. This summary is synthesized in Figure 10.5.

Figure 10.5 Global Economic Classification

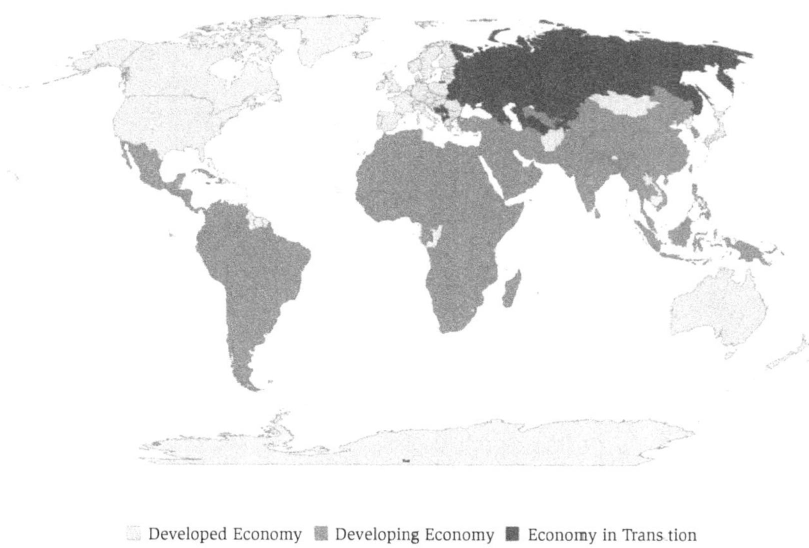

Source: Author's own (2021).

It is evident from the economical classification as set out in Figure 10.5 that a substantial number of global economies are still 'in transition' or 'developing'. As highlighted earlier in this chapter, the digitalization of the economy established a single global economy. This in implies that tax authorities' success does, to a large extent, rely on the efficiency and effectiveness of a fully saturated global interconnected tax ecosystem. Any inefficiencies in such an interconnected tax ecosystem will consequently impact on all other stakeholders that forms part of this ecosystem. Such insufficiencies will be to the benefit of some and detriment of others.

22. United Nations, *World economic situation and prospects.* (Statistical annex, 2020), https://www.un.org/development/desa/dpad/wp-content/uploads/sites/45/WESP2020_Annex.pdf.

This raises the question as to whether all tax authorities globally have undergone – at least to some degree – a minimum level of organizational and digital transformation to standardize and optimize global tax administration and service offerings within a post-digital era.

'Organizational transformation' can be defined as a 'major change in an organization involving a break with existing routines and a shift to new kinds of competencies that challenge organizational knowledge',[23] while 'digital transformation' refers to 'the process of holistic organizational change. This change is driven by changes to organizational means for value creation and appropriation.'[24] Digital transformation, thus, comes from the combined effects of several digital innovations.[25]

'Digital innovation' forms an integral part of digital transformation and can be defined as 'the process of combining digital and physical components to create novel devices, services or business models, bundling them to constitute and enable market offerings, and embedding them in wider sociotechnical environments to enable their diffusion, operation and use'.[26]

Research results highlight a stark contrast between legislative reform, organizational development, and digital transformation among tax authorities from developed and developing economies.[27] The main challenges experienced by tax authorities from developing economies include budgetary constraints, lack of political support, political interference, domestic taxpayer culture, lack of the required skills and competencies, and insufficient digital infrastructure.

Further to the above, no evidence of a defined minimum digital maturity model for global tax authorities – and the independent monitoring of adherence to such a model – could be identified. Such a model might, however, be key to ensuring a minimum global digital and organizational standard, which is relevant in an interconnected globalized post-digital eco-system.

The stark imbalances in digital transformation that currently exist among tax authorities from developed and developing economies raise serious concerns regarding the individual and collective ability of global tax authorities to administer taxes in a globalized post-digital world.

Considerations for a tax administration and a global tax ecosystem fit for a post-digital era are discussed in section 5.

---

23. Aldrich & Ruef, *Organizations evolving* (2nd ed., SAGE Publications Ltd., 2006).
24. Skog, *The dynamics of digital transformation: The role of digital innovation, ecosystems and logics in fundamental organizational change.* (Umeå: Umeå University, Thesis (PhD), 2019), https://www.researchgate.net/publication/330539207_The_Dynamics_of_Digital_Transformation_The_Role_of_Digital_Innovation_Ecosystems_and_Logics_in_Fundamental_Organizational_Change.
25. Hinings, Gegenhuber & Greenwood, 2019. *Digital innovation and transformation: An Institutional Perspective.* (Information and Organization, *2019*) 28:52-61.
26. Skog, *The dynamics of digital transformation: The role of digital innovation, ecosystems and logics in fundamental organizational change.* (Umeå: Umeå University, Thesis (PhD), 2019), https://www.researchgate.net/publication/330539207_The_Dynamics_of_Digital_Transformation_The_Role_of_Digital_Innovation_Ecosystems_and_Logics_in_Fundamental_Organizational_Change.
27. Strauss, *Tax reform within the digitalised economy: Tax, information technology and assurance.* (Potchefstroom: North West University, Thesis (PhD), 2021).

5 REDESIGNING THE TAX ADMINISTRATION SYSTEM

5.1 Legislative and Policy Considerations

There has been a significant amount of international discussion to find a workable solution for tax policy and legislation within the digitalized economy, but no consensus has been reached to date. Current discussion is mostly limited to the principles of traditional tax law and systems, which may well be perceived as an attempt to 'fit a square peg in a round hole'.

The Third and Fourth Industrial Revolutions are known for their innovative and agile natures. The question thus arises as to whether innovation and agility with regard to legislative reform are also required. A new international tax system that takes into consideration the elements and principles of a post-digital era and moves away from some of the traditional tax law principles would be critical for optimized tax administration.

The digitalized economy has two main actors and an universal enabler: users, clients, and consumers; suppliers and service providers with and digital platforms, enabled by cyberspace, to establish interaction and/or transacting abilities among these parties in cyberspace. These users, clients, and consumers have a physical presence and can, to a reasonable extent, be allocated to geographical jurisdictions as required by traditional tax law principles. In contrast, the digital platforms and ecosystems used to deliver the related services and transactions are situated in cyberspace, which is borderless and therefore not defined according to traditional territorial borders and laws.

It is widely acknowledged that the 'back offices' that create and maintain these various platforms and ecosystems do have a physical presence in at least one geographical jurisdiction. These platforms and ecosystems are, however, without value in the absence of cyberspace; cyberspace thus function as a critical enabler to conduct trade and provide services globally. Income generation is thus directly dependent on cyberspace to enable the trade of goods and services. This is comparable to the infrastructure that countries provide to their citizens to enable trade in the traditional economy. Cyberspace is, however, universal, borderless and the 'architects' are not bound to one specific country.

This author thus puts forth the argument that cyberspace should be regarded as a unique environment, jurisdiction, and nexus for tax purposes Similar arguments have been made by Johnson and Post.[28] Such an approach would allow for the design of a tax regulatory environment that is neutral, efficient, certain, simple, effective, fair, and flexible. It also has the potential to equalize or reduce the current imbalances reflected by research carried out into tax authorities from developed and developing economies.

Furthermore, current discussion mainly focuses on the *present* technology, business models, and value created by these models. It is, however, evident that technology and business models will continuously change as digital transformation

28. Johnson & Post, 1996. *Law and borders: The rise of law in cyberspace* (Stanford law review, *1996*) 48(5):1367-1402, https://www.jstor.org/stable/1229390?seq=1.

and innovation continue to evolve. This places doubt on the sustainability of the current international tax policy and legislative reform discussion and considerations.

Should cyberspace, however, be considered a tax jurisdiction on its own, and allocation rights to relevant jurisdictions be regulated in terms of a multilateral agreement, the international tax law and system may well be able to keep abreast of the continuously changing and evolving digitalized economy. The enforcement of these legislative changes and multilateral agreements would, however, require the support of a global tax authority that would form an integral part of the international tax ecosystem.

5.2 A Global Tax Authority and Tax Ecosystem

Cyberspace undermines traditional geographical borders and therefore has a global reach. The tax ecosystem and related tax laws are, however, still bound by geographical borders. This – coupled with the fact that a significant number of tax authorities globally have not transformed in such a way as to equip themselves to be able to optimize tax administration in a post-digital world – is indicative that the support of a global tax authority could well be a welcome solution to the array of current challenges experienced by tax authorities.

An ecosystem whereby a global tax authority integrates with the ecosystems of highly digitalized MNEs, the gig economy, cryptocurrency platforms, and with domestic tax authorities would address a significant number of the challenges experienced with the traditional tax administration model. Furthermore, it would mimic the global structure of a digitally saturated economy and reap the benefits of such a structure should the correct organizational development strategy be implemented.

Functions that could be executed by a global tax authority would include, but are not limited to, data collection, ingestion, analysis, and distribution to domestic tax authorities, (near) real-time tax collection and distribution to the relevant jurisdictions, and international tax arbitration.

Legislative reform to support a global tax authority would include matters such as data privacy, cybersecurity, and mutual legal assistance within cyberspace. This would require both policymakers and lawmakers to broaden their perspectives and move away from traditional territorial borders that currently regulate tax laws.

Critical digital considerations to optimize tax administration in the post-digital world are discussed in section 5.3.

5.3 Tax Authorities' Digital Responses to the Digitalization of the Economy

As pointed out in section 3.2 many tax authorities globally have not undergone the minimum digital transformation that would be required to fulfil their mandates to enforce tax legislation and collect tax revenue in a post-digital era. Technology trends for the last four years are illustrated in Figure 10.6.[29]

29. Accenture, *The post-digital era is upon us, are you ready for what's next?*, (Accenture Technology vision 2019, 2019), https://www.accenture.com/_acnmedia/PDF-94/Accenture-TechVision-20

Figure 10.6 Technology Trends from 2017 to 2020

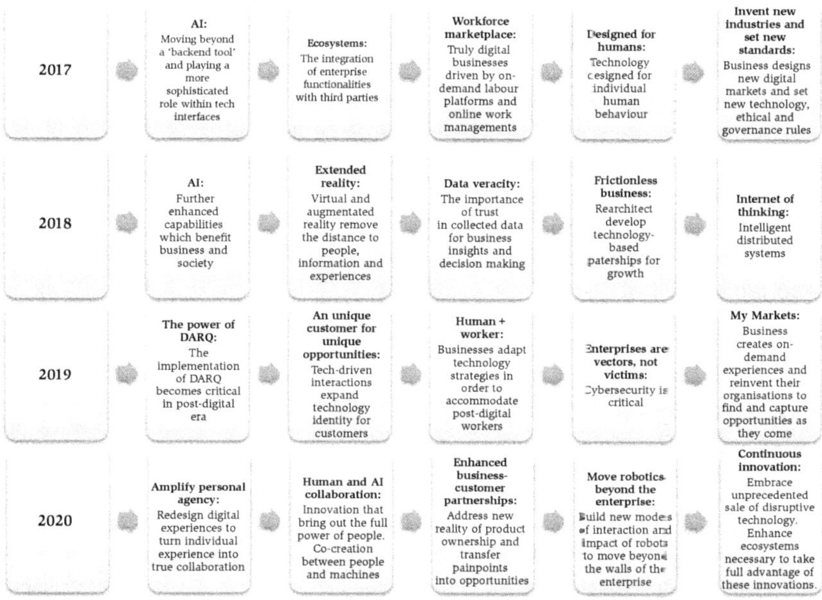

Source: Author's own (2021).

Sections 5.3.1-5.3.10 discuss the ten emerging trends highlighted in Figure 10.6 that are predicted to guide business over the next three years, as well as their applications in the tax administration environment.

5.3.1 DARQ

DARQ is predicted to be the next set of new technologies to ignite improvement and allow businesses to redefine entire industries.[30] Research, however, reflects that a limited amount of tax authorities globally currently implement DARQ technologies to their fullest extent.[31,32] These technologies could, however, form the basis for the

19-Tech-Trends-Report.pdf; Accenture, *We, the post-digital people; can your enterprise survive the 'tech-clash'?*, (Accenture Technology vision 2020, 2020), https://www.accenture.com/us-en/insights/technology/technology-trends-2020.

30. Accenture, *The post-digital era is upon us, are you ready for what's next?*, (Accenture Technology vision 2019, 2019), https://www.accenture.com/_acnmedia/PDF-94/Accenture-TechVision-2019-Tech-Trends-Report.pdf; Accenture, *We, the post-digital people; can your enterprise survive the 'tech-clash'?*, (Accenture Technology vision 2020, 2020), https://www.accenture.com/us-en/insights/technology/technology-trends-2020.
31. Strauss, Schutte & Fawcett, *An evaluation of the digital response of tax authorities to optimize tax administration within the digitalised economy.* (eJournal of tax research, *2020*), https://www.

organizational and digital transformation of domestic as well as of global tax administration (*see* section 3.2). Some possible applications of DARQ technologies within tax administration include, but are not limited to, the following.

Distributed ledger technology:

(a) Global tax authority:
- allocation of taxing rights;
- distribution of collected and sanitized data; and
- allocation and management of global taxpayers' tax ID numbers;

(b) (Near) Real-time tax collection;
(c) Asset management;
(d) Procurement and supplier management;
(e) Smart contracts:
- corporate contract management; and
- deferred payment arrangements;

(f) Tax arbitration; and
(g) Tax collection.

Artificial intelligence:

(a) Global tax authority: allocation of taxing rights;
(b) (Near) Real-time tax collection;
(c) Tax arbitration; and
(d) Standard taxpayer queries.

Extended reality (XR):

(a) Creation of unique customer/taxpayer experiences;
(b) Creation of virtual taxpayer engagements fit for various purposes spanning from complex customer/taxpayer queries, workforce, and taxpayer training to tax arbitration.

Quantum computing:

(a) Global tax authority:
- data ingestion and analysis; and
- intelligence gathering within defined legislative limits.

business.unsw.edu.au/research-site/publications-site/ejournaloftaxresearch-site/Documents/An-evaluation-of-the-digital-response-of-tax-authorities-to-optimise-tax-administration-within-the-digitalised-economy.pdf.

32. Strauss, Schutte & Fawcett, 2020. *Tax risk assessment and assurance reform in response to the digitalised economy.* (Journal of telecommunications and the digital economy, *2020*). Available at: https://jtde.telsoc.org/index.php/jtde/article/view/306.

5.3.2 *Customized Service Offerings and Experiences*

Technology-driven interactions are creating an expanding technology identity for every consumer and customer. This living foundation of knowledge is key to not only understanding the next generation of consumers, but also to delivering rich, individualized, experience-based relationships in the post-digital era. Tax authorities can use this technology to turn taxpayer trust, relationships, and tax experiences into a strategic asset for the organization.

Some considerations regarding this technology trend include:

- use of customer segmentation models and new digital channels to meet the demands and 'channel-of-choice' of taxpayers;
- focus on putting taxpayers/customers at the heart of new system designs: taxpayers' end-to-end journey should be a priority;
- focus on human-centred design;
- proactive encouragement of taxpayers through the use of advanced data analytics to personalize their tax experience: tax authorities should, however, be mindful of the relevant privacy protection and security measures; and
- continuous exploration and implementation of new technologies: the AI ecosystem will play an important role in customizing the taxpayer experience and enhance taxpayer services. Language processing, chatbots, virtual agents, machine learning, and robotic process automation are some examples to consider when designing tax administration systems and related taxpayer experiences.

5.3.3 *The Post-Digital Worker*

A skilled and experienced workforce is one of the greatest assets of any organization. Workforces are becoming 'human plus'. This implies that each individual is empowered by their skillset and knowledge *plus* a new, constantly growing set of capabilities that is made possible through technology.[33] Tax authorities will have to adapt their technology and organizational development strategies to support these new capabilities and new ways of working in the post-digital era as this will ultimately impact taxpayer services, service offerings and its ability to execute its overall mandate.

5.3.4 *Cybersecurity*

While ecosystem-driven tax administrations depends on interconnectedness, those connections significantly increase their information and technology security risks. Leading businesses are recognizing that the investment in top cybersecurity is not optional, but as critical as the rest of the products and services delivered.

33. Accenture, *The post-digital era is upon us, are you ready for what's next?*, (Accenture Technology vision 2019, 2019), https://www.accenture.com/_acnmedia/PDF-94/Accenture-TechVision-2019-Tech-Trends-Report.pdf; Accenture, *We, the post-digital people; can your enterprise survive the 'tech-clash'?*, (Accenture Technology vision 2020, 2020), https://www.accenture.com/us-en/insights/technology/technology-trends-2020.

Tax authorities are the custodians of a significant amount of sensitive taxpayer information and cybersecurity is, therefore, critical in safeguarding taxpayer and other relevant data. International privacy laws also significantly increase taxpayer expectations of stellar cybersecurity and has cybersecurity breaches proven to be detrimental not only to the trust relationship between taxpayer and tax authorities, but also to its ability to execute its mandate.

5.3.5 *Meeting Consumers' Needs in Real Time*

Technology has created a world of highly customized and on-demand experiences. Users, customers, and consumers require services and products that are provided in real time. One of these opportunities for tax authorities is tax administration on a (near) real-time basis which allows taxpayers to meet their tax obligations as and when the qualifying business transactions take place. This significantly reduces the tax authority's risk of non-compliance, reduces tax collection costs, and reduces taxpayers' time and cost burdens in managing their tax affairs.

5.3.6 *Amplified Personal Agency*

A post-digital era requires that digital experiences be modified according to new models that amplify personal agency. This has the potential to turn passive audiences into active participants by transforming one-way experiences into true collaborations. These collaborations, in turn, proof to increase customer loyalty, trust and increased turnover.

Organizations have established robust data-gathering and analytics practices, which largely take place behind the scenes, to determine what customers want and to deliver targeted personalization. As organizations have expanded their experience delivery and customization capabilities, the 'behind-the-scenes' techniques have inadvertently, but increasingly, excluded customers from the feedback loop and, thus, from choosing their own experiences.[34]

This is also true for many tax authorities. They create digital taxpayer "journeys" that enable tax management but, in many instances, fail to involve the taxpayer to customise their tax management experiences. As human behaviour is universal, customised taxpayer experiences might proof to increase taxpayer trust and loyalty and possibly voluntary compliance.

The introduction of customised taxpayer experiences and the related data collection will help tax authorities to understand when to make the process seamless and invisible, and when to step back and give taxpayers control. Tax authorities therefore need to reposition themselves and move from the position of 'administrator' to an 'enabler'.

34. Accenture, *The post-digital era is upon us, are you ready for what's next?*, (Accenture Technology vision 2019, 2019), https://www.accenture.com/_acnmedia/PDF-94/Accenture-TechVision-2019-Tech-Trends-Report.pdf; Accenture, *We, the post-digital people; can your enterprise survive the 'tech-clash'?*, (Accenture Technology vision 2020, 2020), https://www.accenture.com/us-en/insights/technology/technology-trends-2020.

Taxpayers are not always viewed as 'customers' by many tax authorities globally; a view held by some is that taxpayers cannot choose their tax authority in the way that customers can choose their vendors or service providers. Although this may well be the case, global digital saturation has significantly increased the competition between tax authorities to collect taxes due in the digitalised economy. Digitalisation also enables taxpayers to direct their legal tax responsibilities to no or low tax havens.

Further to the above, research reflects a very strong link between trust and voluntary tax compliance, as well as the ineffectiveness of 'enforced' compliance through tax audits and penalties. [35] It may therefore be necessary for tax authorities to reconsider how taxpayers are viewed in a post-digital era.

Krichler[36] refers to a relationship between 'service and customers', where taxpayers and tax authorities work together and trust each other. In terms of this relationship synergy, taxpayers are treated with respect and trusted by the tax authorities (similar to a business-customer relationship) and the taxpayers, in turn, pay taxes honestly, trust the tax authority, and even act as whistle blowers in cases of tax evasion and fraud. Tax authorities that regard themselves as service providers or enablers will also seek more cooperation from taxpayers, which further builds trust between the concerned parties.[37]

Taking all of the aforementioned client/taxpayer expectations into account, there is a major opportunity for tax authorities to utilize technology to align themselves in a way that allows them to build strategic relationships that builds trust and lead to increased voluntary tax compliance in a post-digital era.

Some questions that tax authorities should ask when aligning their organizational and digital reform strategies include:

(a) *To what extent does the tax authority understand taxpayers' trust (perceived or lack thereof) in the organization and the government as a whole?*

Taking the current level of taxpayer trust into consideration will allow the risks and benefits associated with the tax authority developing its personalization strategy to be considered, as well as the methods used to generate those experiences. To do this, a tax authority should:

- seek out opportunities to generate more customer/taxpayer feedback that will build a trust relationship;
- build a holistic understanding of how taxpayers experience digital products or services today, and test this continuously as the services evolve; and
- use these insights to inform the approach to designing future interactions that will enable voluntary tax compliance.

(b) *Does the current method for designing experiences lend itself to sharing control of experience design?*

Tax authorities should identify and invest in technologies that will enable cooperative experiences: scalability, immersion, and participation will

35. Krichler, *The economic phycology of tax behavior* (New York: Cambridge university press, 2007); Faizal, Palil, Maelah & Ramli, 2017. *Power and trust as factors of influencing tax compliance behavior in Malaysia.* (Asian Journal of accounting and governance, *2017*), pp. 79-85, https://core.ac.uk/download/pdf/160010422.pdf.
36. Krichler, *The economic phycology of tax behavior* (New York: Cambridge university press, 2007).
37. Murphy, *Enforcing tax compliance: To punish or persuade?* (Economic Analysis & Policy, *2008*), pp. 113-135.

be key to sharing control and co-creating unique customer/taxpayer engagements. To do this, tax authorities should identify digital experience events within the customers'/taxpayers' journeys over which they may want more control (including the editing and disputing of tax data to ensure accuracy and completeness). Seizing such opportunities to give agency to customers/taxpayers that use digital tax products and services will develop long-term partnerships and trust.

(c) *Is the tax authority preparing for data regulation that impacts customer experiences?*

Tax authorities should prepare themselves to address an increasingly regulated digital landscape. Current data collection and management practices should thus be reviewed to identify and mitigate potential risk areas, such as the ethical and legislative challenges regarding the collection and storing of data, data breaches, and data losses.

Tax authorities should further ensure that their policies for data management are fully documented and made available to customers/taxpayers and regulators. Data collection and storage strategies should be revised to support cooperative experiences while complying with regulation that requires consumer privacy.

5.3.7 Co-creation Between People and Machines

Organizations are expected to implement new approaches that use AI to bring out the full power of people; business is required to move beyond deploying AI for automation alone and push into the new frontier of co-creation between people and machines. Examples of such co-creation applicable to tax authorities include:

- human-machine collaboration that makes use of the machine's ability to mine potentially interesting patterns with potential tax implications from large-scale datasets and the human's unique ability to recognize patterns that generalize; and
- the use of AI to search through large volumes of, for example, tax objections/arbitration to flag certain patterns to be further examined and interpreted by human experts to enhance tax policy and legislation, arbitration processes, and tax risk management.

5.3.8 Business-Customer Partnership

Organizations are expected to address the new reality of product ownership in the era of 'forever beta'. Knowing that technology continuously changes, tax authorities should transform tax administration pain points into opportunities to enhance the taxpayer-tax authority partnership which, in turn, enhance trust and voluntary tax compliance.

5.3.9 Robotics Beyond Enterprise Walls

Organizations are expected to build new models of interaction and impact as robotics moves beyond organizational walls. Organizations across industries are in the process of unlocking new opportunities by introducing robots to enhance service delivery and customer experiences.

Although some tax authorities are making use of robotics, this is not currently the norm and robotics is not utilized to its full extent. Examples where robotics can be deployed both within and beyond the tax authority's walls include:

- standard taxpayer queries, such as tax registration, tax registration numbers, obtaining tax clearance certificates, submission of tax returns, scanning of documents for tax arbitration purposes, and 24/7 telephone and e-mail taxpayer services;
- taxpayer, tax professionals, and workforce education;
- creation of unique customer/taxpayer experiences;
- tax verifications;
- tax arbitration;
- debt collection; and
- customs: border surveillance, and routine inspections.

5.3.10 Innovative DNA

It is expected that organizations will tap into the unprecedented number of disruptive technologies available to remain relevant and competitive in a post-digital era. Building the necessary capabilities and ecosystem partnerships to assemble the tax authorities' unique innovation DNA will thus be critical.

Innovative DNA merge the concepts and processes associated with human innovation with the technological tasks associated with innovation. These concepts are applied in an organizational environment to enable innovation that will support the realization of organizational goals.

Innovative DNA will require a workforce that is creative, able to solve problems, taxpayer-centric, cross-functional, and 'tech savvy'. Since organizational development and digital transformation has a 'top-down' approach, it is critical that a tax authority's leadership embraces, understands, prioritizes, and finances innovation.

Although digital transformation is critical to a tax authority's success in a post-digital era, an equally critical priority for tax authorities is the transformation of the way that tax risks are managed and responded to upon realization of these tax risks. This is dealt with in section 6, which focuses on new models to achieve this goal.

6 TAX RISK MANAGEMENT WITHIN THE DIGITALIZED ECONOMY

6.1 Trust Becomes Currency

Optimized tax risk management and assurance in a digitally saturated era requires tax authorities to adopt a broader perspective. With impact that resonates beyond customers/taxpayers and employees alone, every tax authority and government must hold itself accountable for its role across society and the global economy.

Failure to acknowledge this impact will result in customers/taxpayers rejecting even the best of tax systems, as trust becomes currency in a post-digital era. Governments whose tax policies are perceived to be 'unfair' or 'ineffective' as well as governments that mismanage and misallocate taxpayer funds stand to risk losing a significant amount of tax revenue due to the absence of taxpayers' trust. The digitalization of the economy has made it is easier than ever to legally transfer tax liabilities to a jurisdiction of choice. This means that tax authorities will have to embrace the impact of taxpayer trust on their ability to execute their mandates to enforce tax legislation and collect tax revenue.

6.2 A New Tax Risk Management Model

The inability to adapt and implement new tax risk management and assurance models does not only pose a risk of tax non-compliance and under collection of taxes, but it may also permanently limit the potential for future innovation and growth. The establishment of a global tax authority was discussed in section 5.2. In terms of this new model, taxes due in cyberspace would be collected in (near) real time by the global tax authority and subsequently distributed in terms of law or multilateral agreements to the relevant tax authorities. Tax data and intelligence would be collected, ingested, and analysed by the global tax authority. The data relevant to the specific tax authority would be distributed thereafter for further action.

A global tax authority would allow for optimal utilization of technology, such as distributed ledgers, quantum computing, advanced AI, and automation, and thereby overcome most of the challenges highlighted in sections 3.2 and 3.3. Furthermore, it would expedite the transformation of global domestic tax authorities and their ability to optimize tax administration in a post-digital world. Other benefits of a global tax authority might include, but are not limited to, (near) real-time tax verifications and intermediary services to support international tax investigations.

7 CONCLUSION: MEETING TAXPAYER EXPECTATIONS

It is clear that technology has brought with it a newfound freedom for individuals and businesses alike in terms of the level of 'control' that governments and other institutions have over them. The level of control has significantly diminished. This phenomenon is expected to exponentially increase, while national government control is set to decrease.

The globalization of the economy has significantly increased competition among not only global businesses but also tax authorities. This competitive market has also significantly increased customers, consumers, and taxpayers' influence and expectations. Tax authorities are, thus, left without any other choice but to develop their organizations, service offerings, and taxpayer experiences beyond the mere digitalization of traditional services and service offerings.

Tax authorities that are seeking to meet taxpayer expectations and remain competitive in an ever-changing digital environment should set new priority goals which include:

- **Moving tax administrations' focus to the end**: although the main objective of tax authorities is to enforce tax (and, in some instances, customs) laws, a post-digital society requires tax authorities to reconsider the dynamics with regard to the taxpayer-tax authority relationship, as well as the standard and method of service delivery.

  A taxpayer-centric approach that builds trust, collaborates with customers/taxpayers, and provides a high standard support function might prove to be much more effective for achieving mandates than enforced or 'controlled' tax administration. Such an approach would enhance voluntary tax compliance in a post-digital era where government control is slowly diminishing.
- **Defining what it means for the tax authority to be 'post-digital'**: as tax authorities (and possibly a global tax authority) establish their new objectives and the pathways available to reach these objectives, they must also determine which ecosystem partners they need and where their own place in the ecosystem should be.

  Tax administration is moving to a support function/enabler status where taxpayers expect tax to 'happen' as a natural result of normal business transactions. Taxpayers further expect a service standard equal to that of the private sector which allows them to design their own engagement experiences, to have input with regard to this experience and data collected, and to obtain easy and quick access to, and feedback from, any tax-related service and query. The establishment of interdependent, interrelated experiences that connect with taxpayers will help propel taxpayer engagement.
- **Mastering and embracing technologies associated with a 'post-digital' era**: technology strategies should include a combination of social, mobile, analytics, and cloud (SMAC) to drive organizational development that is fit for a post-digital era. Failure to adopt and master these tools will leave tax authorities unable to serve even the most basic demands of a post-digital society.

DARQ technologies are already impacting disparate areas of enterprises globally. These technologies will drive the post-digital era but optimizing the benefits of these technologies will only be possible with a firm foundation of SMAC. The expectation is that DARQ technologies will enable innovation in such core aspects of the business that *they* will be foundational for any future innovation.[38]

As tax authorities move towards the above-mentioned goals, a new level of responsibility must be accepted: as tax authorities use technologies to reach further into taxpayers' lives, it becomes critical to address the privacy, safety, ethics, and governance questions associated with this level of access.

38. Accenture, *The post-digital era is upon us, are you ready for what's next?*, Accenture Technology vision 2019 (2019), https://www.accenture.com/_acnmedia/PDF-94/Accenture-TechVision-2019-Tech-Trends-Report.pdf.

CHAPTER 11
Electronic Fiscal Invoices

Goran Todorov

1 INTRODUCTION

The registration of taxpayer information is one of the fundamental activities of tax authorities; proper registration drives how the whole tax administration operates. In reality, obtaining the right information in a timely manner is challenging, and an inaccurate taxpayer database will inevitably lead to ineffective compliance efforts.

New legal requirements to fiscalize invoices can accelerate the data cleansing process if a deadline to comply is coupled with mandatory information supply. As part of fiscalization, every transaction – from any business location – must be electronically signed using a digital signature authorized by the taxpayer. In 2012, a Ministerial Order governing the use of Electronic Billing Machines (EBMs) in Rwanda paved the way for the Rwanda Revenue Authority (RRA) to electronically communicate with its customers. Moving towards accepting new technologies is easily possible when 'code' (i.e., 'computer code') is the law.

Fiscalization is enforced[1] in various jurisdictions, but it is important to note that it differs in concept, features, scope of use, and rules per country, and that there is also a misconception related to its definition. In that vein, the author uses the term 'Electronic Fiscal Invoice' to describe a proof of transaction (in printed or electronic form) generated by an Accredited Invoicing System (AIS)[2] operating in accordance with the fiscal law (i.e., the rules of fiscalization) established in a particular country.

1. 'Fiscalization' refers to regulations stipulating the manner in which a transaction is recorded, secured and reported to the tax authorities. It also refers to any sanctions applied for misconduct in relation to avoidance or evasion according to the penalty provisions.
2. An 'AIS' is an umbrella term covering devices and systems capable of producing invoices, normally issued in business-to-consumer (B2C) transactions, as well as those normally issued in B2B transactions. A point-of-sale (POS) system is a specific AIS application. POS and AIS will be used interchangeably in this text.

There is also a common misconception that fiscalization is introduced to prevent fraud only among small and medium-sized enterprises, i.e., usually among retailers and restaurants. For that reason, the author uses the term 'invoice' instead of the more commonly used term 'receipt' to emphasize the importance of fiscalization in relation to monitoring business-to-business (B2B) and business-to-government (B2G) transactions as well; 'invoice' better reflects the totality of fiscalization efforts and brings clarity to the discussion.

From the taxpayer's perspective, fiscalization is all about 'fiscal devices', a term which appears to describe specific physical products, but whose definition also needs elaboration: the term 'fiscal device' actually refers to a system, and not to a unitary device. Different names are used in various jurisdictions to describe fiscal devices (some examples of which are EBMs, Certified Cash Registers, Sales Register Machines, Electronic Tax Registers, and Value Added Tax (VAT) Machines, to name but a few), but probably the most widespread name used is 'Electronic Fiscal Device' (EFD). A comparison of these different fiscal devices and their broader concepts has been attempted on several occasions,[3] but the information available is often found to be incomplete, inaccurate, and related business processes are not fully described.[4] This means that there is currently no public record of updated legislative requirements and technical instructions concerning all fiscalized jurisdictions.

According to one jurisdiction's legislative requirement contained within Fiji's Tax Administration (Electronic Fiscal Device) Regulations 2017[5] stipulating the use of fiscal devices, the definition of 'fiscalization' is the following:

> 'fiscal invoice' means a receipt that –
>
> (a) is issued from an EFD to acknowledge that a transaction has occurred between a business and a customer; and
> (b) has printed on it the fiscal data and other information relating to the transaction specified in regulation 12(2);

2 WHAT ARE THE PREREQUISITES WHEN INTRODUCING FISCALIZATION?

It is relatively easy to justify the need to introduce fiscalization into a jurisdiction from the economic and legal points of view, but more difficult to get a green light from the political side. The evidence of the existence of electronic sales suppression[6] is

3. Peter Casey (30 March 2015), Electronic Fiscal Devices (EFDs): An Empirical Study of Their Impact on Taxpayer Compliance and Administrative Efficiency. International Monetary Fund (9 March 2021, 01:50 PM CET), https://www.imf.org/en/Publications/WP/Issues/2016/12/31/Electronic-Fiscal-Devices-EFDs-An-Empirical-Study-of-their-Impact-on-Taxpayer-Compliance-and-42820.
4. Goran Todorov, Sales Data Controller – (SDC) (9 March 2021, 11:45 AM CET), http://www.salesdatacontroller.com/encyclopedia/.
5. Government of Fiji Gazette Supplement No. 19 (1 June 2017), p. 75 https://www.frcs.org.fj/wp-content/uploads/2018/04/LN-37-Tax-Administration-Electronic-Fiscal-Device-Regulations-2017.pdf.
6. Richard T. Ainsworth (7 January 2016), Sales Suppression: The International Dimension. Boston University School of Law (10 March 2021, 11:35 AM CET), https://www.bu.edu/law/files/2016/10/2-Ainsworth-65-AULR-1241-2016.pdf.

compelling, and this comes in addition to the other non-electronic frauds, making a strong case for why fiscalization is so urgently required.

Once the sought-after political 'green light' has been given, a consultancy period begins that involves all stakeholders in the country, among which are the likes of the chamber of commerce, various commercial associations, consumer protection agencies, certified accounting experts, manufacturers of invoicing software and devices, etc. Often, during this consultancy period, lawmakers accept compromises[7] to lessen the 'burden'.[8] However, little do they know that such compromises can become very costly later on when a resulting lack of functionality creates its own burden on the tax administration. When selecting the fiscalization concept to implement, it must be carefully studied, drawing on the experiences of other countries that have already implemented fiscalization, most of which have had to rebuild their fiscalization concepts (e.g., in the cases of China, Greece, Hungary, Italy, Poland, Russia, and Turkey). Even in their second attempts to improve fiscalization, these countries have faced challenges to level the playing field among all stakeholders in order to mitigate compromises which were initially introduced (and resistance has come especially from vendors and operators who have participated in the process or supplied legacy solutions).

2.1 The Reasons, Requirements and Benefits for Governments

The main reasons why governments want to implement fiscalization, as well as the requirements and benefits the governments are looking to gain from fiscalization, can be summarized as follows.

Why use EFDs in the first place?

Governments choose EFDs because they:

- provide a very easy way to raise more tax revenues;
- create a fair environment for all taxpayers;
- are an effective tool for suppressing the grey economy, preventing all frauds;
- provide a remote communication channel with the tax authorities' system; and
- use the data obtained for investigations and audit operations.

What should governments consider?

Some considerations governments face when deciding on which type of EFD to implement are as follows:

7. Compromises are herein referred to modifications of regulations and instructions on how fiscalization process flows, content of the invoice, security to guard the invoice from alternations and what functionality devices/software need to satisfy each or most of the groups' interests.
8. Burden refers to administrative, monetary, or other inconveniences incurred by stakeholders (taxpayer, vendor, tax administration, etc.) due to regulative mandate, i.e., a taxpayer is required to safekeep paper copies of the journal records when the same can be achieved with electronic records alone or due to the fear of evading privacy; remote audit (transmission) of encrypted files is removed so tax officers must collect data physically (on-site).

- The priority is to achieve the balanced functioning of the whole system using current technological possibilities.
- The administrative burden on taxpayers must be kept to a minimum.
- The cost of implementing the system must be kept to a minimum.
- The simplicity and openness of the system must be considered.
- The entire system should be implemented within the shortest possible time.
- There should be transparent cooperation between the tax authorities, suppliers, and taxpayers.
- There should be public participation in the verification of certified invoices.

What are the expected results of introducing EFDs?

The implementation of EFDs should result in:

- simple compliance in the shortest timeframe;
- minimal costs for all taxpayers to comply;
- security and remote visibility for the tax authorities; and
- cooperation and collaboration of consumers through innovative and attractive invoice verification services.

A properly defined fiscalization process will achieve all of these expectations and overcome some inherent structural challenges that almost all administrations face, the main ones being the digital identity of taxpayers and the registry of all essential taxpayers' records.[9]

The registration of taxpayer information is one of the fundamental activities of a tax authority as it drives the whole operation. But, in reality, obtaining the right information in a timely manner is challenging. Simply put, taxpayers cannot be managed if the tax authority does not know who they are, whether they are active or inactive, and where they are located.

Regulating this inherited problem is simple through the legislation mandating the use of EFDs, which is intended to strengthen tax compliance. According to Article 18(3) Functions of businesses of taxpayers – issue of fiscal invoices of the Tax Administration (Tax Invoice Monitoring System) Regulation 2020 enacted by the Government of Samoa:

> A taxpayer is responsible for giving the Commissioner the following information –
>
> a) the taxpayer's name and address;
> b) the name and address of each business operated by the taxpayer;

9. Tax Commissioners from fifty-three of the most advanced tax administrations worldwide, including all Organisation for Economic Co-operation and Development (OECD) and G20 countries, have endorsed the development, in early 2021, of a roadmap identifying the priority areas for future Forum on Tax Administration (FTA) work, including the identification of areas where international standardization could be beneficial, such as digital identity, e-invoicing and secure mechanisms for the real-time sharing of information across borders. 'Tax Administration 3.0': The Digital Transformation of Tax Administration is a discussion paper published by the OECD's FTA in December 2020, http://www.oecd.org/tax/forum-on-tax-administration/publications-and-products/tax-administration-3-0-the-digital-transformation-of-tax-administration.pdf.

It also includes any change to (a) or (b). Therefore, what used to be voluntary, now becomes mandatory, because without this information the Commissioner is not able to issue a digital certificate to each taxpayer and each EFD, as stipulated by the same law.

The fiscal impacts of introducing a new monitoring system will vary substantially depending on sector of economic activity, and most significantly for companies engaged in IT, construction, and hospitality.[10] A rate of compliance with EFD requirements suggests scope for targeting future implementation activities at specific economic sectors, such as construction, with low adoption rates but high impacts when adopted.

In time, all taxpayers of a particular jurisdiction will have to use EFD-compliant hardware or software to register their sales transactions. The implementation should be rolled out in stages, with groups that are announced by public notices. By the end of all implementation stages, every registered business in a jurisdiction will be legally required to provide a certified and verifiable Electronic Fiscal Invoice for all sales, which will be reported in real time to the tax authorities. Such an implementation plan will eventually lead towards:

- real-time returns;
- real-time payments; and,
- real-time audits.

3 WHAT IS THE DIFFERENCE BETWEEN FISCALIZATION AND E-INVOICING?

Let us forget about 'unstructured' invoices that are in electronic form, such as PDF or MS Word formats, or even scanned paper invoices – none of these invoice types constitute an e-invoice.

An e-invoice is made up of 'structured' invoice data issued in EDI, XML or other machine-readable formats. The idea goes as far back as the mid-1960s[11] when some of the largest multinational enterprises strived to establish paperless communication with their trading partners. Businesses invested heavily in their enterprise resource planning solutions and processors, which enabled them to reduce human involvement (and subsequently human error) in exchanging new document formats, such as e-invoices, and which automatically trigger other business processes necessary to facilitate trade.

Different regulations, technical formats and protocol specifications have been, and are being, introduced on a mandatory basis internationally. These include, for

10. The International Growth Centre (IGC) Rwanda is focussed on research and analysis under a memorandum of understanding with the Ministry of Finance and Economic Planning (MINECOFIN) and has issued several papers on the fiscal impact of EBMs in Rwanda. *See* one of the latest research papers (Victor Steenbergen, Reaping the Benefits of Electronic Billing Machines – Working Paper. ICG 2017, available at, https://www.theigc.org/wp-content/uploads/2017/09/Steenbergen-working-paper.pdf) for an explanation of the EBM journey.
11. *Electronic Invoicing* (10 March 2021, 11:47 AM CET). In *Wikipedia*, https://en.wikipedia.org/wiki/Electronic_invoicing.

example, CIUS-PT in Portugal, Svefaktura in Sweden, FatturaPA in Italy and XRechnung in Germany (*see* Figure 11.1), among others.

Figure 11.1 German ZUGFeRD: Elektronische Rechnungen[12]

```
<ram:SellerTradeParty>
 <ram:Name>Run my Accounts AG</ram:Name>
 <ram:PostalTradeAddress>
  <ram:PostcodeCode>8712</ram:PostcodeCode>
  <ram:LineOne>Grundstrasse 16b</ram:LineOne>
  <ram:CityName>Stäfa</ram:CityName>
 </ram:PostalTradeAddress>
 <ram:SpecifiedTaxRegistration>
  <ram:ID schemeID="VA"></ram:ID>
 </ram:SpecifiedTaxRegistration>
</ram:SellerTradeParty>
<ram:BuyerTradeParty>
 <ram:Name>Mr. Future AG</ram:Name>
 <ram:PostalTradeAddress>
  <ram:PostcodeCode>8000 </ram:PostcodeCode>
  <ram:LineOne>Hans Muster</ram:LineOne>
  <ram:LineTwo>Zukunftstrasse 1</ram:LineTwo>
  <ram:LineThree></ram:LineThree>
  <ram:CityName>Zürich</ram:CityName>
  <ram:CountryID></ram:CountryID>
 </ram:PostalTradeAddress>
</ram:BuyerTradeParty>
```

Modern fiscalization[13] mandates the use of fiscal invoices which are nothing less than structured invoice data issued in electronic formats (*see* Figure 11.2).

12. Translation: E-Bills.
13. Modern fiscalization refers to concepts that involve the digital signing of fiscal invoices. Such a concept first appeared in Sweden with the introduction of the control unit (2008) and Quebec with SRM (2009).

Figure 11.2 Fiji's VAT Monitoring System (VMS). Mapping Fiscal Invoice Requests and Responses

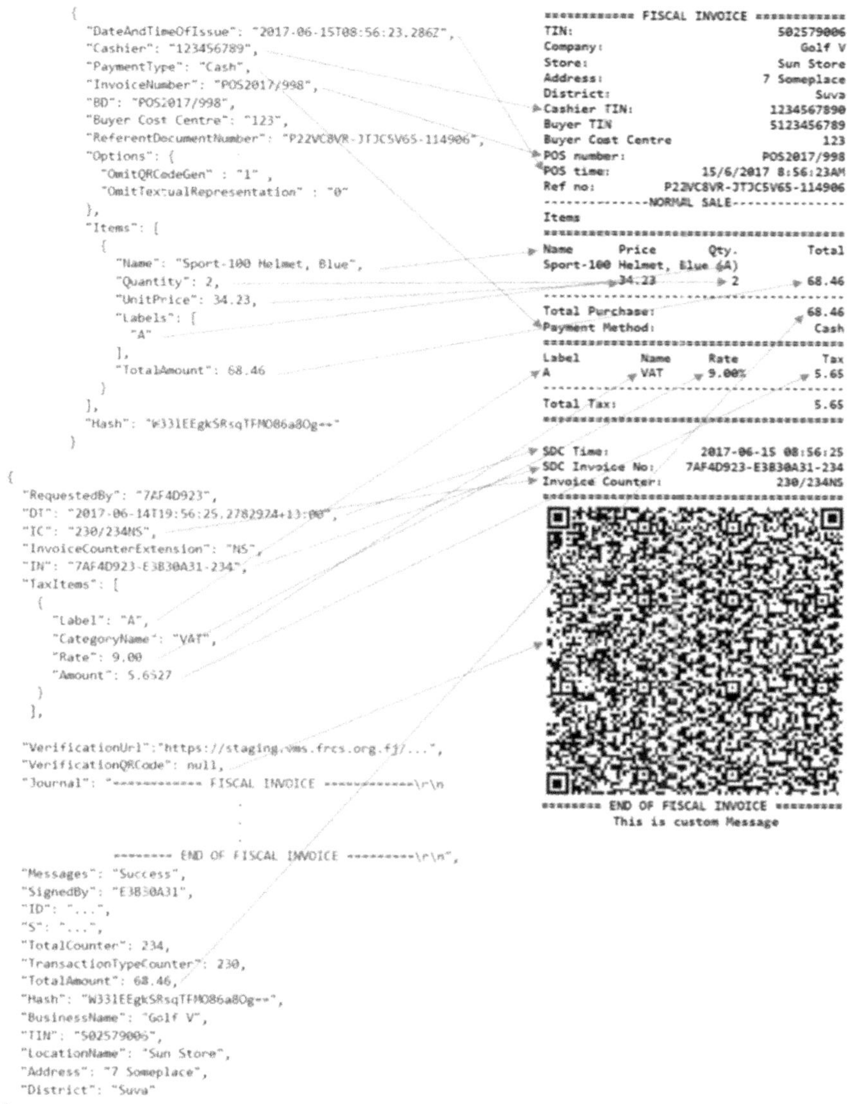

Both e-invoicing and fiscalization come in different formats, but there are a few common principles of the modern approach:

- the content of the invoice and a communication protocol are prescribed by a technical specification;
- information is available to the recipient in real time; and
- a digital signature is applied.

In papers that describe and discuss e-invoicing, two models are identified:

- the clearance model, which is based on the direct involvement of the revenue administration in digitally signing the invoice, and thus verifying the authenticity of the invoice; and
- the post-audit model, where invoices are exchanged directly between the seller and the buyer, and the tax authorities verify transactions after their completion.

Papers on e-invoicing will rarely mention the term 'fiscalization' - perhaps to some it is considered redundant - when in fact fiscalization has been evolving historically, and we are coming to a point where e-invoicing and fiscalization have only minor differences, as Table 11.1 shows.

Table 11.1 E-Invoicing Versus Fiscalization

	E-Invoicing	*Fiscalization*
Mandate:	Business driven	Government driven
Applies to:	B2B and B2G	B2C, B2B and B2G
Facilitated by:	Private intermediaries	Tax authorities
Benefit to:	Recipient	Public
Instant verification:	No	Yes
Reporting:	Real time	Real time & near real time
Dependency:	Internet connection	Secure element by government
History:	Started in the early 1960s as a business initiative to automate information exchange between businesses	Started in the early 1980s as a government initiative to reduce tax evasion through the introduction of invoice monitoring solutions

Some may argue that this comparison (depicted in Table 11.1) is not 100% accurate, and the author can agree with that perspective: these concepts have evolved over time and variations have emerged. In some countries, such as Italy and Mexico, e-invoicing has become a government-driven mandate, merged with fiscalization.

4 THE CASE OF FISCALIZATION IN RWANDA AND THEIR WAY FORWARD

The adoption of EBMs in Rwanda with the enactment of Ministerial Order No. 002/13/10/TC of 31 July 2013[14] has resulted in a revenue increase, boosted the efficiency of the RRA's audits, helped create more accurate taxpayer profiles and reduced the risk of tax fraud.

Under the public financial management (PFM) reform strategy[15] initiated in 2008, the RRA developed a proposal to implement comprehensive tax and customs compliance programmes based on risk analysis. In 2011/2012, the RRA launched tenders for procuring consultancy, devices, and software for data analysis from separate vendors, aimed at maximizing their control through counter-fraudulent measures and technology that captures data at the sales point, i.e., at the level of each transaction made by individuals. Rwanda was looking to be the third country in the East African Community to deploy fiscalization/EFDs after Kenya and Tanzania, but wanted to avoid inheriting the problems caused by placing trust in a single vendor.

In August 2011, two expressions of interest were made: one for a certified invoicing system (CIS) and the other for a sales data controller (SDC). An EBM is composed of these two physically separated components that, in the case of Rwanda, were delivered by two different manufacturers. Procurement of 500 EBM sets was completed, and the pilot phase started in May 2012.

Early in 2011, the RRA management realized that planning, implementing and monitoring such a system requires skilled personnel with adequate knowledge to manage the day-to-day activities and high-level issues. The terms of reference outlined tasks for consultants who assisted the RRA's project management office to implement the EBM project. The author of this chapter was the lead consultant, designing the process and procedures to use devices as well as supervising the development of the software to collect audit data.

The statement of work for consultants required the following:

(1) Project management:
   (a) assist the project office in the planning, managing, and controlling of implementing the EBM system based on the facts provided by the RRA;
   (b) advise the project office on how to enforce technical parameters and standards set as defined in the regulations and the guidelines;
   (c) design and implement work systems, procedures, and manuals supporting the project implementation unit;

14. Rwanda Ministry of Finance and Economic Planning, *Official Gazette No. 34 of 26/08/2013* (11 March 2021, 12:55 PM, CET), https://www.rra.gov.rw/typo3conf/ext/complete/Resources/Public//download/pdf/ogazette.pdf.
15. ECORYS, the Netherlands (2012), Rwanda: Independent Evaluation of the Implementation of the PFM Reform Strategy 2008-2012. Rwanda Ministry of Finance and Economic Planning (11 March 2021, 01:04 PM CET), https://www.oecd.org/derec/unitedkingdom/11_EvaluationSupportPublicFinanceManagement%20ReformRwanda.pdf.

(d) advise on the establishment of an EBM Implementation Committee and its working procedures; train the board members on how to investigate applications, issue accreditations, and evaluate test cases before approval;
(e) review and update CIS specifications;
(f) review and update SDC specifications;
(g) review and update the communication protocol (CIS <-> SDC);
(h) develop a certification method (EBM component accreditation);
(i) provide required business process reengineering for the development of the software to manage the CIS;
(j) conduct software testing;
(k) advise on matters related to awareness creation; and
(l) provide training to staff of the RRA on registration, inspection, and documentation of reports.

(2) Software development:
(a) design and implement work systems, procedures, and manuals supporting the project implementation unit;
(b) develop software to manage the EBM system; the software should include the following:
- security key management software;
- certification software;
- audit software; and
- invoice verification software.

(c) provide mentoring and training to the RRA's IT staff on the development of the system and on point-of-sale (POS) technology and firmware; and
(d) prepare implementation reports with detailed analysis of progress and problems.

Engagement on the project began on 2 February 2012 and ended on 31 January 2014. 'Commissioner General Rules'[16] were developed by the consultants and defined the set of instructions that were essential for the proper implementation of EBMs. These Rules are completely in accordance with the associated Ministerial Order[17] and are accompanied by five annexes defining each technical point.[18]

In January 2012, the RRA concluded a tender process and chose two different suppliers: one for 500 CIS devices and one for 500 SDC devices, which, when connected, comprise the EBM system. Two foreign manufacturers (with their local representatives) were awarded contracts and entered into contractual obligations that

16. Rwanda Ministry of Finance and Economic Planning, *Official Gazette No. 40 of 07/10/2013* (11 March 2021, 01:20 PM CET), https://www.rra.gov.rw/typo3conf/ext/complete/Resources/Public//download/pdf/gasette.pdf.
17. Rwanda Ministry of Finance and Economic Planning, *Official Gazette No. 34 of 26/08/2013* (11 March 2021, 12:58 PM, CET), https://www.rra.gov.rw/typo3conf/ext/complete/Resources/Public//download/pdf/ogazette.pdf.
18. The link with legislative requirements was accessed on 6 January 2020, https://www.rra.gov.rw/index.php?id=301.

stipulated that their products must pass an evaluation, and that the manufacturers must complete installation of the devices before the agreed monetary amount be paid in full. The evaluation process lasted six months due to the continual failure of the SDC supplier to comply with its contracted duties. Having a tender process to supply one set of devices (i.e., the EBMs) but split between two companies (each contracted to supply one component of an EBM device) led to some difficulties: the CIS supplier had the somewhat less demanding task as it had fewer technical features to comply with, yet it was dependant on the supplier of the SDC component before its own evaluation could be completed, as both components had to be tested together. Finally, both components passed the evaluation in mid-June 2012.

The consultants also changed the approach and methodology for software development: during the first phase, development was focussed on the software parts that are independent of the low-level, device-specific implementation, while later all the device-specific parts were implemented. This approach had the effect of minimizing the impacts of third-party delays.

The VAT law amendment (Article 24 – Use of certified EBMs)[19] triggered the roll-out process for EBMs. An action plan was presented to concerned stakeholders (vendors and taxpayers), describing details of the first phase of the implementation process, i.e., the installation of the 500 EBMs procured, which commenced in the second half of 2012. This document contained seven action points, and it was used by the project office to keep track of the progress, and to identify and resolve issues. The action plan outlined that most attention should be given to taxpayer orientation, providing them with operational instructions on how to use EBMs and their obligations regarding their continuous use. Coordination between stakeholders was also carefully planned to optimize the process of installation and training.

Enactment of the Ministerial Order No. 002/13/10/TC of 31 July 2013[20] was delayed in the Parliament of Rwanda and thus caused serious issues with enforcement. By April 2013, a total of only 464 taxpayers had received user training and were equipped with EBMs. The project office faced many challenges, mostly involving taxpayers' compliance. Several shops were shut down based on existing administrative rules which were used as a restrictive measure on those taxpayers who failed to comply. The penalty was temporary as, the day after being shut down, they were offered an opportunity to sign a letter of intent to use an EBM, and subsequent to signing they were allowed to reopen. Resistance to comply erupted, waged by the Private Sector Federation, an association of private businesses, which complained that the EBM devices, despite being provided free of charge, did nothing for their benefit.

Finally, the Ministerial Order was published in Official Gazette No. 34 of 26 August 2013 and gave power to the RRA to use the enforcement methods prescribed in the Order to increase the use of the EBM system. Unfortunately, enforcement was not

19. Rwanda Revenue Authority (11 November 2012), Electronic Billing Machine General Obligation (11 March 2021, 01:33 PM CET), https://www.rra.gov.rw/fileadmin/user_upload/electronic_billing_machine_general_obligation.pdf.
20. Rwanda Ministry of Finance and Economic Planning, *Official Gazette No. 34 of 26/08/2013* (11 March 2021, 12:58 PM CET), https://www.rra.gov.rw/typo3conf/ext/complete/Resources/Public//download/pdf/ogazette.pdf.

strong enough and the project office was continuously challenged by increasing resistance from businesses that refused to fiscalize. By 2015, only 8,000 VAT-registered taxpayers out of 15,000 were using EBMs.

Fiscal invoice verification was introduced to the Rwandan public for the first time with the introduction of the EBM system. Fiscal invoice verification involves checking the content of the invoice using the RRA's public webportal to assess its authenticity by cross-checking invoice content against an electronic signature, making it technically impossible to produce a fake invoice when using an EBM. Details on how this works have been disclosed to the public in the 'Commissioner General Instruction on SDC specification'.[21] Figure 11.3 shows what invoice information is captured in the electronic signature calculation by the EBM system.

Figure 11.3 Mapping Fiscal Invoices in Rwanda[1]

Description	Example
Tax Identification number	Must: "000000000"
Client's Tax Identification number	If exist "000000000"
Tax Rate 1	*exempt = "0"
Taxable Amount 1	"1000"
Tax Amount 1	"0"
Tax Rate 2	*(18%) = "18"
Taxable Amount 2	"5340"
Tax Amount 2	"814,58"
Tax Rate 3	*(0%) = "0"
Taxable Amount 3	"0"
Tax Amount 3	"0"
Tax Rate 4	*(0%) = "0"
Taxable Amount 4	"0"
Tax Amount 4	"0"
SDC Date and Time on the receipt	"25/5/2012 11:07:35"
Sales Data Controller ID	"SDC001000001"
Receipt Type	"N"
Transaction Type	"S"
SDC Receipt Type Counter	"168"
SDC Total Receipt Counter	"258"
Receipt Run Number	"152"
CIS Date And Time on the receipt	"25/5/2012 11:09:32"
Machine Registration Code	"AAACC123456"

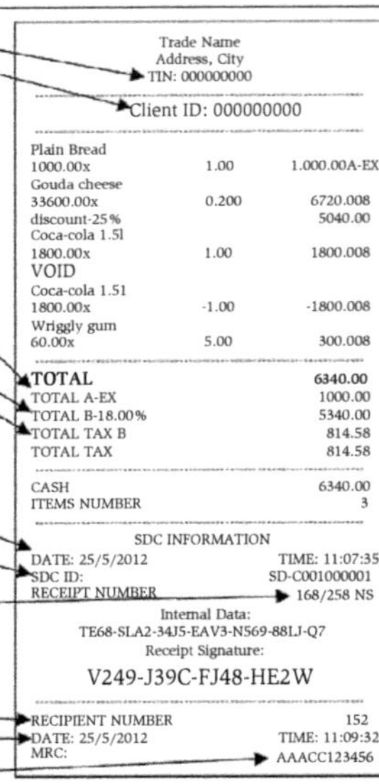

1. Fixed values, in accordance with prescribed legislation.

When used in the prescribed manner, the invoice verification software indicates whether the invoice is valid or not, as shown in Figure 11.4. The message 'Receipt is not valid' indicates that invoice information has been tampered with and the electronic signature is inaccurate or fake.

21. *See* 'SDC Signature data' chapter, https://www.rra.gov.rw/typo3conf/ext/complete/Resources/Public//download/pdf/2._Commissioner_General_Instruction_on_SDC_specification.pdf.

Figure 11.4 Public Verification Portal

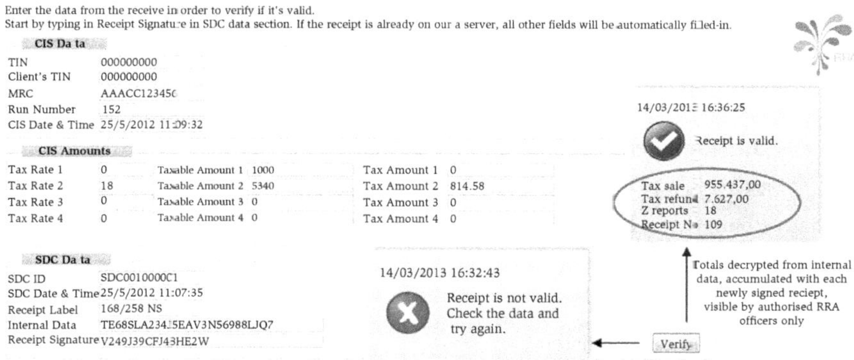

Source: *See* https://ebm.rra.gov.rw/backoffice/Verificator.

The official deadline for the installation and use of the EBM system was 1 April 2014. Just 6 months after its introduction, the RRA reported that the results were impressive, although the number of compliant taxpayers was extremely low. Speaking at the Taxpayers' Day celebration in 2014, the Commissioner General of the RRA at that time, Richard Tusabe, said the machines were helping the government increase its tax base.[22] In 2013, domestic revenue to the budget was RWF 782.5 billion, which is equivalent to 62%. In the financial year 2014/2015, collections were projected at RWF 906.8 billion,[23] which is a 16% increase on the previous year. The average impact of adopting EBMs on an enterprise's VAT payments is estimated to be approximately 8%. These effects vary substantially depending on the sector and the size of the business. In general, the impact of EBMs is greater for smaller firms where the pre-intervention VAT compliance may have been comparatively low.

4.1 Major Challenges

Some of the major challenges faced after implementing the EBM system in Rwanda can be summarized as follows:

- Statistics provided by the RRA indicate that only 8,000 out of the 15,000 registered VAT payers in the country are using EBMs.

22. http://www.newsofrwanda.com/featured1/24681/billing-machines-increase-tax-collection-by-16/.
23. Ministry of Finance and Economic Planning Website (30 April 2014), http://www.minecofin.gov.rw/index.php?id=119&tx_ttnews%5Btt_news%5D=181&cHash=b6041f1042e439073b10581b959a75c7.

- A 'mystery shopper' study[24] found that EBM utilization is low (at least for low-cost goods in retail stores in Rwanda's capital, Kigali), but responsive to consumer requests for formal invoices.
- The lack of quality service management for remote audit facilitation is delaying the schedule of EBM reporting to the RRA's server.
- EBM components are expensive.

4.2 Lessons Learned and Recommendations

Success and failure factors of the EBM system in Rwanda, as well as recommendations for enhancements, can be summarized as follows.

4.2.1 Success Factors

The success factors can be listed as:

- The EBM regulation is well written - the Ministerial Order has not been updated, but it still supports the new generation of EBM (online) systems.
- There is a good technical reference document - manufactures of EBM components benefitted from the open specification and free certification service.
- There has been good planning in terms of the interoperability of EBM components.
- A transparent certification process exists.
- There are unique secure elements for all EBMs.
- A Consumer Compliance Award programme and the EBM Tombola have been established for consumers.
- There are administrative benefits for compliant taxpayers.
- It encourages the B2B invoicing process flow among traders.
- Serious penalties have been introduced for non-compliance.
- Administrative privileges, such as paying taxes in instalments, can be revoked for taxpayers who do not have an active EBM.
- There has been a good communication campaign.

4.2.2 Failure Factors

The failure factors include:

- Remote management of EBMs is weak.
- There is low motivation to use EBMs among traders.
- Devices are expensive.
- The full potential of the EBM system was not fully utilized by the RRA audit team.

24. Andrew Zeitlin, Nada Eissa (9 February 2016), Evaluation of Electronic Billing Machines: Effectiveness of Tax Administration, International Growth Centre (11 March 2016, 01:55 PM CET), http://www.theigc.org/project/evaluation-of-electronic-billing-machines-effectiveness-of-tax-administration/.

- The enforcement of compliance with EBM regulations is low.
- Advertising and communication by the RRA's public relation services is weak.

4.3 Recommendations for Enhancements

On 10 October 2013, a company called Avatar Technologies LTD presented an online invoicing system to the RRA. The successful presentation resulted in a decision by the RRA management to consider a technical evaluation of the solution and conduct a live pilot test of it once the system met with specification requirements stipulated by the existing Commissioner General Rules.[25]

The conditions set by the RRA's certification department were met in January 2014. Avatar Technologies LTD was approved to be a supplier of the equivalent EBM solution (under Article 4 of the EBM Ministerial Order)[26] and submitted a request for the CIS model to be evaluated, while the SDC could not be evaluated as it did not conform with the existing standard. It was therefore proposed, during a meeting held on 24 January 2014 between Avatar representatives and the RRA's technical team, that a virtual SDC (developed by Avatar) could only be considered if it were to be under the administrative control of the RRA with the ability to serve all users. Subsequently, the virtual sales data controller (V-SDC) was introduced.

The live pilot test was launched on 13 February 2014 among taxpayers who accepted to use the online invoicing solution on a voluntary basis. The pilot was successful, but a change of management at the RRA[27] and the expiration of the consultants' contract resulted in efforts to upgrade the EBM system being postponed.

Table 11.2 Key Differentiating Features: Rwanda Upgrade

Functional Requirement	*EBM 1.0*	*EBM Upgrade*
Enhanced Audit Efficiency		
Real-time audit using V-SDC	No	Yes
EBM for mobile operators	No	Yes

25. Rwanda Revenue Authority, Commissioner General Instruction on CIS Specification (11 March 2021, 01:57 PM CET), https://www.rra.gov.rw/typo3conf/ext/complete/Resources/Public//download/pdf/cisspecification.pdf.
26. Rwanda Ministry of Finance and Economic Planning, *Official Gazette No. 34 of 26/08/2013* (11 March 2021, 12:58 PM CET), https://www.rra.gov.rw/typo3conf/ext/complete/Resources/Public//download/pdf/ogazette.pdf. *See* Article 4:

    Article 4: Exemption from the obligations under this Order

    The Commissioner General may exempt from the obligations under this Order, if the need for reliable information on financial supervision may be provided by other means upon an individual case.

27. Ivan R. Mugisha (7 March 2014), New RRA Boss Seeks to Increase Tax Base. The New Times, https://www.newtimes.co.rw/section/read/73680.

Functional Requirement	*EBM 1.0*	*EBM Upgrade*
Enhanced Audit Efficiency		
Prompt invoice verification	No (not for public)	Yes (for all)
B2B invoice for VAT refund notifications	No	Yes
Reduction of the Compliance Cost		
Compliance without the purchase of new hardware	No	Yes
Multiple CIS users - pay-per-invoice model	No	Yes
Possibility of tablet or smartphone to be CIS compliant	No	Yes
Increased Number of EBM Users		
Elimination of all exemption criteria	No	Yes
Activation procedure decentralized (public key infrastructure) and outsourced	No	Yes

Note: Functional enhancements recommended by the lead consultant in January 2014.

4.4 Efforts to Upgrade to EBM Versions 2.0 and 3.0

Based on Article 24 of Law 37/2012 of 9 November 2012 on the code of VAT, the RRA issued a memo to all VAT-registered persons obliged to use EBMs that generate invoices informing them that from 1 March 2015 taxpayers would not be allowed to deduct VAT input tax or a VAT refund upon the presentation of invoices that are not generated by an EBM and bear the other business's tax identification number. This order has resulted in multiple arrests of taxpayers who tried to misuse the EBM system and sold fiscal invoices to other entities who used them to claim fictitious expenses.[28]

This has further resulted in pressure from the private sector on the RRA to find a way to broaden the tax net and offer low-cost compliance tools for those businesses that cannot afford an EBM in order to create a level playing field so that all businesses justify their VAT inputs and outputs transparently using the EBM system.

The RRA management issued a tender seeking to upgrade the EBM solution from Version 1.0 to Version 2.0 in 2015/2016, but the tender process was cancelled on three consecutive occasions by the RRA before the evaluation had been completed.

Since 2016, the RRA has been under a lot of pressure from the public and vendors alike to choose a solution to upgrade to, and after three failed tenders, the RRA finally entered into an agreement with the Korean International Cooperation Agency (KOICA).[29]

The first public manifestation of RRA-KOICA cooperation was in July 2017 when the then Commissioner General, Richard Tusabe, announced that the EBM technology

28. In 2016, the RRA was able to intercept cases of EBM misuse by cross-checking VAT input against VAT output between businesses, https://www.newtimes.co.rw/section/read/203378.
29. Hope Magazine (17 October 2018), EBM Technology Evolves, Boosting Revenue Collection, http://www.hope-mag.com/index.php?com=news&option=read&ca=6&a=3855.

had been upgraded thanks to KOICA[30] after the RRA formed a partnership with a Korean vendor which was eventually funded by KOICA's grant. The result of this venture was EBM Version 2.0, an internet-based CIS. Technical specifications from existing Ministerial Order and Commissioner General Rules did not change, and the CIS designed by the Korean vendor is owned by the RRA and distributed for free to taxpayers who qualify.

Another EBM upgrade (EBM Version 3.0) is currently underway and efforts are being made to outsource online processors (V-SDC) to third-party companies. So far, only a few local companies have been nominated as service providers, and they are currently servicing some taxpayers. Their names have not yet been announced on the RRA's website, and this author therefore believes that the project is still in the pre-production development stage.

5 THE FLEXIBILITY OF SOFTWARE SECURITY AND WHY ONLINE INVOICING IS SO WIDELY ACCEPTED

5.1 The Components of an EFD

An EFD has two parts - an AIS and an SDC - either or both of which may be entirely software based; an accredited AIS[31] must connect with an accredited SDC to issue an instantly verifiable fiscal invoice.

Essentially, the EFD regulation[32] takes a wide (market) view of accreditation. The legislative body should be aware that the AIS market is both diverse and dynamic, that the government needs to work with the market as a regulator of the outcomes, and not as an advocate of a one-size-fits-all POS system. The tax authorities should be dedicated to providing detailed integration instructions to all manufacturers and software developers (EFD component vendors).

The regulation identifies the two avenues for producing a fiscal invoice with an accredited AIS:

(1) A hardware or software solution - uses an external SDC (E-SDC). This is a semi-connected scenario which does not require a permanent Internet connection for normal operations.
(2) A software solution - uses a virtual SDC (V-SDC). This is an internet-connected scenario.

Based entirely on how the taxpayer's business is set up, and how it achieves connectivity with the outside world, a choice can be made by the taxpayer between an AIS plus E-SDC, or an AIS plus V-SDC. But regardless of this choice, the EFD must produce the specified compliance outcomes.

30. IGIHE Network (20 July 2017), RRA Introduces Upgraded EBM. http://en.igihe.com/news/rra-introduces-upgraded-ebm.html.
31. *See supra* n. 2.
32. A legal framework enacted by a jurisdiction to regulate the implementation, technical requirements, and the use of EFD.

To help the market achieve these goals, the regulation tasks the tax authorities with setting up a development environment accessible to all software developers seeking to produce accredited AIS or accredited E-SDC components. By registering on the tax authorities' web page, for example, a developer will be able to receive test certificates, technical documentation and a user manual. The goal in each case is to demonstrate the creation of a fully compliant fiscal invoice.

There are two data-intensive parts to creating a fiscal invoice:

(1) some data is included in the invoice request sent by an accredited AIS to an E-SDC or V-SDC; and
(2) other data is included in the invoice response which is generated by the E-SDC or V-SDC in reply.

Both the request and the response must include specific data points.

The regulation also specifies four types of invoice that an accredited AIS must be able to issue when connected to an accredited SDC: normal invoices, copy invoices, training or pro-forma invoices, and sales or refund invoices. Each test case is set out for all transactions. The expected results are specified in the regulation, making accreditation for vendors very simple.

5.2 Encryption Algorithms and Data Security

Modern fiscalization systems should use well-known and proven encryption mechanisms to secure users, audit data and communicate between different parts of the system, and, to that end, data security for EFDs must be based on public-key cryptography.[33] Such fiscalization should be based on the following principles:

- the taxpayer obtains one digital certificate per EFD;
- the taxpayer (and the taxpayer's software) must carry out the signature protocol properly;
- the private key must remain private;
- the public key owner must be verifiable;
- invoices must be digitally signed by the taxpayer's digital certificate;
- communication between a taxpayer's system and the central server must be confidential;
- communicating parties must be mutually authenticated;
- the taxpayer's data must be encrypted in such a way that no one can access and misuse sales data;
- non-repudiation of issued invoices must be guaranteed; and

33. Public-key cryptography, or asymmetric cryptography, is any cryptographic system that uses pairs of keys comprising a public key, which may be disseminated widely, and a private key, which is known only to the owner. This accomplishes two functions: authentication, where the public key verifies that a holder of the paired private key sent the message, and encryption, where only the paired private key holder can decrypt the message encrypted with the public key.

- invoices must be signed in such a way that they can be instantly verifiable online.

Table 11.3 Some Example Methods of Securing Data Collected Using EFDs, Dating from Oldest Physically Protected Method to Newest Asymmetric Encryption Based Security

Countries with Hardware Security (Data Physically Protected)	*Countries with Software Symmetric Encryption Security*	*Countries with Software Asymmetric Encryption Security*
Romania (since 1998)	Sweden (since 2008)	Belgium (since 2015)
Serbia (since 2003)	Quebec (since 2009)	Russia (since 2016)
Kenya (since 2004)	Rwanda (since 2012)	Fiji (since 2018)
Zimbabwe (since 2010)	Macedonia (since 2015)	Samoa (since 2020)

5.3 Algorithms

Public-key algorithms are fundamental security ingredients in cryptosystems, applications and protocols. The algorithms and keys detailed in Table 11.4 should be used to secure the system.

Table 11.4 Recommended Security Algorithm

Algorithm	*Key Size*	*Usage*
AES-Rijndael	256 bits	Encryption of large chunks of data (audit data)
RSA	2048 bits	Signing, non-repudiation, authentication, integrity

5.4 Certificate Authority

A dedicated certificate authority (CA) provides digital certificate management. Digital certificates are issued to taxpayers and used to sign invoices and authenticate callers, both in online and offline invoice fiscalization scenarios.

Depending on the AIS in use, certificates can be distributed using encrypted files, smartcards or USB tokens. These three methods of certificate distribution will cover all expected usage scenarios for both online and offline EFDs.

5.5 Invoice Verification

Each fiscal invoice issued in online or offline modes must be instantly verifiable on the publicly available website belonging to the tax authorities. Invoice verification provides reassurance to the recipient that all information recorded on the fiscal invoice is true. It also provides an alternative channel to monitor the activity and tax liabilities of taxpayers who fail to submit audit data on a regular basis. Invoice verification is one of the foundations of a Consumer Compliance Award scheme (or 'invoice lottery'), which is a proven mechanism used to stimulate consumers to ask for fiscal invoices and increase the compliance rate.

6 MAIN PRINCIPLES AND BEST PRACTICES IN FISCALIZATION

6.1 The Benefits of EFDs

The use of EFDs will increase both efficiency and revenues. Tax authorities will also benefit by receiving tax returns of higher quality and will see a reduced need to handle individual cases. But focussing on tax collection processes is not only beneficial to the tax authorities; the taxpayer will also benefit in terms of more straightforward administrative procedures, increased certainty, and reduced administrative costs.

Some others benefits of using EFDs include:

- significantly increasing tax collection due to the registration of a taxpayer's turnover;
- decreasing the share of the grey economy due to a more organized approach to providing evidence of registered taxpayers, their activities, and their sales locations;
- suppressing tax evasion due to the comprehensive insight EFDs provide of all taxpayers' activities;
- protecting honest taxpayers from unfair competition;
- minimizing the cost of compliance per taxpayer and per sales point;
- increasing consumer awareness by receiving certified invoices along with purchased goods or services, with a clear and true specification of the tax amount dedicated to the government;
- registering both sales and purchases in B2B transactions, which enables easy cross-checking when processing claims;
- increasing transparency and levelling the playing field for all suppliers of fiscal equipment; and
- modernizing sales outlets with management tools designed to better serve taxpayers' businesses.

6.2 Principles Behind a Good System Design[34]

When introducing a fiscalization system in a jurisdiction, it is important that legislative body and competent authority bear the following principles in mind.

34. The fifteen principles listed in section 6.2 were published in April 2015 by the author with the objective of setting out the minimum requirements for designing anti-sales suppression systems. The author would like to thank the following contributors who observed the need for such a high-level outline, and who also advised the author and endorsed the content:

    (1) Richard T. Ainsworth, Adjunct Professor at the Boston University Law Graduate Tax Program, and the New York University Law Graduate Tax Program.

Anti-sales suppression system design

(1) A fiscal invoice acknowledging that a payment has been made must contain sufficient transactional data to confirm proper tax calculations.
(2) A fiscal invoice must be safeguarded by an electronic signature produced by an associated secure element, which uses encryption to confirm that the issued document is authentic and manipulation free.
(3) A secure element used for signing a fiscal invoice must be independent of the creator of the automated tax calculation system designed to serve the business needs of the user (AIS).
(4) A secure element and invoice system can be used as separate products or integrated into one product and be available in any place at any given time.
(5) Work between the secure element and invoice system must be optimized in a way to avoid any delay in producing the document.
(6) The system must be personalized in such a way that the fiscal invoice clearly identifies the issuer.

Verification of document integrity, inspection and audit

(1) An inspection conducted in the simplest form must immediately provide information about the integrity of the fiscal invoice.
(2) Simple on-the-spot inspection does not require authorized personnel or sophisticated technical knowledge to perform verification of encrypted data.
(3) Authorized personnel follow a unified method of inspecting the secure element. Information about each transaction can be extracted from the secure element, preferably in encrypted form.
(4) Electronic journal records, in human-readable form, must be provided for the user through the invoice system or made available through a secure element data collector.
(5) Verification services to authenticate documents, for both authorized personnel and the public, must be available at any time, preferably online, and in various media types.

Levelling the playing field for all suppliers

(1) Requirements for compliance must be transparent to allow a level playing field for all suppliers to offer their products.
(2) A variety of models of invoicing systems must be made available to accommodate different business needs.

(2) Ben Kagarama, Commissioner General of Rwanda Revenue Authority from 2011 to 2014.
(3) Francois Dugue, co-founder of Avatar Technologies LTD.
(4) Ivan Pavlovic, CTO and co-owner of Data Tech International.

This list can also available and can be accessed in six different languages at, https://dti.rs/english/.

User acceptance

(1) Information on a fiscal invoice, in both printed and electronic form, has to be unequivocally presented to the customer.
(2) In B2B transactions, the unique identity of the purchasing party must be safeguarded from any modifications by an electronic signature.

Index

www.ingramcontent.com/pod-product-compliance
Lightning Source LLC
Chambersburg PA
CBHW071330230926
51849CB00002B/363
* 9 7 8 9 4 0 3 5 3 4 0 3 9 *